Runaway Inequality

An Activist's Guide to Economic Justice

Revised, Updated Third Edition

Les Leopold

Labor Institute Press

The first printing of 30,000 copies of *Runaway Inequality* sold out in six months. The Revised, Updated Edition sold 20,000 copies in two years. It turns out the data, themes and many of the solutions proposed in *Runaway Inequality* were central to the presidential campaign of 2016 and the subsequent fall out. This book is now being used extensively to help build an on-going political movement — a "political revolution" — involving labor unions, community organizations, religious groups and thousands of individuals who want to reverse runaway inequality. Tens of millions of Americans truly want to take on the shameless financial strip-mining perpetuated by Wall Street and the country's top CEOs. We hope that this book can help us all build a sustainable mass movement to take back our country from the billionaire class. All proceeds from sales of the book go to the Labor Institute's National Economics Educational Campaign — not to the author personally.

Labor Institute Press
817 Broadway, New York, NY 10003

TheLaborInstitute.org

runawayinequality.org

ISBN 978-0-9990954-2-3

Library of Congress Cataloging-in-Publication Data

Leopold, Les.
    Runaway inequality : an activist's guide to economic justice / Les
Leopold.
        pages cm
Includes index.
ISBN 978-0-9990954-2-3 (pbk.)
    1. Income distribution—United States. 2. Equality—United States.
3. Wealth—United States. 4. United States—Economic policy—2009-
5. United States—Social policy—1993- I. Title.

HC110.I5L45 2015
339.20973--dc23

                                                    2015035233

Printed in the USA by Kay Printing

Contents

Part Four: Solutions

Stepping It Up

About 120 years ago, small farmers, black and white, in the South and Midwest joined with other social activists across the nation to wage an epic battle against the moneyed interests. These home-grown progressive populists (not to be confused with the current type of xenophobic, racist populists) wanted a new economic system based on public ownership of railroads and banks, and cooperatives that would serve the needs of small farming communities and factory workers. To build their movement, the populists sent out 6,000 educators to help small communities learn how to reverse runaway inequality.

Because of their combined efforts, a powerful movement grew to take back our country from the corporate and financial elites. *And it succeeded*: This progressive populist movement ultimately culminated in Social Security, the 8-hour day, the weekend, the regulation of Wall Street and large corporations, and protections for working people on the job.

That earlier populist movement has inspired and informed this book and the groundswell of activism that has been built around it.

Runaway Inequality, newly revised and updated, is now in its third printing, with more than 50,000 copies sold, including Spanish language print and e-book editions. Labor unions, church groups, immigrant worker centers, and environmental organizations have grabbed hold of *Runaway Inequality* and used it to educate and acti-vate a new generation of progressive populists through workshops, conferences, and discussion groups.

The project began in 2015, when the Communications Workers of America (CWA) asked the Labor Institute to conduct five half-day sessions for 30 Verizon workers based on a draft of *Runaway Inequality*. At the end of the course, participants wanted to take action. They asked if they themselves could become runaway inequality trainers. The CWA said yes! The union partnered with the Labor Institute to train 60 workers as trainers who in turn would conduct 8-hour runaway inequality workshops for 1,000 CWA members from around the country. That train-the-trainer network continues to spread across the country.

The CWA moved beyond its own membership to organize train-the-trainer programs for Citizen Action New York, Jobs for Justice in Detroit, community allies in Buffalo, and a joint train-the-trainer program with the United Steelworkers, the CWA, and the Sierra Club in California. The union sponsored an 8-hour course in Spanish and English for 150 United Automobile Workers from New England, New York, and Puerto Rico. In the coming year, the CWA will help more community groups and unions start their own runaway inequality networks.

The New Jersey Educational Association has joined with the New Jersey Work Environment Council to conduct more train-the-trainer programs. Their goal: to reach 2,000 New Jersey labor and community activists who are joining to fight for a new state public bank. Meanwhile, National Nurses United distributed 5,500 copies of *Runaway Inequality* to bolster activists at the 2016 and 2017 Peoples Summit in Chicago.

Hundreds of people around the country have asked to become runaway inequality trainers, and we've stepped up our trainings to meet that demand. We created the runawayinequality.org website to recruit and train new trainers, and to make our curricula available for free at www.runawayinequality.org. Royalties from book sales go to support these efforts.

I hope you'll consider becoming a trainer yourself, if you aren't already.

Because training hundreds of trainers and putting 50,000 books in circulation is not enough. We need 50,000 *educators* to engage their friends, co-workers, and neighbors in this discussion. We need to reach out to all those who are left behind by our economic and political system, and help them see that runaway inequality is not an act of God, but rather the willful result of corporate and financial greed.

To do all this, and to build the kind of massive organized movement we need to once again take back our country from the financial and corporate elites, we'll have to confront some engrained ideas and habits that have been holding us back.

Sustained movement building on a large scale is foreign to most of us. For more than a generation, we've grown accustomed to the neoliberal free-market vision that has narrowed our sense of the possible. It taught us that it's okay for students to go deeply in debt; that it's natural to have the largest prison population in the world; that it's inevitable to have a crumbling infrastructure; and that it is impossible to prevent corporations from shifting our jobs to low-wage areas with poor environmental protections.

We've grown accustomed to waiting and hoping that the next elected leader will rescue us – even though history tells us that major social change comes not from great leaders, but from great movements.

Even those of us who are actively working for change are often isolated in our own "issue silos." We've been conditioned to think small about movement-building – to drill down in our own areas of work and not link up together. Now more than ever, we've got to get active and get together. Here's why:

- The economy is now structured so that financial and corporate elites will continually gain more and more wealth and power at our expense – unless *we* put a stop to it. There is no hidden mechanism that will right this ship. That's *our* job.
- The financial strip-mining of our economy (which is how economic elites siphon wealth from our workplaces, families, and communities) impacts all of us and all of our issues – from climate change, to mass

incarceration, to job loss, to declining incomes, to labor rights, to student loans.

- That means that no matter what our individual identity (labor unionist, environmentalist, racial justice activist, feminist, etc.), we also need to take on the identity of movement builder. We all must come together or we all lose.

- To build a powerful and diverse movement that can challenge the economic elites, we also must fight discrimination and raise our own awareness related to race, ethnicity, gender, sexual orientation, and other differences. The denial of respect and basic human rights to any group divides us and cripples our movement-building efforts.

It's on us. We get to choose whether to keep our heads down and work only in our issue silos or whether to look up and join others to build a broader, bolder movement.

This book, and the spreading network of trainers surrounding it, are part of the vast educational infrastructure we'll need to build that bigger, bolder movement. Please go to www.runawayinequa lity.org to join the project and spread the word!

I'm honored to join you and thousands of others in this national collective effort.

Les Leopold
Executive Director,
The Labor Institute
May Day 2018

Introduction

The United States is among the richest countries in all of history. But if you're not a corporate or political elite, you'd never know it. In the world working people inhabit, our infrastructure is collapsing, our schools are laying off teachers, our drinking water is barely potable, our cities are facing bankruptcy, and our public and private pension funds are nearing collapse. We – consumers, students, and homeowners – are loaded with crushing debt, but our real wages haven't risen since the 1970s.

How can we be so rich and still have such poor services, so much debt and such stagnant incomes?

The answer: runaway inequality – the ever-increasing gap in income and wealth between the super-rich and the rest of us.

This isn't the first time that a tiny elite has gained extraordinary control over economic and political life. Ancient Egypt had the Pharaohs. Medieval Europe had feudal lords and kings. We Americans had industrial robber barons.

And today, we've got financial and corporate elites.

Runaway inequality is upending how we see ourselves and how we govern. It is upending the American Dream (the cherished idea that life gets better and better with each generation). And it is upending the practice of democracy and the very idea that each of us has roughly equal influence in governing our country.

It's time to face up to runaway economic inequality – what causes it, what it's doing to us, and what we can do about it.

This book has four aims:

1. Shine a light on economic inequality: It's worse than you think

For all the talk about economic inequality, most of us have no idea how bad it really is. It's as if our native sense of justice won't let us comprehend how outrageously unequal our economy has become and how much worse it's getting day by day. Maybe we're just too fair-minded to wrap our minds around the level of systematic greed that now permeates society's top echelons.

We'll look at just how wide the gap is between the super-rich and the rest of us, and how rapidly it is accelerating. A very small group of economic elites is accumulating more and more of the country's resources while the rest of us stand still or fall further behind.

But the problem goes beyond how many dollars we have (or don't): Runaway inequality is tearing apart the fabric of our society. The super-rich live in a world that no longer requires mutual reliance on common public services. Elites generally don't use our schools, our roads, our airports. They don't really care if our infrastructure collapses. We are cracking into two separate societies.

At the same time, the super-rich are able to park trillions of dollars far from the reach of the tax collector. By avoiding and evading taxes, with help from an army of lawyers and bankers, the rich are undermining the government services that the rest of us need. So our roads and bridges crumble, our environment becomes contaminated, our children crowd into our rundown schools. We pay a fortune out of pocket for higher education and poor quality health care. And some of us with darker pigmentation are targeted for arrest and fines in order to help fund local government, while also facing poverty and police violence.

Runaway inequality undermines the practice of democracy. As the rich get richer and richer, it gets easier and easier for them to buy political favors. They can twist the media, elected officials, and government agencies to do their bidding. They vote with their money, which makes a mockery of our democratic "one vote, one person" creed. We'll see data showing that elected officials rarely act on the agenda most Americans support. Instead they represent the wishes of the affluent.

Using over 100 easy to read charts and graphs as well as text, we will demonstrate that as bad as you think it is, it's worse.

2. Examine the Fading American Dream

We'll take an honest look at how we compare to other developed nations.

Most of us still view our country through the lens of the American Dream and American "exceptionalism." We see ourselves as leading the world in just about everything that is good and just. As virtually every politician likes to say, we are the shining light of freedom and prosperity, blessed by God.

Most Americans believe that the U.S. has the most upward mobility and highest standard of living in the world. We think that the U.S. is the fairest nation on Earth, offering the best prospects for everyday people. (And for anyone who isn't moving up, it's their own fault.)

But the facts in this book will undermine that perspective. While America may have had the most prosperous working class from World War II to 1980, it doesn't anymore. In fact, today the U.S. is the most unequal country in the developed world. We have the most child poverty and homelessness. We have more people in prison than China and Russia. And Americans are less upwardly mobile than most Europeans.

We'll see that our public services don't stack up either. Our health care costs more, covers fewer people and produces worse outcomes. And we are nearly last among developed nations in energy efficiency and overall infrastructure.

No question about it, the top 1 percent never had it so good. But the rest of us are losing sight of the American Dream as runaway inequality accelerates.

3. Empower ourselves with the big picture

From years of conducting economic workshops for adults, we've learned that having a clear overview of what is going on is remarkably empowering for people. When you can step back and see how it all fits together, the world makes more sense.

We'll work hard at presenting that big, wide view, because most of us never have a chance to see it. You just can't get an accurate picture of the economy as a whole through the everyday media or the jumble of internet sources. We hear snippets about stock markets, government debt, trade, unemployment and inflation. What we don't hear about is the context, substantive explanation, or critical questioning about why any of this is happening and how it relates to our daily lives.

Most of all, the media turns a blind eye to the fact that we live in a capitalist system. We're never allowed to get outside that box so we can look at it and see how it ticks. So we never hear about the fundamental conflict that capitalism creates between the needs and wishes of privately owned corporations and our health and well-being – or the well-being of the planet that sustains us. We don't hear about how the corporate owners' and financiers' insatiable drive for profits is eroding our standard of living. Yet these conflicts are key to understanding our new era of runaway inequality.

The picture of the economy that nearly all of us share turns out to be wrong. We are told in many different ways that the economy is like a complex machine that functions beyond the reach of human control. This machine metaphor frames our view of the economic world: It makes us think that everyone is just doing their thing in the machine, and that we each get what we deserve, more or less. It obscures the reality that there is, in fact, a fundamental conflict between employees and owners, between the rich and the rest of us.

The big picture we'll present makes a lot more sense than the chopped up version that bombards us each day. Yes, the economic system is complex and yes, it is very hard to control. But its fundamental direction is set by humans who serve particular interests. We will see how powerful people chose to dramatically change the economy's direction a generation ago, and how working people have been paying the price ever since. Runaway inequality is not an act of God. It is the result of a system designed by and for wealthy elites.

4. Come to a common understanding so we can build a common movement
We offer this, our most ambitious goal, with the utmost humility: We aim to help build a broad-based movement for economic and environmental justice.

Right now, we lack a robust mass movement with the power to reclaim our economy and our democracy to make it work for the 99 percent. Although the Bernie Sanders campaign for president in 2016 shows us it is possible.

Instead, we have thousands of individual groups working on every issue from fracking to a living wage. We have unions fighting for their members and worker centers fighting for immigrant rights. We have protests ranging from Occupy Wall Street to Black Lives Matter to climate justice. We have hundreds of progressive websites and journals to cover all this activity. But we do not have a coherent national movement with a clear and bold agenda that links us together.

We will show that runaway inequality is at the root of many of the problems we face, including the meteoric and disastrous rise of the financial sector, defunding of the public sector, environmental destruction, increased racial discrimination, the gender gap in wages and the rise of our mammoth prison population. And we will posit that if we share a clear understanding of runaway inequality – and the basic economic situation we face – we can begin to build a common, broad-based movement for fundamental economic justice that will take on America's economic elites.

The political system will not move unless we organize on a mass level like the Populists did over a hundred years ago, like the trade union movement did in the 1930s and like the Civil Rights movement did in the 1950s and 1960s. Is it time for a political revolution?

Some liberal economists and politicians appeal to the self-interest of the super-rich. They argue that the rich would be (even) better off if they would just allow a fairer distribution of income and wealth. We disagree. Expecting the wealthy to help us secure basic fairness is a losing proposition.

Economic elites will only give up power and wealth when they're forced to do so by a powerful social movement.

So this book has far-reaching but difficult to achieve goals. It outlines an economic analysis and economic solutions that can connect us and enable us to build a broad, common movement. Such a common economic analysis does not by itself bring us together. But it will be very hard to create a powerful mass movement without one.

To achieve these goals the book is divided into four parts:

> **Part 1: Causes of Runaway Inequality** analyzes how wealth is extracted from all of us by Wall Street.
>
> **Part 2: The Decline of American Exceptionalism** examines America's ranking on key economic and social issues in comparison to other developed nations.
>
> **Part 3: Separate Issues, Common Cause** shows the major impact of runaway inequality on a series of issues that often are viewed independently.
>
> **Part 4: Solutions** reviews a range of policies and actions that will be needed to bring more economic and social justice to America.

In the end this book makes one essential point again and again. Runaway inequality comes at a steep price. The money that enriches the few is extracted from all that we hold dear – our public life, our incomes, our health and the education of our children. It is making poor the richest country on Earth. . . . Until we do something about it.

PART ONE

Causes of Runaway Inequality

It's as Bad as You Think
It Is . . . . And Worse!

Please take a moment to write down the answers to two basic questions:

- How much do you think the CEO of a large corporation makes in a year, on average?
- How much do you think an entry-level (unskilled) factory worker earns in a year, on average?

Your answers allow us to construct an important statistic about inequality – the wage-gap ratio.

For example, let's say your answer is that the typical CEO makes about $500,000 per year, while the factory worker earns about $25,000 per year. That gives us a wage-gap ratio of 20 to one – that is, for every one dollar earned by the worker, the CEO earns $20 (500,000/25,000 = 20/1).

If you said one million dollars for the CEO and $25,000 for the factory worker, then the ratio jumps to 40 to one.

What ratio did you come up with?

How Americans view the wage gap

These same two questions were asked of more than 50,000 people around the world, of whom 1,581 were Americans of all stripes. [1]

---

1 The data comes from the International Social Survey Programme: Social Inequality IV - ISSP 2009 on the website Gesis. If you do research or educational work, you can sign up for free and examine the amazing array of data collected here:

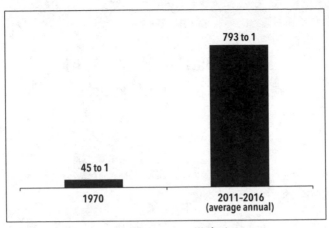

Chart 1.1: Wage Gap: Top 100 CEOs vs Average Worker*

*Average worker is production or nonsupervisory worker, based on weekly wages multiplied by 52 weeks.

Sources: CEO pay from CEO compensation surveys, *Forbes*, April/May issues, 1971-2011 and "The New York Times/ Equilar 200 Highest-Paid CEO Rankings," 2012-2017; Worker earnings based on U.S. Bureau of Labor Statistics data, http://www.bls.gov/data/#wages.

It turns out that the median American response – that is, the response that is exactly in the middle of survey results from Americans – estimated that a CEO of a large company earned about $900,000 per year and that the average factory worker earned about $25,000. That makes for a wage-gap ratio of 36 to one.

But how close are these estimates to reality? Not very.

Charts 1.1 and 1.2 give us a pretty good estimate of the growing gap between total compensation[2] for the top 100 and top 200 CEOs and the pay of a typical worker.[3]

In 1970, for every dollar earned by the average worker, the top 100 CEOs earned on average $45. From 2011 to 2016, the average ratio had jumped to 793 to one.

More amazing still is that on average Americans think CEOs of

---

http://zacat.gesis.org/webview/index.jsp?object=http://zacat.gesis.org/obj/fStudy/ ZA5400.

2 Total compensation includes salaries, bonuses, stock options and deferred compensation.

3 The number for worker's pay was derived by using the average wages of production or nonsupervisory workers, which includes workers in the service sector as well as other private industry sectors.

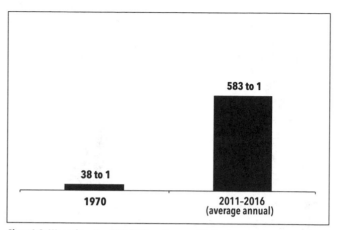

Chart 1.2: Wage Gap: Top 200 CEOs vs Average Worker*
*Average worker is production or nonsupervisory worker, based on weekly wages multiplied by 52 weeks.

Sources: CEO pay from CEO compensation surveys, *Forbes*, April/May issues, 1971-2011 and "The New York Times/ Equilar 200 Highest-Paid CEO Rankings," 2012-2107; Worker earnings based on U.S. Bureau of Labor Statistics data, http://www.bls.gov/data/#wages.

large companies receive about $900,000 per year in compensation, when in reality they receive nearly $30 million!

It's as if our perception of the income gap was frozen in 1970. We just have not caught up with the realities of runaway inequality.

What do we think the wage gap should be?

Ok, let's try these two questions again. But this time, let's come up with what we think should be the fair and just compensation for CEOs of large corporations and for unskilled factory workers.

- How much do you think the CEO of a large corporation *should* earn per year?
- How much do you think an entry-level factory worker *should* earn per year?

Please take a moment to jot down your answers.

Now let's go back to the survey information to see how the typical American answered these same questions.

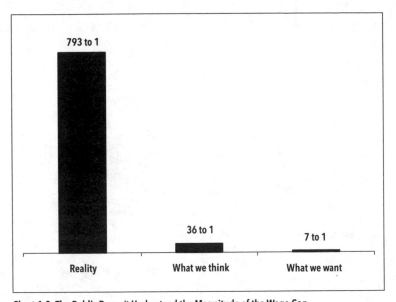

Chart 1.3: The Public Doesn't Understand the Magnitude of the Wage Gap
Sources: Opinion data from International Social Survey Programme: Social Inequality IV-ISSP 2009; author's calculations based on data for 2011–2016 from "The New York Times/Equilar 200 Highest-Paid CEO Rankings," 2012–2017; and average wages from Bureau of Labor Statistics, http://www.bls.gov/data/#wages.

This time it turns out that Americans' median response – the one smack in the middle of all the responses – is that a CEO of a large corporation *should* earn about $200,000 a year and that an unskilled factory worker should earn about $30,000. This produces a wage-gap ratio of about seven to one.

Let's pause for a moment to consider how jarring this result is (see Chart 1.3). The actual wage gap between a CEO and the average unskilled worker is 793 to one. Yet Americans believe it should be only seven to one. This is an enormous difference. It suggests that if the typical American knew the real numbers, they would be outraged by this glaring example of runaway inequality.

Do our estimates vary by political affiliation or educational level?

The survey also asks questions about political affiliation so that we can see whether those who call themselves "Strong Democrats" have significantly different beliefs than those who call themselves "Strong Republicans." We can also see how the responses vary between people who didn't finish high school and those who have graduate degrees.

Remarkably, the responses hardly vary at all. All of us, on the right and the left – high school dropouts and PhDs – have two things in common: 1) We all grossly underestimate the size of the wage gap; and 2) We all want a much, much smaller wage gap.

As Table 1.1 shows, "Strong Democrats" estimate that the *actual* ratio between the pay of a CEO of a large corporation and an unskilled factory worker was about 36 to one. "Strong Republicans" said it was 40 to one. Not much of a difference.

When it comes to offering opinions about what the wage gap *should* be, the Strong Democrats thought five to one was about right, while the Strong Republicans thought it should be about 12 to one. The two political extremes obviously are far closer to each other than to the current reality of 793 to one.

And how much did the responses vary based on people's educational attainment? Again, not much. Those who didn't finish high school thought the *actual* gap was 60 to one, while those with

Table 1.1: Americans Estimate What the Ceo/Worker Pay Gap Actually Is, and What It Should Be*		
	What we think the pay gap actually is**	What we think the pay gap should be
Strong Democrat	36 to 1	5 to 1
Strong Republican	40 to 1	12 to 1
< High School degree	60 to 1	5 to 1
Graduate Degree	40 to 1	12 to 1
Actual	793 to 1	

* All estimates are calculated for the median respondent - the mid-point in the array of responses.
** The ratios are calculated by creating a ratio of responses to two survey questions: "How much do you think a chairman of a large national corporation earns?" divided by "How much to you think an unskilled worker in a factory earns?" The "should be" wage gap comes from similar questions in the survey that ask how much a chairman and an unskilled worker should earn.
Source: Leibniz Institute for the Social Sciences, International Social Survey Programme: Social Inequality IV-ISSP 2009, http://zacat.gesis.org/webview/index.jsp?object=http://zacat.gesis.org/obj/fStudy/ZA5400.

graduate degrees thought it was about 40 to one (both compared to the reality of 794 to one).

Those who didn't complete high school thought the ideal pay gap should be about five to one, while those with graduate degrees thought it should be 12 to one. These ratios are identical to those offered by the Strong Democrats and Strong Republicans.

When it comes to our ignorance of the pay gap, there are no blue states, no red states – only misinformed states of mind.

Why are we so blind to runaway economic inequality?

Most of us have no idea that our golden land of opportunity is the runaway leader among developed nations when it comes to inequality (see Chapter 5). Of course this runs completely counter to the American Dream, that persistent belief that America is the fairest nation of them all – the most just and upwardly mobile country in history.

That core belief about America's superiority seems to make it hard for us to take in this contradictory information. As social scientists have established, we tend to tune out information that challenges our deep-seated beliefs. In this case, absorbing this new data is just too jarring to our long-held sense of national identity.

Our misreading of inequality also may be a legacy of the post-World War II economic boom. During that time, our working class had the highest global standard of living in the world, with ever increasing yearly real wages (which we'll see in greater detail in Chapter 2).

From the New Deal through the Cold War (1933 to 1990), it was American policy to boost job and income levels as much as possible to make sure our workers and middle class were "the envy of the world." That's a half century of rising prosperity for working people. Also during this period, income taxes on the wealthy were extremely high, more than 90 percent for people at the highest income bracket during World War II and the 1950s. As a result, the

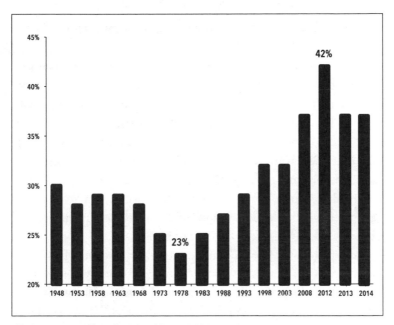

Chart 1.4: Top 1% Share of U.S. Wealth, 1948-2014

Sources: Emmanuel Saez and Gabriel Zucman, *Wealth Inequality in the United States Since 1913*, National Bureau of Economic Research, October 2014, Appendix Table B-1, http://gabriel-zucman.eu/files/SaezZucman2014.pdf; and World Wealth and Income Database, http://wid.world/data/.

top 1 percent, while living extremely well, saw their share of total U.S. wealth decline (see chart 1.4).[4]

So it's little wonder that the massive baby boom generation grew up with both the ideal and the reality of relative equality – at least for Caucasians. Of course, there were wealthy people all over America even then, but life was getting better and better for the vast majority of Americans.

It seems we're still living with this cultural hangover, clinging to a societal self-image from yesteryear. Although runaway inequality is our new economic reality, many of us still look in the mirror and see the fairest of them all looking back at us.

---

4   Emmanuel Saez and Gabriel Zucman, "Wealth Inequality in the United States Since 1913," October 2014, http://gabriel-zucman.eu/files/SaezZucman2014Slides.pdf.

Both political parties refuse to address inequality

Perhaps the biggest reason we are so misinformed is that it is not in the interests of our political parties for us to see the truth. Neither political party has addressed rising inequality in a meaningful way. Yes, the Democrats tend to support modest rises in the minimum wage that do make a difference to those stuck in the lowest-paying jobs. But they won't go near the revolutionary idea of placing a legal limit on what the CEO/worker pay gap should be.

Why don't our politicians propose to limit the CEO/worker pay gap to, let's say, 12 to one, a ratio that even Strong Republicans and the well-educated think would be fair and just?

Perhaps because they live in fear of a different revolution – a massive revolt from their elite corporate donors, who wouldn't dream of earning so little. In fact, the elite establishment – in finance, the corporate world, the higher levels of government, academia and the media – have no intention of limiting their incomes, no matter what the public believes to be just and fair. Here lies the very essence of class struggle between the 99 percent and 1 percent, and neither party wants any part of it.

What will it take to wake us up to inequality?

The good news is that Americans of all genders, shades, incomes, education levels and politics think on average that the wage gap should be about seven to one, not 793 to one. That's a pretty good place to start. Imagine if the only real economic debate was between the Strong Democrats who thought a fair wage gap should be five to one versus the Strong Republicans who thought it should be 12 to one. A broad movement for economic justice should be able to build on this shared sense of basic fairness. It's light-years ahead of what elites expect and feel is their due.

For about six months, Occupy Wall Street touched this nerve and put inequality on the agenda. "We are the 99 percent" became the national anthem for many Americans. For the first time in a generation, the country was talking about the gap between the super-rich and the rest of us.

Roughly at the same time, the Tea Party emerged with a different message. They also sensed that something was profoundly wrong. But for them the problem was (and is) big government, not inequality. They and their political allies tend to blame inequality on low-income families themselves (the "takers"), while heaping praise on the wealthy ("the makers").

Others, including some liberals, blame inequality on new technologies that require skills workers don't have. The implication is that those at the bottom could close the wage gap if they could just get that college degree or advanced skill. This self-help message resonates with most Americans, and access to (free, high-quality) education would certainly help.

But it will take a different kind of education to reduce the wage gap. We no longer have 900 Occupy encampments around the world to remind everyone that inequality is our new way of life. But each day millions of Americans face the stark reality of trying to survive on low pay and porous benefits, and pressure for increasing wages and benefits is growing. And so is the level of anger and frustration.

We need to relearn the skills of building a mass movement. That includes educating ourselves about the realities of growing economic inequality. Only then can we break through the faulty self-image of America that is crippling us.

Spread the word: We are the most unequal society in the developed world, and we can change that.

Discussion Questions:

1. In your opinion, is the growing wage gap between CEOs and the rest of us an important issue? Why or why not?

2. Why do you think that Americans underestimate the wage gap between CEOs and the rest of us?

3. Do you think it would make a difference to spread the word about how extreme the CEO/worker wage gap has become? Why or why not?

CHAPTER 2

Wage Theft Comes to America

In Denmark, companies like McDonald's and Burger King pay workers $20 an hour[1] plus benefits with no complaint. These same companies, which are actually based in the U.S., pay American workers less than $9 with no benefits.[2]

What is going on here?

The answer is simple and painful – wage theft. In America, corporations can get away with stealing our wages, but in Denmark (and elsewhere), they can't. Virtually the entire bottom 95 percent of American wage earners are victims of wage theft ... perhaps including you!

Wage theft is a reality understood by every immigrant day laborer standing on a street corner looking for a job with a drive-by construction or landscaping contractor. Far too many contractors "hire" these workers and then simply refuse to pay after the work is done.

Workers who are undocumented have little recourse. If they report the theft, they might be turned in to U.S. Immigration and Customs Enforcement (ICE). So most people just try a different corner, hoping to luck out with a more scrupulous contractor the next time around. Workers who are lucky and resourceful enough to be affiliated with an immigrant worker center like the Workers Justice Project[3] in Brooklyn, NY, can find jobs through its hiring

---

1   Liz Alderman and Steven Greenhouse, "Living Wages, Rarity for U.S. Fast-Food Workers, Served Up in Denmark," *New York Times*, October 27, 2014, http://www.nytimes.com/2014/10/28/business/international/living-wages-served-in-denmark-fast-food-restaurants.html?_r=3.
2   A Big Mac in Denmark costs $5.60 compared to $4.80 in the U.S., Ibid.
3   David Gonzalez, "Job Center Gives a Voice, and Fair Wages, to an 'Invisible' Work Force," *New York Times*, October 12, 2014, http://www.nytimes.com/2014/10/13/nyregion/giving-a-voice-and-fair-wages-to-an-invisible-work-force.html.

hall, where contractors agree to pay decent wages and provide safer working conditions.

Fast-food franchise managers sometimes steal wages by fiddling with workers' time logs, erasing any evidence of overtime. So much for the time-and-a-half pay workers are entitled to by law for OT.[4] You don't like it? Leave.

However, if the Fast Food Forward campaign[5] has your back, the threat of protest and legal action might force your boss to pay up. Managers who try stealing OT in Denmark have to worry that the union will respond by shutting down the entire chain.

You might think that U.S. workers could go to court to claim their stolen wages. Sometimes they do. Sometimes they even win... and then are unable to collect. Employers go out of business, hide assets or find other ways to worm their way out of paying what they owe. According to a 2015 report about wage theft in New York City by a coalition including the Legal Aid Society, the Urban Justice Center and the National Center for Law and Economic Justice, "Our research identified at least $125 million in judgments and orders, providing a glimpse into the scope of the wage collection problem in New York."[6]

And then there are the Amazon warehouse workers who must line up for 25 minutes to pass through "egress security" screeners to prevent "inventory shrinkage." Does Amazon pay people for this time? No, says Amazon, because this activity is not "integral and indispensable" to the job. The Supreme Court now agrees.[7] So time

---

4   Hunter Stuart, "An Overwhelming Number of Fast Food Workers Report Getting Ripped Off by Their Bosses: Poll," *The Huffington Post*, April 11, 2014, http://www.huffingtonpost.com/2014/04/11/fast-food-wage-theft_n_5085502.html.

5   See information from Fast Food Forward on Facebook, https://www.facebook.com/FastFoodForward.

6   Jim Dwyer, "Awarded Stolen Wages, Workers Struggle to Collect," *New York Times*, February 19, 2015, http://www.nytimes.com/2015/02/20/nyregion/awarded-stolen-wages-workers-struggle-to-collect.html?ref=todayspaper&_r=0.

7   Robert Barnes, "Supreme Court Rules Amazon Doesn't Have to Pay for After-hours Time in Security Lines," *Washington Post*, December 9, 2014, http://www.washingtonpost.com/politics/courts_law/supreme-court-rules-amazon-doesnt-have-to-pay-for-after-hours-time-in-security-lines/2014/12/09/05c67c0c-7fb9-11e4-81fd-8c4814dfa9d7_story.html.

workers spend helping the company reduce theft moves into the legalized wage theft column.

Grand Larceny?

How would you feel about losing 15 percent of your wages to theft? According to the report "Broken Laws, Unprotected Workers,"[8] that's the norm for low-wage workers in New York, Chicago and Los Angeles. The authors write:

> The average worker lost $51, out of average weekly earnings of $339. Assuming a full-time, full-year work schedule, we estimate that these workers lost an average of $2,634 annually due to workplace violations, out of total earnings of $17,616. That translates into wage theft of 15 percent of earnings.

The Economic Policy Institute (EPI) uses those numbers to provide a national estimate:

> The total annual wage theft from front-line workers in low-wage industries in the three cities approached $3 billion. If these findings in New York, Chicago, and Los Angeles are generalizable to the rest of the U.S. low-wage workforce of 30 million, wage theft is costing workers more than $50 billion a year.[9]

---

8   Annette Bernhardt, et al., *Broken Laws, Unprotected Workers: Violations of Employment and Labor Law in American Cities* (New York, NY: National Employment Law Project, 2009), http://www.nelp.org/page/-/brokenlaws/BrokenLawsReport2009.pdf?nocdn=1.

9   Brady Meixell and Ross Eisenbrey, *An Epidemic of Wage Theft Is Costing Workers Hundreds of Millions of Dollars a Year*, Report, Economic Policy Institute, September 11, 2014, http://www.epi.org/publication/epidemic-wage-theft-costing-workers-hundreds/#_ref1.

If this is true, then wage theft is the largest form of larceny in our economy – more than the $13.6 billion we lose each year in stolen cars, other larcenies, burglaries and robberies (using 2012 figures from the FBI[10]). Fifty billion dollars a year is enough to provide over 1.2 million people with jobs – and pay them $20 an hour.

Not me?

You may be thinking "Thank God I'm not a low-wage worker. Nobody is stealing my pay."

Or are they?

It may be that your employer isn't tampering with your overtime records or flat-out stiffing you. But your wages are being stolen nonetheless – subtly. Employers and their Wall Street backers have developed sophisticated legal ways to remove dollars that should be in our paychecks. And not just a few dollars, but about half of what we've earned.

Exhibit #1: The productivity/wage gap

To expose this hidden larceny, we need to understand the concept of productivity and how we measure it in our economy.

Productivity, a word near and dear to every manager's heart, has nothing to do with how much we are paid. It's a measurement of how much we *produce* in a given hour. We make managers happy when we produce a lot every hour, either individually or collectively. In general, in a productive economy, we collectively have the knowledge, skill, technology and organization we need to produce more each hour. Productivity is the key to the wealth of nations: The more goods and services we produce per hour, the higher our standard of living.

---

10 Federal Bureau of Investigation, "Crime in the United States 2012," Uniform Crime Reports, http://www.fbi.gov/about-us/cjis/ucr/crime-in-the-u.s/2012/crime-in-the-u.s.-2012.

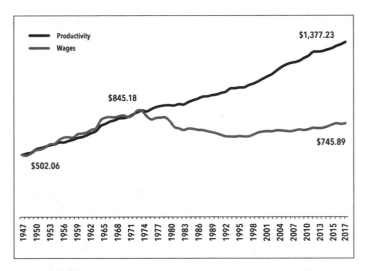

Chart 2.1: Average Weekly Wages and Productivity, 1947-2017 (Adjusted for inflation in 2017 dollars)

Sources: Average weekly wages for production and nonsupervisory workers based on Bureau of Labor Statistics data, http://www.bls.gov/data/#wages; productivity data based on Bureau of Labor Statistics, http://www.bls.gov/data/#productivity.

Of course, this crude measurement doesn't account for important qualities that don't have price tags – like a sustainable environment and a general sense of well being. But usually, countries with the highest level of productivity are better able to protect the public's health and the environment.

As Chart 2.1 shows, productivity in the U.S. economy (the line on top) has risen steadily since WWII, climbing in 65 of the last 70 years. Today we produce two and a half times more goods and services per hour of labor than we did in 1947.

For generations, as productivity increased so did real wages (that's the line at the bottom of the graph). "Real wages" is what we earn after accounting for inflation over time. As we can see, from WWII until the mid-1970s, productivity and wages were virtually insepa-rable. As productivity increased, so did wages.

In fact, in universities across the country, economists once taught that this entwinement was an economic law. They thought that if wages started to drop relative to productivity, competitive market forces would push them back up again. But, alas, as we can see, during the mid-1970s, this iron law was repealed.

But until then, wages rose steadily for a quarter century. And because they rose in tandem with productivity, profits did just fine: About two-thirds of workers' productivity gains (that is, the value of the goods they produced) went to wages, but the rest went to profits, research and development, and the replacement of plant and equipment.

Since the late 1970s, the average real wage for most of us has stalled. Productivity is still rising at a healthy pace, but we workers aren't getting our share of the value of what we produce. Corporate elites are siphoning off revenues for themselves – and cutting their investment in facilities, equipment, research, and workers. Had we continued to get our fair share of productivity gains, the average American non-supervisory production wage would be $1,377 per week in 2017. That's almost double the current average weekly wage of $746 (measured after inflation in 2017 dollars).

Think about how you'd be living with twice your current wages (like a Dane!).

What happened? Where did all that productivity money go?

We can directly blame this wage theft on Wall Street. The U.S. government began deregulating the financial industry in the late 1970s. (We'll look at why and how that happened in Chapter 4.) Under the new laws and regulations, financial maneuvers that once would have landed financiers in jail now put them in penthouses.

The new rules gave financiers a myriad of ways to siphon wealth away from corporations – that is, from our pockets to theirs. And they were outrageously successful, as Charts 2.2 and 2.3 show: From 2011 to 2016, the top 100 CEOs were able to siphon away enough of our wages to make an average of 793 times more than the average worker each year.

So where did our productivity money go? They took it.

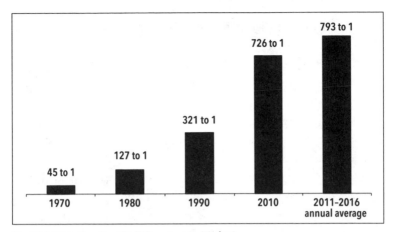

Chart 2.2: Wage Gap: Top 100 CEOs vs Average Worker*
*Average worker is production or nonsupervisory worker, based on weekly wages multiplied by 52 weeks.

Sources: CEO pay from CEO compensation surveys, *Forbes*, April/May issues, 1971-2011 and "The New York Times/Equilar 200 Highest-Paid CEO Rankings," 2012-2017; Worker earnings based on U.S. Bureau of Labor Statistics data, http://www.bls.gov/data/#wages.

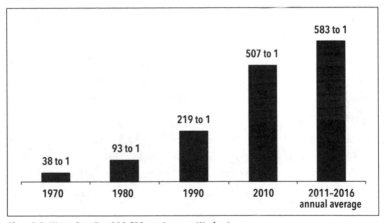

Chart 2.3: Wage Gap: Top 200 CEOs vs Average Worker*
*Average worker is production or nonsupervisory worker, based on weekly wages multiplied by 52 weeks.

Sources: CEO pay from CEO compensation surveys, *Forbes*, April/May issues, 1971-2011 and "The New York Times/Equilar 200 Highest-Paid CEO Rankings," 2012-2017; Worker earnings based on U.S. Bureau of Labor Statistics data, http://www.bls.gov/data/#wages.

But is this really theft?

Many people might think it's extreme to call the disappearance of our productivity increases a form of theft. Wouldn't that require breaking the law?

According to the dictionary, theft is defined as:

> the act of stealing, the wrongful taking and carrying away
> of the personal goods or property of another; larceny.[11]

What bosses are doing when they abscond with our productivity gains might not be illegal. But a very good case could be made that it constitutes "wrongful taking."

Just about everything that's bad about our economy stems from this "wrongful taking." As economic elites siphoned off our wages, our standard of living stopped improving – and by many measures, worsened. After capturing all that income, Wall Street went on a gambling spree, stoking the most profitable financial casino in world history. And then came... the crash of 2008. Eight million blameless workers lost their jobs in a matter of months. Long-term unemployment reached the highest levels since the Great Depression. The government spent trillions in cash and loans to bail out the biggest casino banks, the ones that had caused the crash in the first place. And meanwhile, inequality just kept on rising.

As we will see, the American Dream that so mesmerized working people around the globe is no more. And it will not return until we start doing something about that "wrongful taking."

Next, we travel back to the 1970s, to the pivotal years when those two lines – wages and productivity – pulled apart. What happened back then that so drastically changed the course of American lives?

---

11 Dictionary.com, http://dictionary.reference.com/browse/theft.

Discussion Questions:

1. In your opinion, why did the productivity and average wage lines separate in the late 1970s?

2. Why do you think the CEO/worker wage gap is growing more and more extreme?

3. How important do you think the issue of rising economic inequality is for our country?

CHAPTER 3

What Happened?

Something of great importance took place in this country around 1980, something that set runaway inequality into motion.

In a few short years, rising productivity and average wages pulled apart: Worker wages went flat and stayed flat for more than a generation. Yet both productivity and CEO salaries soared.

As we'll see in future chapters, many other important economic trends began at this same moment – and in general these trends continue today: rising consumer debt, student debt, government debt, prison population, homelessness, and child poverty.

What happened around 1980 that sparked this momentous change?

Here are some common responses we've all heard:

- Growing global competition, new advanced technologies and attacks on labor drove wages down and put workers on the defensive.
- Companies shifted production overseas to meet the competition, causing factory closures and layoffs. Those good-paying union factory jobs were replaced by low-wage service jobs especially in fast food and retail.
- Globalization, automation and the new employer offensive all made it much harder for unions to bargain for higher wages and organize new workers.
- In 1982, President Reagan fired more than 11,000 striking air traffic controllers. This gave a green light to corporations everywhere not only to resist union demands, but to crush the unions altogether.

All these things did happen. But they weren't random events. And they weren't automatic, unavoidable consequences of blind market forces. Rather, we will argue, all these events resulted from conscious human decisions. They were part of a clear, intentional shift in the fundamental philosophy driving American economic policy.

Curing the ills of the 1970s

To understand this shift we need to go back into the 1970s, a turbulent decade of global economic instability.

From WWII until the late 1960s, the U.S. economy was the envy of the world. Unemployment was low, profits were robust and wages were rising. Since the Great Depression, the U.S. government had used Keynesian policy tools to avoid deep recessions. These tools, named for British economist John Maynard Keynes, included targeted government spending, relatively high taxes and careful federal reserve policies. Through these measures, policy makers believed they could avoid depressions, maintain growth, curtail inflation, increase average wages and ensure jobs for those willing and able to work. For more than two decades it looked like they had succeeded.

But by the early 1970s, none of these policies seemed to produce the desired results. Economic historians are still debating exactly what went wrong. But they've pointed to culprits including:

- Vietnam War and Cold War military spending "overheated"[1] the economy.
- The 1973 and 1979 Arab oil boycotts quadrupled oil prices and then quadrupled them again. This sparked a dramatic rise of all prices.

---

1   In the 1960s, the economy was at full capacity, with nearly all factories and workers going at full tilt. When the government tried to increase production even further to support military operations, the economy overheated, resulting in increased prices for labor and goods.

- Europe and Japan had recovered fully from WWII, and were competing with the U.S. globally, which put pressure on U.S. markets and corporate profits. U.S. corporations responded by cutting costs, including through layoffs and sending U.S. jobs overseas.
- The political and social turmoil of the 1960s spurred the government to increase domestic spending to improve the lives of low-income Americans.

Whatever the precise causes, for the first time in American history we saw both rising unemployment and rising prices – something that Keynesians had always said was impossible. The media called it "stagflation."

The old Keynesian policies that seemed to have served the world so well after WWII came under severe attack, especially from conservative economists. They argued that freer markets would cure all our ills.

Policy makers and corporate leaders were hungry for something new and they got it. We call it the Better Business Climate model.[2]

The Better Business Climate model prescription for increasing profits, investments, jobs and incomes

The Better Business Climate model, which the U.S. adopted around 1980, has three major economic prescriptions:

1. *Cut taxes, especially on the wealthy and large corporations.*
   If we cut their taxes, the super-rich and largest corporations will have more money to invest in new ventures

---

2   Academics call the new economic philosophy neo-liberalism. In this book we will refer to it as the Better Business Climate model, which better reflects the aims of this approach. Special thanks to economist Ken Peres who first came up with this phrase and model when working on policy issues in Montana during the early 1980s. After meeting there to do various public educational programs, I adopted his model and have been using it ever since.

and improvements. And this will yield stronger, more competitive industries, more jobs and higher wages. In the 1980s, cutting taxes became the mantra of the new economic order. It still is.

Back then, there was much to cut: Tax rates on the super-rich hovered over 70 percent. (This meant that for every extra dollar the rich earned over about $800,000 a year, 70 cents would go to taxes.) Even accounting for all the deductions and loopholes the super-rich used to evade that high rate, their effective tax rate still ranged from 40 to 45 percent. Corporate tax rates stood at similar levels. They soon would come crashing down.

2. *Cut government regulations, especially on high finance.* In 1975, more than 11 percent of the U.S. economy was regulated by governmental agencies. Conservative economists argued that these regulations increased the cost of doing business and decreased efficiency. And besides, they said, if we eliminated those inefficient regulations, it would spur competition between companies, driving innovation, expansion and lower prices. And all this would reduce inflation. Our economy didn't need government policing, these economists argued. Free markets with intense competition would police themselves.

For many corporations, labor regulations were the most onerous of all, since unions and the rules that protect them limit management's ability to maximize production and profits. So the Better Business Climate plan called for weakening the rules that govern collective bargaining, union organizing, and union rights during mass layoffs, plant closings and bankruptcies. They called this "labor flexibility."

High finance was particularly interested in deregulation. Since the Great Depression, the federal government had actively limited financial maneuvers, aiming to prevent a repeat of the 1929 stock market crash. The

New Deal severely curbed speculation, stock issuance, bank competition, interest rates and many other aspects of high finance. Wall Street desperately wanted to escape from these rules so they could boost their profits.

3. *Reduce government social spending and weaken unions.* The third pillar of the plan was to weaken the governmental social safety net. Cutting social programs like food stamps and welfare payments would force more low-income people into the workforce, thus increasing the supply of low-cost labor for a growing economy.

And since the plan was to cut taxes drastically, government spending obviously had to be sliced as well – at least some kinds of government spending. The Better Business Climate advocates agreed that military spending should be protected and even increased, because fighting the Cold War was essential for global economic growth. Besides, the military establishment had very strong corporate and political backing.

So in summary the plan looks like this, at least in theory:

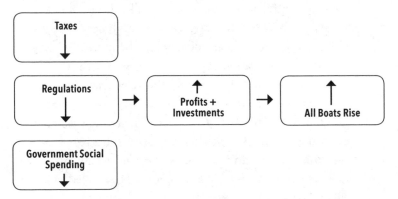

Does this cure work?

The Better Business Climate model was much more than an academic idea. It actually became the operating policy for all Republican and Democratic administrations since 1980, and it still is. We now have a great deal of information about how each element of the plan worked.

Cutting taxes

The U.S. fully enacted the tax cut component of the Better Business Climate model. As Charts 3.1 and 3.2 make clear, our political leaders have slashed effective tax rates (the rates actually paid after all deductions and loopholes) on large corporations and the super-

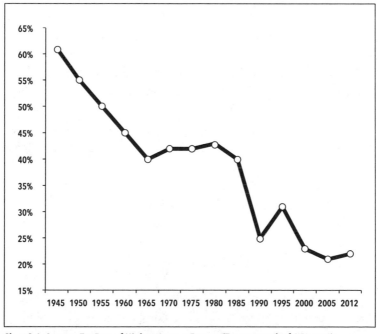

Chart 3.1: Average Tax Rate of Highest Income Earners (Top one-tenth of 1 Percent)
Source: Thomas L. Hungerford, "Taxes and the Economy: An Economic Analysis of the Top Tax Rates Since 1945 (Updated)," Congressional Research Service, December 12, 2012, http://fas.org/sgp/crs/misc/R42729.pdf.

Chart 3.2: Corporate Taxes as Percent of Corporate Profits, 1945–2015
Source: Federal Reserve Bank of St. Louis, FRED Economic Data, http://research.stlouisfed.org/fred2/graph/?g=aWA.

rich. Note that the effective tax rates on the richest Americans were already coming down after WWII. But from 1965 to 1980, these rates held steady at around 40 to 45 percent after all deductions. After that, the Better Business Climate model sent tax rates plummeting.

The story for corporate tax rates is much the same, except that the major drop started in the late 1980s. Corporate tax rates have been falling ever since. (In reality, as we'll see in Chapter 7, corporations and the wealthy have developed new strategies to avoid nearly all taxes, mostly by parking their money abroad.)

Cutting regulations

Again, mission accomplished. As Table 3.1 shows, the percent of the U.S. economy that was regulated dropped from 11.52 percent in 1975 to 2.96 percent in 2006.

Note that the financial sector was deregulated year after year

Table 3.1: Percent of the Economy that Is Regulated				
	1975	2006	% of Economy Regulated in 1975	% of Economy Regulated in 2006
Oil and Gas Extraction (1980)	Yes	No	.89%	0%
Railroads (1976, 1980)	Yes	No	.25%	0%
Airlines (1978)	Yes	No	1.02%	0%
Trucking (1980)	Yes	No	1.25%	0%
Pipelines (1978, 1985)	Yes	Yes	.07%	.07%
Electricity (1992)	Yes	Yes	1.19%	1.19%
Telecom (1984, 1996)	Yes	Partially	2.10%	.70%
Radio/TV (1985,1987)	Yes	Partially	.70%	.23%
Finance (1978, 1980, 1982, 1987, 1989, 1994, 1996, 1998, 2001, 2003)	Yes	No	3.28%	0%
Insurance	Yes	Yes	.77%	.77%
Totals			**11.52%**	**2.96%**
Percent Decline				**-74.0%**

Source: Robert W. Crandall, "Extending Deregulation: Make the U.S. Economy More Efficient," Brookings Institution, http://www.brookings.edu/~/media/research/files/papers/2007/2/28useconomics-crandall-opp08/pb_deregulation_crandall.pdf.

after year. Wall Street bankers longed to be free from New Deal era financial controls so they could expand and merge their institutions, and develop highly profitable (but risky) new forms of investment. Bankers wanted liberation from Glass-Steagall, a law that prevented them from combining federally insured banking with much riskier investment activities. The Better Business Climate model came to Wall Street's rescue, opening a path to economic freedom. As we'll see in future chapters, this deregulation was the key to runaway inequality. It still is.

Reducing government social spending

This part of the Better Business Climate plan reduced the social safety net that protects workers and families in hard times, especially

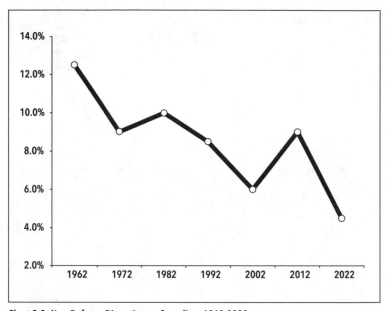

Chart 3.3: Non-Defense Discretionary Spending, 1962-2022

Source: Committee for a Responsible Federal Budget, "President's Budget Calls for Record Low Discretionary Spending, Record High Revenue," Blog, March 19, 2014, http://crfb.org/blogs/president%E2%80%99s-budget-calls-record-low-discretionary-spending-record-high-revenue.

recessions. A tattered safety net forces people to work on the employer's terms. This chart shows that non-defense discretionary spending, which includes the social safety net, has dropped since 1980, with one exception: spending on unemployment insurance and food stamps spiked after the Wall Street crash in 2008.

Unions and the Better Business Climate

The Better Business Climate model aims to weaken the power of organized labor and increase labor flexibility. After all, unions are the most potent regulatory force corporations face. In unionized facilities, each and every day, management has to live under the union contract's rules and regulations, all backed up by labor laws. Management also faces the threat of strikes and other collective action.

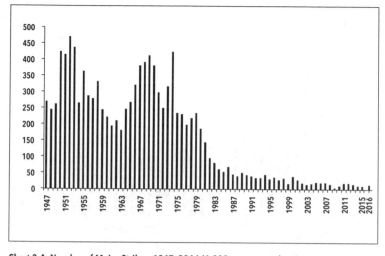

Chart 3.4: Number of Major Strikes, 1947-2016 (1,000 or more workers)
Source: Bureau of Labor Statistics, News Release, "Work Stoppages Involving 1,000 or More Workers, 1947-2016," http://www.bls.gov/news.release/wkstp.t01.htm.

When unions are strong, they can bargain for and win better wages, benefits and working conditions. And since the Better Business model's goal is to put money into the hands of corporations and wealthy investors, undermining unions was a top priority of the plan's proponents back in the 1980s and still is today.

Their plan is succeeding.

One way to measure union strength is to look at how often labor is able to use its ultimate weapon, the strike. Historically, during periods when there is lots of strike activity, wages and unionization levels rise. But since 1980, as Chart 3.4 shows, work stoppages involving 1,000 or more workers have virtually disappeared, leaving labor toothless.

The Reagan administration did indeed send a clear message to corporate America when it replaced 11,000 striking air traffic controllers in 1982. And the message was: go ahead, break that strike and send in the replacement workers – even the government is doing it. Meanwhile, courts across the land were busy weakening labor laws with rulings that made it much harder for workers to organize and win.

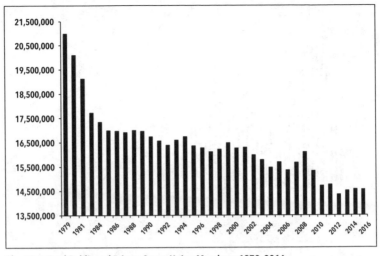

Chart 3.5: Total Public and Private Sector Union Members, 1979–2016
Source: Barry Hirsch and David MacPherson, "Union Membership and Coverage Database," http://unionstats.com/.

As a result, the number of dues-paying union members dropped, draining union strength and coffers, even as the workforce was growing (see Chart 3.5).[3]

All boats rise?

The Better Business Climate model has achieved its goals when it comes to taxes, regulations, government safety net spending, unionization and strikes.

But all this was supposed to lead to something else: rising boats for everyone. The yachts of the super-rich certainly were crafted and took sail. But we working people are still in our dinghies, and they're taking on water. Chart 3.6 shows how the super-rich have been doing under the Better Business Climate model. The line at the bottom represents the average incomes of the bottom 90 percent of Americans during the same period.

---

3   Many refer to "union density" – that is, the percent of all workers who are in unions – to measure how unions are doing. Union density has declined from a high of 35 percent of all private sector workers in 1955 to under 7 percent today. But we think the more telling number is the absolute decline in union members. That's what unions most notice and what most undermines their effectiveness.

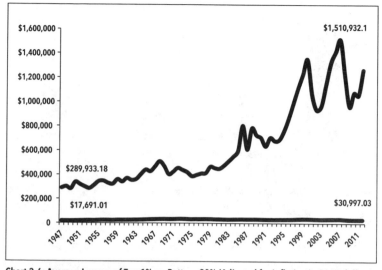

Chart 3.6: Average Income of Top 1% vs. Bottom 90% (Adjusted for inflation in 2012 dollars)
Source: Alvaredo, Facundo, et al., "The World Top Incomes Database," http://topincomes.g-mond.parisschoolofeconomics.eu/.

What's the main cause of runaway inequality?

The Better Business Climate model has clearly led to runaway inequality. But a new study suggests that one element of the model bears more responsibility for inequality than all the others.

In its *Global Wage Report 2012/13*,[4] the International Labor Organization produced an eye-popping study of 71 countries that tested the relative significance of these possible causes of wage inequality: globalization, new technology, and cutbacks in government support for workers and unions. They also added another possible explanation to the list: "financialization" – that is, how much of a nation's economy is devoted to Wall Street-like financial activities.[5] It's all about financial strip-mining.

---

4   International Labour Office, *Global Wage Report 2012/13: Wages and Equitable Growth* (Geneva: ILO, 2013), Figure 38, p. 52, http://www.ilo.org/wcmsp5/groups/public/---dgreports/---dcomm/---publ/documents/publication/wcms_194843.pdf.

5   Professor Gerald Epstein, one of the first economists to use this term, writes in 2001 that "Financialization refers to the increasing importance of financial markets, financial motives, financial institutions, and financial elites in the operation of

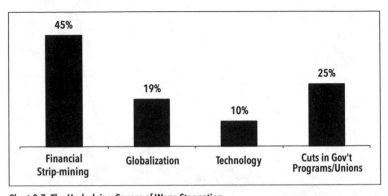

Chart 3.7: The Underlying Causes of Wage Stagnation
Source: International Labour Organization, *Global Wage Report 2012/13: Wages and Equitable Growth* (Geneva: ILO, 2014), http://www.ilo.org/global/research/global-reports/global-wage-report/2012/WCMS_194843/lang--en/index.htm.

They compared data from different countries to assess which factors contributed most to wage stagnation (and resulting inequality). For example, do countries with more global trade have more or less inequality? Do countries with more advanced technology see workers' wages rise or fall? Do countries with large labor movements have higher wages than those with smaller labor movements?

Chart 3.7 summarizes the ILO's startling results for developed economies.

Occupy Wall Street apparently had it right: Financial activities are an important factor, perhaps even the *most* important factor, in the rise of runaway inequality.

Financial strip-mining as the hidden driver of the Better Business Climate model

The ILO study suggests (at least to us) that the deregulation of Wall Street beginning in the late 1970s is the main culprit in our story.

In upcoming chapters we'll take a closer look at financialization and how it propels runaway inequality.

---

the economy and its governing institutions, both at the national and international levels." "Financialization, Rentier Interests, and Central Bank Policy," paper prepared for the PERI Conference on Financialization of the World Economy, December 2001, http://www.peri.umass.edu/fileadmin/pdf/financial/fin_Epstein.pdf.

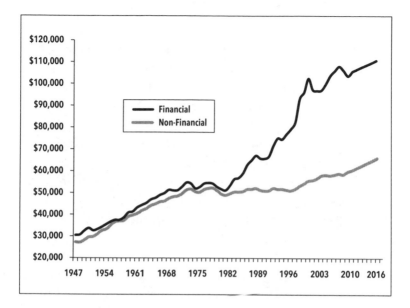

Chart 3.8: Financial Sector vs. Non-Financial Sector Yearly Compensation, 1947–2016 (Adjusted for inflation in 2010 dollars)
Source: Data compiled by the author from Bureau of Economic Analysis, "National Income and Product Accounts Tables, Section 6 - Income and Employment by Industry," http://www.bea.gov/iTable/iTable.cfm?ReqID=9&step=1.

But first, we'll look at a few more clues about what really happened in 1980.

Chart 3.8 compares incomes in the financial sector[6] to incomes in all the other sectors of the economy. The average income for the financial sector includes everyone working there, from CEOs to administrative assistants.

The chart reveals three new clues:

- From WWII until around 1980, there was nothing special about a job on Wall Street. Given your experience, educational background and skills, your income would be about the same whether you worked for a big bank or a big car company.

---

6 The financial sector includes banks, insurance, and all kinds of investment firms.

- From 1980 on, financial incomes soared while non-financial incomes leveled out. Something major must have changed in the economy to create such a wage premium for financial employees. And most likely, that something had a lot to do with the workings of the financial sector.
- Notice that this chart has nearly the exact same shape over the same timeframe as the productivity/wage chart (Chart 2.1) in Chapter 2. Its remarkable similarity strongly suggests a relationship between financial deregulation and the decoupling of productivity and workers' wages.

This we do know. Something profound did indeed happen around 1980: The Better Business Climate model took hold of government policy. Deregulation, tax cuts, and social spending cuts soon followed. Unions were stifled and Wall Street was unleashed. And that, according to the ILO study, may have had the biggest impact of all.

Let's now look at how Wall Street produces runaway inequality in our workplaces.

Discussion Questions:

1. What are the basic elements of the Better Business Climate model? What was it designed to cure?

2. In your opinion, how successful has the Better Business Climate model been in cutting taxes, regulations, and social spending?

3. What has been its impact on unions?

4. What does the ILO report say is the main cause of wage stagnation?

The Financial Strip-mining of America

Ever since our political leaders began deregulating the financial industry back in the late 1970s, people on Wall Street have gotten richer, while regular Americans have fallen further and further behind. This is not a coincidence: Income and wealth are in fact being transferred from us to Wall Street. How did the CEO/worker pay gap jump from 45 to one in 1970 to a whopping 793 to one by 2016? And what does deregulation have to do with it?

From "Retain and Reinvest" to "Downsize and Distribute"

Economics professor William Lazonick of the University of Massachusetts-Lowell provides brilliant insight into this.[1] He observes that the dramatic jump in the CEO/worker pay gap coincides with an equally dramatic change in the fundamental structure and ethos of the modern corporation.

When you think about it, looking inside the corporation makes sense: If our wages have stopped rising while productivity and CEO incomes have soared, it must have something to do with the fundamental structure of where we work.

Until the 1980s, the basic philosophy of corporate America was "retain and reinvest." Corporate survival and prosperity depended on plowing back most of a corporation's profits into increased worker wages and training, research and development, and new plant and equipment. Banks provided loans for expansion and for mergers.

---

1   William Lazonick, "Profits Without Prosperity," *Harvard Business Review*, September 2014, https://hbr.org/2014/09/profits-without-prosperity.

Meanwhile, stringent New Deal regulations kept high finance in check. And so, as we saw in the previous chapter, working on Wall Street was not more lucrative than working anywhere else.

Then came financial deregulation, when Wall Street escaped from its New Deal shackles. Almost immediately a new breed of financiers appeared to buy up companies. Instead of creating new value *within* the corporation, these corporate raiders (today called private equity and hedge fund managers) wanted to extract value *out and away from* the corporation and into their pockets.

What they did was nothing short of revolutionary. It *should* have been nothing short of illegal. They transformed the corporate ethos of "retain and reinvest" into "downsize and distribute."

Here's how downsize and distribute works:

Step 1: Buy a company with borrowed money and then use earnings from the company to pay back the loans. With money they've raised from wealthy backers, pension funds and banks, the corporate raiders buy a company they judge to be "undervalued" (that is, they think they can extract more money from the company than are its current managers).

As Chart 4.1 shows, mergers and acquisitions weren't very common around the world at the beginning of the 1980s. But once the U.S. began deregulating financial markets, these deals became hugely popular – and their value rose sky-high. Their rise matches the dramatic jump in income for financial elites.

Step 2: Take a hefty fee for pulling off the deal. The corporate raiders use some of the borrowed money to pay themselves enormous fees, right off the top. This provides a quick return on their investment, but does nothing to improve the acquired company.

Step 3: Change the way CEOs are paid. This is a game changer. The new investors hire a CEO who will do their bidding. This requires rewarding the CEO with a new form of pay – stock options or similar schemes that tie compensation to the value of the company's

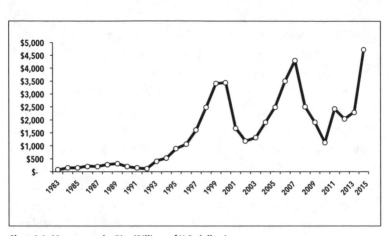

Chart 4.1: Mergers on the Rise (Billions of U.S. dollars)
Source: U.S. Bureau of the Census, *Statistical Abstract of the United States*, various years, based on Thomson Financial; and Thomson Reuters, *Mergers & Acquisitions Review*.

stocks. The more the company share price rises, the more money for the corporate raiders and the CEO.

Step 4: Raise the stock price by using corporate revenues to buy back the company's own stocks. If you can reduce the number of shares in a company, the value of each remaining share must increase. So one of the quickest ways to drive up the price of your company's own stock is to buy back as many shares as possible. By taking those shares out of circulation, each outstanding share is worth more.

The new CEO incentive

The CEO's new top goal is to raise the stock price, so they're eager to plow the firm's revenues into buying up as many of the company's own shares as possible. And if profits are slim, they borrow more money to buy even more shares.

As Chart 4.2 shows, buying back your own stock became the new corporate way of life. (Many thanks to Professor Lazonick for providing the raw data.)

Let's go over this chart carefully. Before around 1980, when Wall

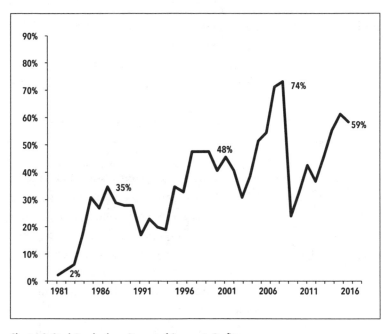

Chart 4.2: Stock Buy-backs as Percent of Corporate Profits
Source: S+P Compustat, compiled and corrected by Mustafa Erdem Sakinç.

Street was still tightly regulated, there were virtually no stock buy-backs. Corporations didn't do that kind of thing because CEOs were not paid in stock options. Instead, they relied on salaries – really good ones that paid 20 to 40 times what the average worker earned. Instead of buying back shares, CEOs generally invested corporate earnings in their workers' skills and wages, hoping to retain a productive workforce that would make their business prosper over the long haul.

But as deregulation set in, the corporate raiders began snatching up companies and changing their corporate culture. They didn't care about the long haul, they just wanted to drive up the value of their new companies as quickly as possible. The more CEOs were paid through stock options, the more corporate revenues were diverted to buy back shares.

As the chart shows, by the time of the 2008 Wall Street crash, CEOs were using 75 percent of their companies' revenues to buy back their own stocks. At the same time, CEOs piled up loans to buy up even more stock. After buying the stock and paying off the loans, only a trickle of corporate revenue was left for reinvesting in the company. (The loan payments and fees, of course, went to Wall Street banks and investment firms.)

So how do today's CEOs ever run a prosperous company if they use most of the revenues for share buy-backs?

Step 5: From "retain and invest" to "downsize and distribute." The answer is extraction. CEOs make their companies profitable by extracting as much value as possible. They cut worker training, wages and benefits, R&D and new plant and equipment to the bone. They eliminate older plants. They outsource production to low-wage areas around the world. They replace permanent employees with temporaries. They reduce or eliminate benefits like health care and pensions. They undermine unions, and sometimes use bankruptcy to break contracts, further reducing employee costs. The fees for all this "financial engineering" go to Wall Street.

These stock-option-loaded CEOs have become a vital part of Wall Street – they are its on-site, wealth extraction overseers. Nearly all corporations, whether raided or not, now follow this lucrative model. Call it corporate strip-mining.

Back in the 1950s, people were actually appalled when then GM CEO Charles E. Wilson was misquoted as saying: "What is good for GM is good for the country." The public wondered, How dare he be so self-centered! (Wilson's actual words were "...what was good for our country was good for General Motors, and vice versa.")

But today Wilson seems community-spirited compared to hedge fund and private equity corporate raiders. Wilson may have been arrogant, but at least he believed that his company was vital to society's well-being. He seemed proud that GM's wages and expenditures enriched workers and local communities.

The motto for today's corporate raiders is more like, "What's good for me is all that counts." Corporate raiders wouldn't dare claim that their slash-and-burn policies and billion-dollar incomes are good for the thousands of communities that lost facilities and jobs.

Where did the stock buy-back idea come from?

The Better Business Climate model doesn't call for rewarding CEOs with stock options or for corporate raiding. It doesn't tell CEOs to shift from "retain and reinvest" to "downsize and distribute." So how exactly did these practices catch on?

The story of how our economy was financialized actually has two intermingled currents. One features the corporate raider and his (yep, pretty much all men) team of bankers and corporate CEOs hungry to unlock "hidden value," one raid at a time. The other current features a different kind of CEO who wants to do his own dirty work. These CEOs, like the raiders, want to make their companies lean and mean so they can enrich themselves. But rather than wait for a raider to do the slicing and dicing, these managers wield the knife themselves.

No one was a more masterful knife-wielder than Jack Welch, the CEO of General Electric. In a briefing for financial analysts in New York in 1981, "Growing Fast in a Slow-Growth Economy," Welch declared that the only true measure of corporate and CEO success is maximizing the return to shareholders. Many credit the talk with launching the "shareholder value" movement. Welch argued that companies like GE (which had become a vast conglomerate producing many different products in many different markets) should sell off any subsidiaries that were not number one or two in their respective markets. He advocated ruthlessly cutting costs by laying off employees and slashing research and development.

Welch was true to his word. In just five years (1980 to 1985), he reduced GE's workforce from 411,000 to 299,000 and cut back on basic research. Welch also developed a highly profitable financial wing (GE Finance) that went on to generate more than a third of the company's profits. The market value of GE skyrocketed. Welch proved that you could make more money – much more money – by producing fewer tangible goods.

In 1979, before Welch took a hatchet to his company, only four U.S. corporations netted more profit than GE. The company was staid, but successful. But that wasn't going to yield the hundreds of millions in stock options Welch and his officers coveted.

Word of Welch's thesis spread through the upper corporate echelons: Corporate managers must align their interests with the short-term interests of stockholders; not workers, not consumers, not the future of the company, and not society. (Academics call this the "agency theory.")

This was an enormous shift. There is nothing in corporate law that says a corporation's primary goal must be to maximize short-term shareholder value. In fact, short-term shareholder value is an unstable thing. It is measured by short-term stock prices, which often gyrate based on expectations of what a stock will do in the future, rather than what it actually does.

Here's an analogy: Stock prices are to the real value of a company as the betting line for football games is to the real score. People bet on football based on expectations. But those bets don't determine the real score.

But if you are rewarded with stock-options, then the short-term fluctuations (the betting line) are much more important to you than the real value of the company (the real score).[2]

Top corporate managers become financial strip-miners

To make this new idea work, top managers had to become members of the investor class. They were rewarded with stock options, mega-salaries and golden parachutes (lavish retirement packages) that often matched or exceeded the exploding earnings of Wall Street elites.

---

2   Steve Denning, "The Dumbest Idea in the World: Maximizing Shareholder Value," *Forbes.com*, November 28, 2011, http://www.forbes.com/sites/stevedenning/ 2011/11/28/maximizing-shareholder-value-the-dumbest-idea-in-the-world/.

Corporate managers became obsessed with cashing in on those stock options. Growing profits through slow and steady corporate growth – the old capitalist way of doing business – was too slow and unpredictable. Instead, managers could spike stock prices by cutting wages, slashing the workforce, raiding pensions, starving R&D, outsourcing jobs, reducing capital expenditures, and using borrowed money and retained earnings to buy back existing shares to drive up their short-term price. And then collect on their hefty stock options.

The two economists whose 1976 paper on the "agency theory" laid the foundation for using stock options to compensate executives, Michael Jensen and William Meckling, actually had a slightly different idea in mind. They had the quaint notion that top managers should suffer the consequences of corporate losses and failures along with workers, not just capture the upside through short-term stock manipulation. If CEOs were paid through stock options, Jenson and Meckling reasoned, then when the company did well, the CEO would gain income. But when the company did poorly, the CEO's compensation would drop. To these academics this sounded both fair and practical.

But Wall Street investment bankers and their corporate management partners aren't dummies. They constructed incentives that insured that managers would always come out on top: If shareholder value increased, management's stock options would soar in value. If the firm crashed, managers found ways to protect themselves from losing income. And if the managers were ousted during a corporate raid, they would float away to retirement with enormous golden parachutes, all in the name of shareholder value. In short, there was no downside for CEOs and other top managers. Little wonder that these days CEOs make 793 times more than workers.

The big payoff for corporate invaders

In the 1980s, financiers everywhere took careful notice of a remarkable leveraged buyout (purchase of a corporation using mostly borrowed money) engineered by William Simon. Simon was Treasury Secretary under Nixon, Ford and Carter. Some people also remember him as the guy who cheered on the murderous Pinochet regime in Chile, who convinced Gerald Ford not to save New York City from its 1975 fiscal crisis, and who then went on to run the ultra-conservative Olin Foundation.

In 1982, Simon and two partners put up $1 million and borrowed another $79 million to buy (and take private)[3] Gibson Greetings, the third-largest greeting card company in the U.S. This deal was the equivalent of putting a 1.3 percent down payment on your home. Sixteen months later they sold it for an incredible $290 million, transforming Simon's initial $333,000 investment into a $66 million fortune.

This was the largest payout anyone had ever heard of on Wall Street. What did Simon and friends do to earn all that money? Some credited Simon's excellent reputation and many VIP contacts for giving him and his partners this exceptional opportunity. Others said that Simon and company were just lucky – they bought low during a recession and sold high when the stock market turned around. In any case, the deal left the company with massive debt. And it left Simon and friends with millions in extracted profits.

Michael Milken, Ivan Boesky, Henry Kravis, T. Boone Pickens and a slew of corporate raiders were enthralled. Clearly, billions could be made by buying up American companies and loading them with mountains of debt. In the new deregulatory environment, they were free to float unrated high-yield bonds (junk bonds) to finance hundreds of corporate takeovers. And wonderfully for them, all the interest on that debt was tax-deductible.

---

3   Taking private means buying all the company's shares so that they are no longer available for the public to buy on stock markets.

With every large takeover the raiders and their compatriots raked in hundreds of millions of dollars in fees. There were fees for the bankers who advised the various parties, for Michael Milken who created (and illegally manipulated) the market for the junk bonds, for the arbitragers (like Boesky) who used insider information to buy up the stock before the raids, for the corporate managers who either received stock options to stay on to manage the purchased company or golden parachutes to leave, and for the big investors who bought in early. Even the existing shareholders made out, since their stocks were bought up at a premium. Companies that had been limping along were turned into money factories – at least for a while. No one worried much about the dislocated workers and devastated communities left behind after these companies were sucked dry.

While the raiders were getting rich off the deindustrialization of America, their apologists heralded them as the new champions of modern capitalism. These financialists weren't really raiders, the apologists argued. They were agents of change, bringing about much needed restructuring that would increase corporate efficiency. They were shaking up fat and lazy managers who were content with their perks and weren't doing a thing to squeeze more money out of their firms. The corporate raiders were market-makers whose drive for corporate control was disciplining the managers, teaching them the importance of maximizing shareholder value. They cleaned away the old dead wood and made room for new managers, new products, and new jobs.

Over time, the targeted companies grew in number and variety. And in the process, the surpluses these companies generated in the real economy – money that once would have been used to grow the firm, improve working conditions and increase wages – was siphoned away to the financial sector. Corporate taxes and employee income taxes from these companies, which had helped fund public education and other social priorities, shrank, while tax-exempt interest payments to financiers grew.

Thanks to a handful of prosecutions and the movie *Wall Street*, we all came to blame "greed" for these ills. To be sure, there were many bad actors, some of whom went to jail. But many of the people who legitimized financial strip-mining and put us on the path toward runaway inequality didn't go to jail. Many even thought they were helping to build a new economy.

Even after the Great Recession began in 2008, people continued to view our economy as a set of assets whose value can be unlocked through financial engineering. The raiding continues to this day. The "corporate raiders" now have more pleasant-sounding titles: They're hedge fund managers and lead private equity firms. But their goal is the same: buying up companies and siphoning off as much value as possible.

Raiding has become so commonplace that most financial writers just assume that buying up companies and grabbing their cash-flow creates new value. The enormous sums these new raiders pocket are their just rewards for their astute investment management. It's the new conventional wisdom. Few people notice that the money is not adding new wealth to our society; it is simply being transferred from the real economy to the financial elites.

The collapse of the Better Business Climate model

Recall that the stated goal of the Better Business Climate model was to create a massive investment and profit boom to make all boats rise. By now we're starting to see why that didn't work:

- Unleashing Wall Street from its New Deal controls (a Better Business Climate model goal) ultimately enabled corporate raiders to buy up companies, load them up with debt and extract their revenues – with economically devastating effects.
- Paying CEOs with stock options created a new corporate culture focused on increasing short-term shareholder value through stock buy-backs, layoffs, and wage and benefit cuts.

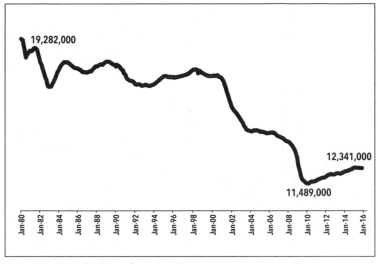

Chart 4.3: Decline of U.S. Manufacturing Jobs
Source: U.S. Bureau of Labor Statistics, "Employment," http://www.bls.gov/data/#employment.

- Compensation for corporate raiders, investment bankers and CEOs soared while worker pay stagnated.
- Financial strip-mining eliminated millions of better-paying U.S. manufacturing jobs (see Chart 4.3), dragging down average worker wages.

The Better Business Climate model does indeed create an investment and profit boom, but the lion's share of those profits come from financial strip-mining and go to Wall Street and CEOs. This is trickle-up economics: The money flows from the bottom to the top.

As Chart 4.4 shows, since 1980 the financial sector has been gobbling up more and more of all corporate profits, reaching a peak of 42.5 percent by 2002. The 2008 crash crushed Wall Street profits, but they're back up to more than a quarter of all corporate profits as of 2017.

Even more amazing: In 1970 and 1980, the financial sector accounted for about 10 to 15 percent of all corporate profits, but only about 5 percent of all U.S. jobs. Today, the financial sector

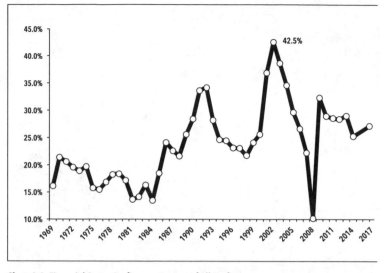

Chart 4.4: Financial Sector Profits as a Percent of All Profits
Source: Author's calculations based on Bureau of Economic Affairs, National Income and Product Accounts Tables, Table 6.16, "Corporate Profits by Industry," http://bea.gov//national/nipaweb/DownSS2.asp.

reaps more than 25 percent of all profits. And as for jobs? Only about 6 percent of U.S. jobs are in the financial sector. No wonder financial incomes are exploding.

At best, the Better Business Climate model is now a fragile veneer for policies that inevitably result in higher CEO and Wall Street compensation and stagnating incomes for the rest of us. It covers up financial strip-mining.

So whenever you hear a politician or an economist say we need to "boost business confidence" or create a "better business climate," think: "runaway inequality."

Discussion Questions:

1. Why did corporations go from "retain and reinvest" to "downsize and distribute?"

2. Has your company been bought and sold in the last ten years?

3. Does your company buy back its stock?

4. What has happened to your wages, benefits and working conditions over the past decade?

PART TWO

The Decline of
American Exceptionalism

CHAPTER 5

We're Number One! (or are we?)

Americans tend to overestimate the U.S.'s position in the world, partly because we underestimate runaway inequality. In the next two chapters, we'll explore the impact of runaway inequality on how we rank compared to other developed nations. Our goal is to grasp how runaway inequality has changed our country – and see the limits of what historians call "American exceptionalism."

Who are we?

American exceptionalism forms the core of our national self-image. Most of us believe that our country does just about everything better than everyone else – that we're blessed with enormous resources, talented people and more political freedom than any other nation in history. Our forefathers, we are taught, built a new nation far advanced from the decaying European feudal order. They constructed a society and a political system that made the ideal of upward mobility a reality.

Our open democracy and vast opportunities drew peoples from all over the world. With them came the talent and vitality to build an exceptional nation. Of course, slaves and Native Americans didn't get to partake in this advancement, and women were second-class citizens. Jim Crow denied African-Americans any access at all to the American dream until the civil rights movement finally broke through. But we also use our narratives of slavery and freedom to validate our greatness as a nation: What other society has such diversity and opportunity for its minorities?

Along the way, we saved the world from fascism and communism and flooded the universe with our technological wonders as well as our music and film. We are the richest, most productive people on the planet, and we should embrace our exceptional role in the world.

As the Pew Research Center results in Table 5.1 make clear, as of 2017 this belief was deeply embedded.

However, more recent polls find that fewer Americans are buying into this idea. When asked if "the U.S. stands above all other countries," the Pew Research Center (Table 5.2) found a sharp overall drop in those who agreed.

What's most interesting is how much the responses vary by age. The younger you are, the less likely that you buy into the overall idea of American exceptionalism. Those over 65 are almost twice as likely to agree (40%) that the "U.S. stands above all other countries" than those between 19 and 29 years of age (28%).

There are many possible reasons for this variation by age.

One might be that people over 65 grew up in an era when wages and productivity rose together, and they probably saw their own family's standard of living rise. (We certainly did in our working class family.) When these folks came of age, the CEO-worker wage gap was no more than 45 to one. They have, in fact, lived in a country whose standard of living and social mobility were envied around the world.

The younger generation, however, has grown up in an era of runaway inequality. Upward mobility, as we will see, is no longer assured. Wages are frozen. And the super-rich are growing vastly richer. No wonder young people have more doubts about American exceptionalism. They're just not feeling it in their daily lives.

Before proceeding further, a word of caution: A good deal of what follows might rub against the grain of some readers (especially old folks like me). However, our goal is not to denigrate America. Rather, it is to help us become a more caring and just society. Hopefully we can get beyond the conversation stopper – America: Love it or Leave it. If we truly love our nation and believe it to

Table 5.1: 2017 Pew Research Center Poll "U.S. stands above all other countries in the world"		
	% Yes	% No
All Americans	85	14
Democrats	79	20
Republicans	93	7

Source: Laura Thorsett and Jocelyn Kiley, "Most Americans Say the U.S. Is Among the Greatest Countries in the World," Pew Research Center, June 30, 2017, http://www.pewresearch.org/fact-tank/2017/06/30/most-americans-say-the-u-s-is-among-the-greatest-countries-in-the-world/.

Table 5.2: 2017 Pew Research Center Poll Young People Least Likely to Say U.S. Is Greatest Country in World			
% who say U.S. "stands above all other countries."			
Age	2011	2014	2017
18-29	27%	15%	12%
30-49	38%	26%	27%
50-64	40%	33%	33%
65+	50%	40%	44%

Source: Alec Tyson, "Most Americans Think the U.S. Is Great, But Fewer Say It's the Greatest," Pew Research Center, July 2, 2014, http://www.pewresearch.org/fact-tank/2014/07/02/most-americans-think-the-u-s-is-great-but-fewer-say-its-the-greatest/; and Laura Thorsett and Jocelyn Kiley, "Most Americans Say the U.S. Is Among the Greatest Countries in the World," Pew Research Center, June 30, 2017, http://www.pewresearrch org/fact-tank/2017/06/30/most-americans-say-the-u-s-is among-the-greatest-countries-in-the-world/.

be exceptional, we need to become exceptionally good at taming runaway inequality.

We lead the world in inequality

This is a very odd headline for someone in my generation to write. I grew up in a white, working class family in the 1950s and '60s. We grew up believing that America was one of the fairest nations in world history, not the most unequal. No, we were never a purely egalitarian society, nor did we profess to be. But we seemed to be committed to giving a fair shake to working people. Certainly, we were the antithesis of a European aristocracy. We believed we could rise as high as our talents and hard work could take us. We didn't

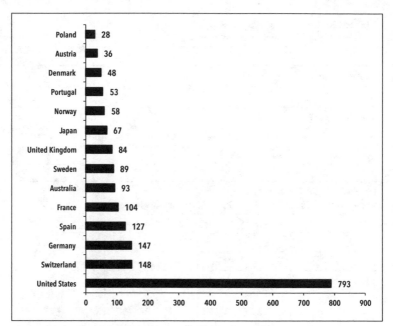

Chart 5.1: CEO-Average Worker Wage Gap: International Comparison
Sources: Data from Sorapop Kiatpongsan and Michael I. Norton, "How Much (More) Should CEOs Make?" *Perspectives on Psychological Science*, Vol. 9 (2014); and author's research for United States gap.

need to be born rich to make it. (Granted, if we had grown up in a black, working class family during the same period, our outlook might have been a little less optimistic.)

The data suggest that we're living in a very different America today.

Of course, the U.S. isn't the only country in the world struggling with rising inequality. The process of financialization we reviewed in Chapter 4 has encircled the globe. Nearly every country over the last three decades has accepted some financial deregulation, and suffered its consequences. But deregulation has had a bigger impact here in the home of Wall Street than in any other country. And as we'll see in later chapters, the growing political power of Wall Street has deepened the impact of deregulation here in the U.S.

So it should come as no surprise that we lead the world when it comes to the CEO/worker wage gap (see Chart 5.1).

Poorer than Taiwan?

We know that in the U.S., workers' wages have stagnated. So how is the average American worker doing these days, compared to workers in other countries? The answer may surprise you.

The first astounding statistic is wealth – that is, how much we own (house, car, bank accounts, stocks, bonds, etc.) minus what we owe (credit card debt, loans, mortgages, etc.). Here we look at the "typical" American – the median person smack in the middle of the wealth distribution, with 50 percent of the population above, and 50 percent below. Median is a more telling statistic than average, because the average lumps in the very, very rich, which pulls up the numbers. If the top 1 percent have most of the nation's wealth, then the average will be much higher than the median.

As Chart 5.2 shows, the median wealth for the "typical" American is $26,687. The median American is even poorer than his

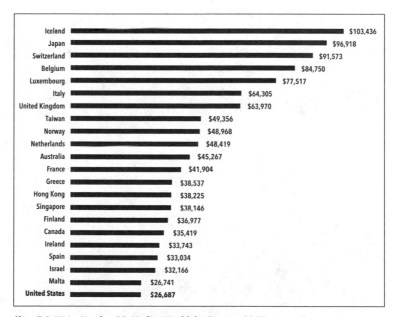

Chart 5.2: We're Number 22: Median Wealth by Country, 2015
Source: Credit Suise, *Global Wealth Data Book, 2016*, http://economics.uwo.ca/people/davies_docs/global-wealth-databook-2014-v2.pdf.

or her equivalent in Taiwan. The median Icelander is four times wealthier. The Swiss are more than three times as wealthy.

After 30 years of runaway inequality in the U.S., we rank 22nd among nations in median wealth.

Meanwhile, we rule the world when it comes to billionaires: We scored 565 billionaires in 2017. China was a distant second, with 319 billionaires.[1]

We also lead the world when it comes to super-millionaires, also known as "Ultra High Net Worth" individuals. To make this list you need to have over $50 million in wealth (assets minus liabilities). Of the 128,220 super-millionaires in the world, 49 percent are Americans. The next highest is China with 6 percent.

The top 1 percent share of all income

Another way to rank inequality by nation is to look at how much of the total income pie goes to the top 1 percent. The more the top 1 percent gets, the less there is to spread over the bottom 99 percent. In a perfectly egalitarian society the top 1 percent would receive 1 percent of the country's income.

Table 5.3: Top 1% Share of All Income			
United States	**19.34**	Australia	9.17
United Kingdom	12.93	Spain	8.20
Germany	12.71	New Zealand	8.13
South Korea	12.23	France	8.08
Canada	12.22	Norway	7.80
Ireland	10.50	Finland	7.46
Portugal	9.73	Sweden	7.13
Japan	9.51	Denmark	6.41
Italy	9.38	Netherlands	6.33

Source: Facundo Alvaredo, et al., "The World's Top Income Database," Paris School of Economics, http://topincomes. parisschoolofeconomics.eu/.

1 Louisa Kroll and Kerry Dolan, "Forbes 2017 Billionaire List," *Forbes*, March 20, 2017.

As Table 5.3 shows, by this measure the Netherlands and Denmark are the most egalitarian countries: There, the top 1 percent receive less than 6.5 percent of the national income. Once again, we are world leaders with our 1 percent receiving almost 20 percent of all U.S. income. We are far more unequal than the U.K., which comes in at number two on this list.

Getting the Gini back into the bottle?

Economists' favorite measure of inequality is called the Gini coefficient, named after the Italian statistician and demographer Corrado Gini (1884–1965). A Gini coefficient score of 0 means that everyone in the country has exactly the same income. A score of 100 means that one person has all the income. Obviously, every nation is somewhere in between. However, once again, among the industrialized countries, we rank number one when it comes to the Gini score of inequality (see Table 5.4). Out of 150 countries, the United States is the 40th most unequal (110 countries are more equal than us).

Table 5.4: Inequality Rankings: Gini Coefficient			
United States	**45.0**	Ireland	31.3
Israel	42.8	Australia	30.3
Russia	41.2	Netherlands	30.3
Japan	37.9	Switzerland	29.5
New Zealand	36.2	France	29.2
Spain	35.9	Austria	29.2
Korea (S)	34.1	Denmark	28.8
Portugal	33.9	Germany	27.0
United Kingdom	32.4	Norway	26.8
Canada	32.1	Sweden	24.9
Italy	31.9	Finland	21.5
Source: Central Intelligence Agency, "Country Comparison: Distribution of Family Income, GINI Index," Most recent data available, *The World Factbook*, https://www.cia.gov/library/publications/the-world-factbook/rankorder/2172rank.html, accessed October 9, 2017.			

CHAPTER 5

The world's fastest sprinter in the runaway inequality race?

Those who believe that the free market can cure all ills might hope that runaway inequality in America would slow down as the natural forces of economic competition reduce the income gap. Perhaps soon we won't be the most unequal country on earth, and other countries will catch up. Or maybe inequality swings like a pendulum, and now it's swinging back to less inequality when compared to other countries.

So we want to find out which countries experienced the greatest *increases* in inequality in recent years. Given the global power of high finance and the spread of financial deregulation around the globe, we would expect that inequality has increased not just in the U.S. but around the world. Is it now escalating faster in those other countries?

To find answers we turn to the Organisation for Economic Co-operation and Development's 2011 report, *Divided We Stand: Why Inequality Keeps Rising*.

Let's go over the OECD chart (Chart 5.3) carefully. It measures the share of all income in a country that goes to the top 1 percent – just as we saw in Table 5.3. But this time it takes this measurement at two points in time – in 1990, when financialization was just blossoming in the U.S. and England, and in 2007 just before the Wall Street crash, when financialization was in full bloom all around the world.

If the line is small or non-existent, then inequality didn't change very much between 1990 and 2007.

Notice that the Netherlands saw a decline in the share going to the top 1 percent. Germany, Belgium, Denmark, France, and Spain changed very little. So it would be reasonable to say that these countries are not experiencing runaway inequality. The country with the most dramatic increase by far in the share going to the top 1 percent was the United States.

Once again, the U.S. leads the pack not just in the absolute size of inequality but also in its increase. By 1990, the U.S. already was

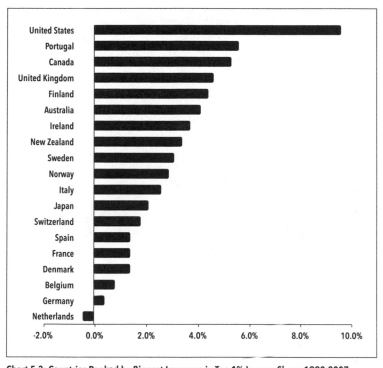

Chart 5.3: Countries Ranked by Biggest Increases in Top 1% Income Share, 1990-2007
Source: OECD, *Divided We Stand: Why Inequality Keeps Rising* (OECD Publishing, 2011), https://dx.doi.org/10.1787/9789
264119536-en.

the most unequal country on this list. It then proceeded to become
even more unequal more quickly than all the other nations.

Clearly we are truly exceptional when it comes to runaway
inequality. In the next chapter we'll see if this exceptionalism
carries into our quality of life.

Discussion Questions:

1. Is America the greatest country in the world? Why or why not?

2. Why are young people less certain about American exceptionalism?

3. Why do you think economic inequality is so much higher in the U.S. than other developed nations?

4. What do you think is the best measure of economic inequality?

We're No Longer Number One

Clearly, we lead the world in just about every significant measure of inequality. But what does that really have to do with the way we lead our lives?

Better Business Climate-oriented economists would argue that we're making way too much of inequality – after all, rising inequality is what creates a wealthier economy that helps us all. People work harder to get richer and richer, and that makes the economy grow. Inequality drives us toward a better standard of living for ourselves and our children for generations to come.

If that's the case, then the U.S. should lead the world when it comes to health, happiness, well-being, the environment, upward mobility, education and other measures of our quality of life.

Let's then look at the data. Are we number one in something other than inequality?

Longevity and happiness

Arguably, one of the best measures of a country's greatness is whether its residents lead long and fulfilling lives. So where do we rank on longevity? Unfortunately, we're number 20 when it comes to average life span among the 22 most developed nations (see Table 6.1).

But the outlook for low-income Americans is even worse. A study by Professor Justin Denney of Rice University found that in the U.S., the affluent live five years longer than the poor, on average.

Table 6.1: Average Life Expectancy			
1 Japan	85.00	12 Austria	81.50
2 Switzerland	82.60	13 Netherlands	81.30
3 Israel	82.40	14 New Zealand	81.20
4 S. Korea	82.40	15 Belgium	81.00
5 Australia	82.20	16 Finland	80.90
6 Italy	82.20	17 Ireland	80.80
7 Sweden	82.10	18 Germany	80.70
8 Canada	81.90	19 United Kingdom	80.70
9 France	81.80	**20 United States**	**79.80**
10 Norway	81.80	21 Denmark	79.40
11 Spain	81.70	22 Portugal	79.30

Source: Central Intelligence Agency, "Country Comparison: Life Expectancy at Birth," Most recent data available, *The World Factbook*, https://www.cia.gov/library/publications/the-world-factbook/rankorder/2102rank.html, accessed October 9, 2017.

His research also shows that as inequality increases, so does the life-expectancy gap.[1]

And what about happiness? A growing field of academic research measures how citizens of various nations perceive their own happiness and well-being. Each year, Columbia University's Earth Institute uses these measures to produce a *World Happiness Report* that ranks nations in order of happiness. The report notes that Americans' sense of happiness has stagnated over the past few decades of runaway inequality. The U.S. now is ranked number 14 after Norway, Denmark, Iceland, Switzerland, Finland, Netherlands, Canada, New Zealand, Australia, Sweden, Israel, Costa Rica, and Austria. [2]

---

1 Justin T. Denney, "Stagnating Life Expectancies and Future Prospects in an Age of Uncertainty," *Social Science Quarterly*, 94(2), (June 2013): 445–461, http://www.ncbi.nlm.nih.gov/pmc/articles/PMC4264628/.

2 John Helliwell, et al., eds., *World Happiness Report 2017*, Sustainable Development Solutions Network, http://worldhappiness.report/wp-content/uploads/sites/2/2017/03/HR17-Ch2.pdf.

Health care

Access to affordable health care is certainly key to our well-being. At first glance, the U.S. appears to be in the lead here, since we're certainly number one when it comes to overall spending on health care. It accounts for more than one-sixth of our entire Gross Domestic Product or GDP (17.1 percent as of 2014). The next highest nation is France at 11.5 percent of GDP. All the other developed nations spend between 8 and 11.5 percent of their GDP on health care.[3]

And yet, as we've seen, all that money isn't buying us longer lives. So it seems we're not getting a lot of bang for our health care buck during this era of runaway inequality.

Our enormous health care spending bill also isn't keeping our infants alive. The odds of an infant dying is almost three times higher in the U.S. than Japan.[4]

Once again these aggregate figures mask the impact of extreme inequality in the U.S. According to multiple studies, the poorer the mother, the greater the chance of troubled pregnancies and deaths. For instance, the U.S. Centers for Disease Control found that for women living below the poverty level, "the infant mortality rate was 60 percent higher and the post-neonatal mortality rate was twice as high as those for women living above the poverty level."[5]

---

3   World Health Organization, "Health Expenditure, Total (% of GDP)," in The World Bank, *DataBank*, http://data.worldbank.org/indicator/SH.XPD.TOTL .ZS/countries/1W?order.

4   Central Intelligence Agency, "Country Comparison: Infant Mortality Rate," *The World Factbook*, https://www.cia.gov/library/publications/the-world-factbook/ rankorder/2091rank.html.

5   "Poverty and Infant Mortality – United States, 1988," *Morbidity and Mortality Weekly Report*, Vol. 44, No. 49, pp. 923-927 (December 15, 1995), Centers for Disease Control, http://www.cdc.gov/mmwr/preview/mmwrhtml/00039818.htm.

Upward mobility

If longevity, health and well-being vary by income, then one obvious antidote is upward mobility. And isn't America the land of opportunity? Don't we have a better chance to move up the income ladder than anyone else? Our people have always been willing to endure hardships and glaring inequality of wealth and income, so long as we can clearly see that pathway to upward mobility.

Most Americans still expect that their children will do better than them economically. Most of us also believe that you can go as far as your talents take you.[6] If you work hard you can make it to the top whether you're descended from a slave, an immigrant or a factory worker. Since the American dream looms so large in our popular culture, we must be number one in social mobility, no?

No. Actually, we're almost first when it comes to the *lack* of social mobility. Chart 6.1 shows that the odds of rising above your father's economic position is about 50/50 in the U.S. In Denmark, you have about a seven to one chance of doing better.

But if you're rich, Chart 6.1 is very good news. Because for you, being "stuck in the same class as your parents" means you'll almost certainly stay rich. You'll be part of the new American aristocracy of wealth.

6 "Where Do We Stand in the Wake of the Great Recession? Economic Mobility and the American Dream," Research and Analysis Report, Pew Charitable Trusts, May 19, 2011, http://www.pewtrusts.org/en/research-and-analysis/reports/2011/05/19/economic-mobility-and-the-american-dream-where-do-we-stand-in-the-wake-of-the-great-recession1.

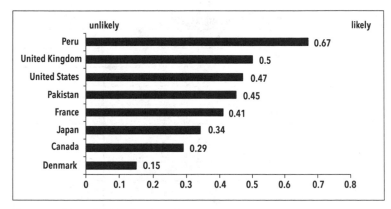

Chart 6.1: Odds You'll Be Stuck in Same Class as Your Parents
Source: CNN Money, "Here's the Likelihood You'll Be Stuck in the Same Economic Class as Your Parents," https://twitter.com/cnnmoney/status/410198127736406016.

Immigration

But something doesn't quite add up here. If our path to upward mobility is blocked, we die early and aren't happy, why does everyone in the world want to come here? Aren't people voting with their feet? Don't millions of others want to come here in the worst way? That by definition must make America the most exceptional country on earth.

What's more, maybe the U.S. doesn't do so well on those other measures because we are such a polyglot. With all our recent immigrants, of course we'll have disparities when it comes to health and well-being. No wonder people in mono-cultural countries like Sweden or Japan live longer and have lower infant mortality: they have virtually no immigrants. And now that they are allowing a few more immigrants, they're seeing a backlash against them.

That's why America must be number one when it comes to immigration and diversity, no?

Well, the story is complex. The U.S. does indeed have the highest *number* of foreign-born immigrants (40 million, including 11 to 12 million who are undocumented). But when we look at the

Table 6.2: Countries by Percent of Immigrants, 2015			
1 Switzerland	29.4	12 United Kingdom	13.2
2 Australia	28.2	13 Spain	12.7
3 Israel	24.9	14 Belgium	12.3
4 New Zealand	23.0	15 France	12.1
5 Canada	21.8	16 Netherlands	11.7
6 Austria	17.5	17 Denmark	10.1
7 Sweden	16.8	18 Italy	9.7
8 Ireland	15.9	19 Portugal	8.1
9 Germany	14.9	20 Finland	5.7
10 **United States**	**14.5**	21 Korea	2.6
11 Norway	14.2	22 Japan	1.6
Source: United Nations, Department of Economic and Social Affairs, "Trends in International Migrant Stock: The 2015 Revision," 2015, https://reliefweb.int/sites/reliefweb.int/files/resources/MigrationWallChart2015-2.pdf..			

percent of immigrants, the U.S. ranks tenth among nations, with 14.5 percent (see Table 6.2).[7]

Americans might be shocked to learn that we're only in the middle of the pack among developed countries in our percentage of foreign-born residents. Israel allows all Jewish people in the world automatic citizenship, so of course it has a high percentage of immigrants. But Germany and Norway have about the same percentage of foreign-born residents as we do – and yet those countries do much better on measures of longevity, health and well-being.

So what justifies our near certain belief that we're the most diverse country in the world? We must be the most diverse country when you count *both* immigration and what we call "racial" background. Or are we?

Researchers have studied ethnic and cultural diversity in various countries in great detail. One particularly rigorous study by James D. Fearon found that the U.S. is the 85th most diverse nation in

---

7   Source: United Nations, Department of Economic and Social Affairs, "Trends in International Migrant Stock: The 2015 Revision," 2015, https://reliefweb.int/sites/reliefweb.int/files/resources/MigrationWallChart2015-2.pdf.

the world. Among developed nations, we're number five, below Canada, Switzerland, Belgium, Israel and Spain.[8]

Paid vacations, paid leaves and hours of work

Imagine this: You work for McDonald's and you've finally earned two weeks of paid vacation. You set out on a fabulous bike trip. On the first day in the saddle, you hit a pothole and crash, cracking your collar bone. You sit on your couch for the rest of your vacation watching the Tour de France. Tough luck.

Okay, change the scene. Now you work for McDonald's in Europe. You get about four weeks of vacation, and when you crash your bike, no worries. You are entitled to a fully paid do-over. According to a ruling of the Court of Justice of the European Union, the highest court in Europe, after an accident during vacation, all European workers are entitled to their full vacation after they have healed:

A worker who becomes unfit during his paid annual leave, is entitled at a later point to a period of leave of the same duration as that of his sick leave.[9]

This means that European workers can take their paid sick leave during their paid vacations, and then take their vacations all over again. And American corporations that do business in Europe – like McDonald's – have to pay for it!

American corporations that provide little or no vacation for employees in this country are on a short leash in Europe: They're

---

8   James Fearon, "Ethnic and Cultural Diversity by Country," *Journal of Economic Growth*, Vol. 8, pp. 195–222, http://www.jstor.org/stable/40215943?seq=1#page_scan _tab_contents.

9   Court of Justice of the European Union, Press Release No. 87/12 Luxembourg, June 21, 2012, "Press and Information Judgment in Case C-78/11 Asociación Nacional de Grandes Empresas de Distribución (ANGED) v Federación de Asociaciones Sindicales (FASGA) and Others," http:, http://curia.europa.eu/jcms/ upload/docs/application/pdf/2012-06/cp120087en.pdf.

Table 6.3: Annual Leave and Paid Holidays by Country		
Country	Statutory Minimum Annual Leave	Paid Holidays
Australia	4 weeks (5 for shift workers)	8
Austria	30 calendar days (22 working days); 36 calendar days after 6 years	13
Belgium	20 work days	10
Canada	2 weeks (3 with seniority)	9
Denmark	25 work days	0
Finland	25 work days (30 after 1 year)	0
France	30 work days	1
Germany	20 work days (up to 30 for young workers)	10
Greece	4 weeks (plus 1 work day after the 2nd and 3rd years)	6
Ireland	4 weeks	9
Italy	4 weeks	10
Japan	10 work days (plus 1 work day after the 2nd – 10th years)	0
Netherlands	4 weeks	0
New Zealand	4 weeks	10
Norway	25 work days	2
Portugal	22 work days (20 in the first year)	13
Spain	30 calendar days	12
Sweden	25 work days	0
Switzerland	4 weeks (5 for young workers)	0
U.K.	28 work days	0
U.S.	**0**	0
Source: Rebecca Ray, et al., "No-vacation Nation Revisited," Center for Economic and Policy Research, May 2013, http://www.cepr.net/documents/publications/no-vacation-update-2013-¬05pdf.		

required *by law* to provide paid vacations of a month or more for their European employees.

In the U.S., financial strip-mining impels corporations to squeeze more labor time from their workers than in any European country. So we have no laws requiring paid vacations and leaves. If you get a paid vacation it's either because the company "gave" it to you or because you achieved it through collective bargaining. It's not considered a right. Table 6.3 compares developed nations by statutory minimum annual leave and paid public holidays.

Table 6.4: Average Annual Hours Actually Worked per Worker, 2016			
Germany	1,363	Canada	1,703
Denmark	1,410	Japan	1,713
Norway	1,424	Italy	1,730
Netherlands	1,430	New Zealand	1,752
Luxembourg	1,512	Hungary	1,761
Belgium	1,551	Czech Republic	1,770
Switzerland	1,590	**United States**	**1,783**
Austria	1,601	Portugal	1,842
Sweden	1,621	Estonia	1,855
Finland	1,653	Iceland	1,883
Australia	1,669	Israel	1,889
United Kingdom	1,676	Poland	1,928
Spain	1,695	Greece	2,035
Source: Organisation for Economic Co-operation and Development, OECD.StatExtracts, http://stats.oecd.org/.			

So if you work at McDonald's in Vienna, Austria, by law you get a full month off (22 work days) in your *first* year plus 13 paid public holidays for a total of 35 days. And after six years of flipping burgers, you get 36 days of paid vacation plus 13 paid public holidays for a total of 49 paid vacation and public holidays – that's more than two months off, paid! (That's in addition to your paid sick leave, maternity and paternity paid leave, and paid leave to care for a sick relative.)

In the U.S., McDonald's "gives" its full-time workers a total of 20 paid days of vacation/holidays. Same company, same product, but U.S. workers get inferior treatment. And can you imagine what a McDonald's manager would say if you asked to start your vacation again because you got sick just after it began. (A *do-over*? Are you kidding me?)

You're also out of luck if you're a part-time worker in the U.S. In Europe, part-time workers are entitled by law to the same paid vacations as full-timers. But in the U.S., only 36 percent of part-time workers have any paid vacation at all, and only 37 percent receive any paid holidays. So when you combine full-time and part-time workers in America, on average we receive only nine days of paid annual leave (vacation/sick days) and six paid holidays. It's a hard work life in the land of runaway inequality.

Those extra hours we're working contribute mightily to making us the most unequal country on earth.

Education expenditures and outcomes

Education is the key to the American Dream, right? It is supposed to provide enormous opportunities for people from all walks of life who are willing to study hard. For the 25 years after WWII, education was indeed the pathway to success, first through the GI Bill of Rights and then through enormous investments in public education at all levels.

Unfortunately, runaway inequality is shattering our educational system. Elites, of course, have access to the very best private schools and colleges. But the rest of us struggle through crippled public school systems that do not compare well with those of other nations.

A report from the Organisation for Economic Co-operation and Development (OECD) compares the educational systems of over 30 developed nations.[10] Again, we're not very exceptional, except for our failures.

First of all, the report confirms the notion that runaway inequality has undermined the ability of our educational system to serve as the conveyer belt for upward mobility. According to the OECD report, "The odds that a young person in the U.S. will be in higher education if his or her parents do not have an upper secondary education are just 29 percent – one of the lowest levels among

---

10   The Organisation for Economic Co-operation and Development, "Education at a Glance: OECD Indicators 2012, United States," http://www.oecd.org/united states/CN%20-%20United%20States.pdf.

OECD countries." When it comes to this kind of educational mobility, we rank third from the bottom among 28 countries listed.

The report also refutes the current notion that our teachers are underworked and overpaid. Actually, they're overworked and underpaid. "Teachers in the U.S. spend between 1050 and 1100 hours a year teaching – much more than in almost every country," according to the report. Of the 38 countries surveyed, only two had teachers who worked more hours – Argentina and Chile. And our primary school teachers work more hours than those in any other country surveyed.

What's more, we don't pay teachers well. The report says that although we spend a lot on education overall, "teacher salaries in the U.S. compare poorly. While in most OECD countries teacher salaries tend be lower, on average, than the salaries earned by other workers with higher education, in the U.S. the difference is large, especially for teachers with minimum qualifications."

Despite all the talk about early childhood education, we're behind in that category as well. Blinded by the anti-government ideology of the Better Business Climate model, we fail to notice that the rest of the world invests much more heavily in their young people, especially the very young: "On average across OECD countries, 84 percent of pupils in early childhood education attend programs in public schools or government-dependent private institutions," according to the report. But in the U.S., only 55 percent of early childhood students attend public school programs; 45 percent are in private programs. What's more, in the U.S. the typical starting age for early childhood education is four years old, while in 21 other OECD countries, kids start pre-K at age three or younger.

Even more telling: Here in the U.S. early childhood teachers are often poorly trained and poorly paid. In contrast, as the report delicately puts it: "early childhood programs in other countries are usually delivered by a qualified teacher and have a formal curriculum, while in the U.S., the situation can vary." Vary indeed.

So where are we ranked?

- 3-year-olds (in early childhood education): 25th of 36 countries
- 4-year-olds (in early childhood education and primary education): 28th of 38 countries
- 5- to 14-year-olds (all levels): 29th of 39 countries

And on to higher ed, where the U.S. is struggling on several fronts. First, we force students and their families to pay more for higher education than students in almost any other OECD country, even though the U.S. government spends a lot of money on higher ed overall. "In the U.S., 38 percent of higher education expenditures come from public sources, and 62 percent are from private sources. Across all OECD countries, 70 percent of expenditures on higher education come from public sources, and 30 percent are from private sources." Little wonder that America leads the world in student debt.

The high cost of college may help explain why the U.S. "ranks 14th in the world in the percentage of 25-34 year-olds with higher education (42 percent)." The richest country on Earth is making a decidedly unexceptional choice about our young people and our future.

Our poor showing on higher ed represents a dramatic shift: After WWII, the U.S. had a higher percentage of high school graduates than anyone. That's why the U.S. is still number one among nations in the percentage of 55- to 64-year-olds who finished high school. We boomers – or at least 90 percent of us – finished high school, compared to the OECD average of 65 percent.

That last statistic about baby boomers is enormously revealing. It lays bare a fault line that runs throughout this book. On one side of the fault line is the post-WWII era, when the U.S. invested generously in the common good, putting the brakes on inequality. On the other side of the divide is the post-1980 era of runaway inequality, when we began catering to our richest elites. It's not an accident that there's an age divide in educational statistics.

During the post-WWII era, the United States invested heavily in public education and guaranteed free higher education to more than 3 million returning GIs through the GI Bill of Rights. Enormous investments in education helped America out-muscle the Russians after Sputnik, and win the symbolic Cold War race to the moon. High taxes on the super-rich helped pay for education, a national highway system, and enormous military budgets. Unions, supported by the federal government and the courts, moved wages up across the board for union and non-union members alike, expanding the middle class. And the burgeoning civil rights movement helped open the promise of America to African Americans. The U.S. had the fairest income distribution in our history.

And then came runaway inequality.

Worker rights

The Better Business Climate model argues that businesses need maximum "labor flexibility." Legal restrictions on employer-employee relations put a damper on business. The more flexibility, the more economic efficiency, the more economic growth. Supposedly, that growth means that the pie gets bigger and everybody gets a bigger slice. Of course we already know that last part hasn't happened.

So restricting worker rights is a key ingredient of runaway inequality. And how are we doing on that?

The Organization for Economic Cooperation and Development ranks 43 nations by how well the government protects workers. To do it, the OECD looks at 21 measures, including each country's laws governing unfair dismissals, protections during mass layoffs, the use and abuse of temporary workers, and whether workers get severance pay based on seniority. Then the OECD ranks countries on a scale of zero to six, with six going to those who provide the most legal protections for workers and zero for those with the least. As Table 6.5 reveals, we're second to last on

Table 6.5: OECD Ranking of Countries by Degree of Employee Protection
(0 is the lowest ranking)

1 Turkey	3.19	23 Iceland	2.32
2 Luxembourg	3.18	24 Brazil	2.29
3 Belgium	3.14	25 Hungary	2.29
4 France	3.14	26 Denmark	2.27
5 Argentina	3.06	27 India	2.27
6 Italy	2.92	28 Korea	2.22
7 China	2.85	29 Sweden	2.18
8 Mexico	2.80	30 Switzerland	2.15
9 Germany	2.77	31 Ireland	2.07
10 Latvia	2.75	32 Japan	2.05
11 Slovenia	2.73	33 Russia	2.02
12 Greece	2.66	34 Finland	2.01
13 Spain	2.63	35 Israel	2.01
14 Norway	2.61	36 Australia	1.86
15 Netherlands	2.53	37 Chile	1.69
16 Indonesia	2.51	38 South Africa	1.63
17 Austria	2.49	39 Saudi Arabia	1.55
18 Portugal	2.48	40 United Kingdom	1.54
19 Slovak Repub.	2.46	41 Canada	1.40
20 Poland	2.45	42 **United States**	**1.22**
21 Czech Repub.	2.45	43 New Zealand	0.83
22 Estonia	2.43		

Source: Author calculations based on data from Organisation for Economic Co-operation and Development, "OECD Indicators of Employment Protection," http://www.oecd.org/employment/emp/oecdindicatorsofemploymentprotection.htm#data.

this list, meaning that we have among the fewest regulations to protect employees – union, non-union, management, full-time and temporary workers alike.

Environment

The Better Business Climate model doesn't like tough environmental regulations either. And under the model, we don't have money to enforce environmental regulations anyway – or invest in other environmental goals. Not with our reduced tax revenues.

Table 6.6: Yale Environmental Performance Index, 2016			
1 Finland	90.68	16 Switzerland	86.93
2 Iceland	90.51	17 Norway	86.9
3 Sweden	90.43	18 Austria	86.64
4 Denmark	89.21	19 Ireland	86.60
5 Slovenia	88.98	20 Luxemburg	86.58
6 Spain	88.91	21 Greece	85.81
7 Portugal	88.63	22 Latvia	85.71
8 Estonia	88.59	23 Lithuania	85.49
9 Malta	88.48	24 Slovakia	85.42
10 France	88.2	25 Canada	85.06
11 New Zealand	88.0	**26 United States**	**84.72**
12 United Kingdom	87.38	27 Czech Republic	84.67
13 Australia	87.22	28 Hungary	84.60
14 Singapore	87.04	29 Italy	84.48
15 Croatia	86.98		
Source: Yale Environmental Performance Index, 2016, http://epi.yale.edu/country-rankings.			

So we'd expect that the U.S. would not make a good showing when it comes to environmental well-being.

The most comprehensive ranking of nations in this area comes from Yale University's *Environmental Performance Index* which looks at a range of indicators of environmental and public health and ecosystem vitality.

And sure enough, we're near the bottom of the list (see Table 6.6).

Child poverty

Nothing reflects the values of a country more than the way it treats its children. And nothing is more painful and inexcusable than children living in poverty.

The countries of northern Europe – Iceland, Finland, Netherlands, Norway, Denmark and Sweden – have nearly eradicated childhood poverty. As we saw in the previous chapter, these also are the countries that have the lowest levels of inequality. These

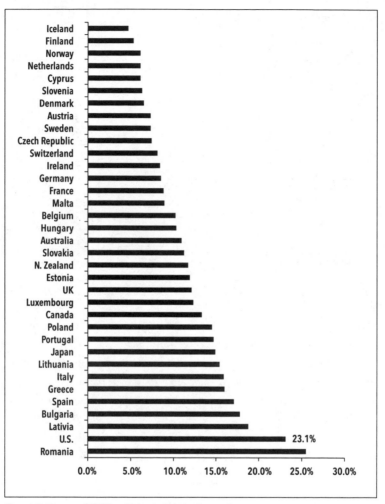

Chart 6.2: Percent of Children Living in Relative Poverty*

* Data is for children younger than 18 years old living in households at less than 50 percent of median household income for the country.
Source: UNICEF Innocenti Research Centre, *Measuring Child Poverty*, 2012, http://www.unicef-irc.org/publications/pdf/rc10_eng.pdf.

countries have made a conscious choice: less inequality, less childhood poverty.

But in a country like ours that is committed to runaway inequality, child poverty becomes the responsibility of the poor. In other words, if your kids are poor it's your fault. Don't expect society to feed them.

By adopting the Better Business Climate model and promoting runaway inequality, we have made our choice about children, and it shows by our pitiful ranking. We almost top the charts when it comes to childhood poverty in an advanced country (see Chart 6.2).

Freedom of the press

> Congress shall make no law respecting an establishment of religion, or prohibiting the free exercise thereof; or abridging the freedom of speech, or of the press; or the right of the people peaceably to assemble, and to petition the Government for a redress of grievances.

We are the first country to enshrine freedom of the press into its most fundamental law. And we have been praised the world over for our free and open press. Less so today.

Reporters Without Borders, an international organization that protects journalists, has ranked 170 countries on their press freedoms since 2002, using the following criteria: Pluralism (different opinions), Media Independence, Environment and Self-Censorship, Legislative Framework (impact of legislative framework on news and information activities), Transparency, Infrastructure (supporting production of news), and Abuses (violence and harassment of news media).[11]

Our self-image concerning freedom of the press may need a bit of adjustment. In 2015, the United States ranked 41st.[12] Interestingly the top four countries in press freedom (Finland, Netherlands, Norway and Denmark) also have the lowest gap between rich and poor.

To explain the low rankings the previous year when the U.S.

---

11   Reporters Without Borders, "2016 World Press Freedom Index: Detailed Methodology," https://rsf.org/en/detailed-methodology.
12   Reporters Without Borders, "2016 World Press Freedom Index," https://rsf.org/en/ranking_table.

ranked 49th overall, Reporters Without Borders cited the U.S. government's persecution of *New York Times* reporter Jim Risen (for refusing to name his sources for a book about the CIA), the U.S.'s aggressive actions against WikiLeaks, and arrests of journalists covering the police protests in Ferguson, Missouri (including *The Intercept's* Ryan Devereaux, who was tear-gassed and shot with a rubber bullet prior to his arrest).[13]

Piercing the veil of runaway inequality

A generation ago, the U.S. led the world with its high standard of living, and its excellent education and health systems. Then, we tossed it away in the name of deregulation, tax cuts and the wild pursuit of profit. We quickly forgot the lessons of the Great Depression as well as the sense of collectivity we developed during WWII. Instead, we followed the Better Business Climate model and deregulated the rich, setting in motion runaway inequality.

As a result, the wealthy have no experience of the statistics and rankings we have just reviewed. Their kids get plenty of high-quality early childhood education. They will never lack for food, clothing or shelter. They don't attend run-down schools. They don't run up debt to go to college. They get the world's best health care and have all the employee rights and vacations that they desire.

Frankly, they care little about our international rankings. Though perhaps they'd prefer that we not focus on them. They'd like us to swallow the myth of American exceptionalism, even when the facts show how exceptionally bad we are at ensuring the well-being of all of our people.

In the next chapter, we'll take a look at something else that the ultra-rich would probably prefer we didn't examine too closely: how tax evasion enables their good fortune.

---

13   Glenn Greenwald, "U.S. Drops to 49th in World Press Freedom Rankings, Worst Since Obama Became President," *The Intercept*, February 12, 2015, https://first look.org/theintercept/2015/02/12/u-s-drops-49th-world-press-freedom-rankings-second-lowest-ever/.

Discussion Questions:

1. If you were to choose one indicator by which to compare the U.S. to other countries, what would it be (Longevity? Happiness? Inequality?, etc.)?

2. Of the comparisons covered in this chapter, which one was most unexpected or shocking to you? Why?

3. Why do you think we've fallen so far behind on paid time off from work?

4. Do you think it is useful for organizing for the American people to know where we really stand in comparison to other countries? Why or why not?

PART THREE

Separate Issues, Common Cause

Runaway Taxes and Runaway Inequality

America is the most unequal country in the developed world. We also pay the lowest taxes in the developed world (see Chart 7.1). Is there a connection?

To review, after the oil boycotts, high unemployment and even higher inflation rates of the 1970s, the policy establishment was hungry for a new plan that would bring renewed prosperity.

Enter the Better Business Climate model, which promised deliverance with this simple formula:

1. Cut taxes on corporations and the super-rich
2. Reduce regulations, especially on Wall Street
3. Pare government social services

The idea was to encourage the rich to invest, which would lead to more jobs and rising incomes for all. A massive boom would ensue, making all boats rise.

But as we painfully learned, tax cuts and the unleashing of Wall Street led to luxurious yachts for the few and leaking skiffs for the rest of us.

Mind-altering tax cuts

The massive tax cuts ushered in by the Better Business Climate model in the early 1980s changed the way we perceive government and how we think about taxes. Because we all dislike paying taxes,

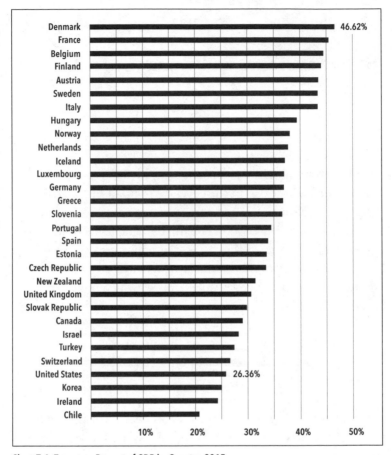

Chart 7.1: Taxes as a Percent of GDP by Country, 2015

Source: Organisation for Economic Co-operation and Development, "Total Tax Revenue by Country as percent of GDP," https://data
.oecd.org/tax/tax-revenue.htm.

many of us were seduced by the idea that tax cuts would actually
be good for the economy.

It's easy to forget that before the Better Business Climate model
slashed taxes, we had something of a national consensus that the
super-rich and corporations should carry a disproportionate share
of the tax burden. It was generally understood that if the wealthy
had too much money, they would eventually gamble it on Wall
Street, creating bubbles that put us at risk of a stock market crash
like the one that led to the Great Depression.

We used money from taxes on the wealthy to fight WWII and the Cold War, and to build the American Dream. Through high taxes on the largest corporations and on the wealthiest Americans, we paid for a new national highway system, nearly free public higher education, affordable housing, AND financed the largest military establishment in the history of the world . . . all creating jobs and leading to what economists call "full employment."

The Great Depression and a monumental world war cast a sobering shadow, and left most Americans craving economic stability, even if it meant high taxes. Never again would we allow mass unemployment. Never again would we allow obscene and illegal financial speculation to take down the economy (or so we thought).

Our tax-the-rich national mindset was so pervasive that both Democratic and Republican administrations from Roosevelt to Nixon supported high taxes on the wealthy.

For example, during WWII all income over $2.6 million (in today's dollars) was taxed at a 94 percent rate (at least officially). Think about that for a moment. Basically we were placing a cap on elite compensation, since once Wall Street executives hit $2.6 million, they only held onto 6 cents on the next dollar.

In 1956, during the Eisenhower administration, which was then considered to be conservative, the tax rate was still 91 percent of all income over $3.4 million. In 1976, 70 cents of every dollar of income over $807,000 went to federal income taxes.

Of course, after deductions and loopholes, the effective tax rates on the super rich were lower. But as we saw in Chart 3.1, the real average rates of the super-rich (top 1/100th of 1 percent) were still far above what they are today. The drop in taxes on the super-rich was extremely steep after 1980, when the Better Business Climate model kicked in.

At the same time, the U.S. was cutting corporate taxes. This had a major impact on state and local finances. As Chart 7.2 shows, corporate taxes as a percent of state and local revenues fell by nearly half as Better Business Climate polices took hold in the early 1980s.

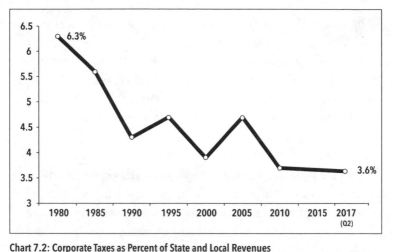

Chart 7.2: Corporate Taxes as Percent of State and Local Revenues

Source: Bureau of Economic Affairs, National Income and Product Accounts, Table 3.3, "State and Local Government Current Receipts and Expenditures," http://www.bea.gov/iTable/iTable.cfm?ReqID=9&step=1#reqid=9&step=3&isuri=1&904=1945&903=88&906 =a&905=2014&910=x&911=0. Fourth quarter, unless otherwise stated.

In sum, in the quarter century following WWII, we had a national consensus that high tax rates were both necessary and proper. We shared a sense of justice: To promote the general good, we needed to limit what the wealthy could earn.

Today, some elites think it's fine that the rich manipulate the tax code so that they can pay lower tax rates than the rest of us. In those postwar days, this would have been unthinkable and revolting. And downright stupid, since runaway inequality would surely lead to calamity.

Currently, the average top effective tax rate is about 20 percent (and even that only applies to the money that rich people aren't hiding offshore). For many of the super-rich the rate is much lower. In fact, an IRS study found that almost 1,500 millionaires paid no tax at all in 2009.[1]

America reached its peak of fairness during that postwar period of high tax rates, as Thomas Piketty, et al. demonstrate in their

---

1   Amy Bingham, "Almost 1,500 Millionaires Do Not Pay Income Tax," ABC *News*, August 6, 2011, http://abcnews.go.com/Politics/1500-millionaires-pay -income-tax/story?id=14242254.

excellent charts on U.S. wealth and income distribution.[2] Yes, there were still plenty of rich people and they still lived damn well. But most Americans experienced a rising standard of living year after year.

However, as soon as tax rates on the super-rich and corporations declined, inequality took off again.

Runaway inequality and runaway democracy

Every nation has a long and sordid history of money buying political favor. But rising inequality creates a downward spiral of corruption that puts democracy itself in danger.

Many of us have an intuitive grasp of how elites translate their increasing wealth into political power, which in turn brings them more tax breaks, more money, and even more political power.

As the tax cuts associated with the Better Business Climate model began piling more money into the bank accounts of the ultra-rich, both political parties saw a fundraising opportunity. That's why we now have the "money primaries" – the period before the actual primaries when political candidates scramble for contributions from the super-rich. We now accept this blatant rush for cash as politics as usual.

The money primaries can determine who wins the election. But that's not the only outcome of this corrupt process: We're letting the rich buy politicians with money that they should have paid in taxes – taxes that we need to support essential public services. (For a more in-depth discussion, see chapter 14.)

---

2   Facundo Alvaredo, et al., "The World Top Incomes Database," http:// topincomes.parisschoolofeconomics.eu/.

Zero sum taxation

When the few are able to buy political favor, it leads to more hardship for the many. As the corporate share of federal taxes dropped from 32 percent in 1952 to only 9 percent in 2016, individual taxpayers had to make up the difference. The super rich did all they could to avoid picking up that tab, leaving it instead for working people to pay.

One subversive way that corporations and the wealthy have reduced their share of the tax burden is to move money offshore. This practice, which would have been frowned on after WWII, is now common. Large corporations simply keep their global profits in foreign subsidiaries. This can be as easy as switching accounts in Wall Street banks. As Chart 7.3 shows, this practice is growing rapidly.

Of course, fans of the Better Business Climate model would like us to believe that cutting taxes on the rich helps the rest of us. Sadly, it doesn't: the less the rich pay, the bigger the tax bill for working people.

Of course working people don't want to pay higher taxes, especially in an era of flat wages and declining benefits. So they fall prey to politicians arguing that we just can't afford public services. First on the chopping block are services for poor people, but the axe strikes us all as public jobs disappear and services deteriorate. The spiral goes like this:

- When people feel they're getting less and less for their tax dollars (which they are, since the rich and corporations aren't paying their share), they turn increasingly against government.
- When people suffer declining services, they succumb to calls for more tax cuts, which further erode government services.
- When private sector workers see their wages stagnate and benefits deteriorate, they sometimes turn against public sector workers, who seem to have it better.

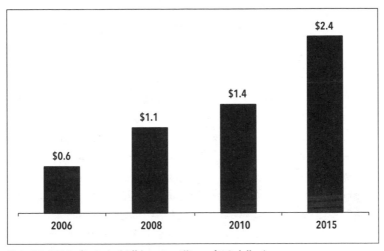

Chart 7.3: U.S. Profits Parked Offshore (In trillions of U.S. dollars)
Sources: Tim Dickinson, "The Biggest Tax Scam Ever," *Rolling Stone*, August 27, 2014, http://www.rollingstone.com/politics/news/the-biggest-tax-scam-ever-20140827; and Audit Analytics, blog, "Indefinitely Reinvested Foreign Earnings Still on the Rise," http://www.auditanalytics.com/blog/indefinitely-reinvested-foreign-earnings-still-on-the-rise/ .

- Corporations then swoop in to privatize public services. These privatized services often cost us more and deliver less.

The net result is ever more money for those at the top and ever declining services for the rest of us.

The Black Hole of runaway tax dollars

Perhaps the biggest tax crime against American working people is perpetrated by rich people who park their wealth abroad. It is now considered normal practice for people to take money they made in the USA and hide it offshore where the IRS can't get to it. The numbers, compiled by the Tax Justice Network, are staggering:

A significant fraction of global private financial wealth – by our estimates, at least $21 trillion to $32 trillion as of 2010 – has been invested virtually tax free through the world's still expanding black hole of more than 80 "off shore" secrecy jurisdictions. We believe the range to be conservative . . .[3]

We don't know precisely how much of this global offshore wealth is owned by Americans. But we can assume that most of it comes from the U.S., since we have nearly half the world's "Ultra High Net Worth" individuals (UHNW) – people with more than $50 million in wealth.

Even more sickening, we taxpayers are actually helping these UHNW people hide their money. According to the Tax Justice Network, "the top 10 players in global private banking all ... received substantial injections of government loans and capital during the 2008-2012 period. In effect, ordinary taxpayers have been subsidizing the world's largest banks to keep them afloat, even as they help their wealthiest clients slash taxes" by hiding their money offshore. What's more, says the Tax Justice Network:

> Many of these market leaders in global pirate banking –
> the practice of hiding and managing offshore assets for
> the world's elite – have also been identified lately as the
> market leaders in many other forms of dubious activity,
> from the irresponsible mortgage lending and high risk
> securitization that produced the 2008 financial crisis,
> to the very latest outrageous scandals involving LIBOR
> rate rigging and money laundering for the Mexican
> cartel.[4]

The U.S. Public Interest Research Group (PIRG) reports that we're losing about $184 billion a year to corporate and individual

3   James S. Henry, "The Price of Offshore Revisited," Tax Justice Network, July 2012, http://www.taxjustice.net/cms/upload/pdf/Price_of_Offshore_Revisited _120722.pdf.
4   Ibid.

offshore tax evasion.[5] That's enough money to cover tuition for students at every public university, college and community college in the country.

The world's most outrageous tax loophole?

Under runaway inequality, the richest of the rich exploit the most outrageous tax loopholes, and they have all the money and power they need to keep politicians from closing those loopholes. The most egregious example is the "carried interest" loophole. This allows billionaire hedge funds and private equity managers to avoid billions in taxes by allowing them to declare ordinary income as capital gains. This drops their top rate from 39.6 percent to 20 percent. We're talking big money.

Here's how it plays out. The top 25 hedge fund managers in 2013 collectively took in $24.3 billion dollars. Please note: this means that these people make an average of $467,000 *an hour*. They make as much in *one hour* as the typical American makes in *nine years*!

The carried interest loophole reduces their taxes by about $4.8 billion a year. That's enough money to hire 175,000 pre-school teachers a year or 76,000 registered nurses. Instead, it goes into the pockets of just 25 billionaires for no reason at all, except one: They feel it is their due. Eliminating the loophole would have no effect on the economy or on these super-rich individuals. Between 2008 and 2010, when the Democrats controlled Congress and the White House, they refused to eliminate this loophole. Of course the Republicans also refuse to touch it. It stands to reason: Both parties are competing for donations from the billionaires they are protecting.

---

5   U.S. Public Interest Research Group, "Offshore Tax Havens Cost Average Taxpayer $1,259 a Year, Small Businesses $3,923," Press Release, April 15, 2014, http://www.uspirg.org/news/usp/offshore-tax-havens-cost-average-taxpayer-1259 -year-small-businesses-3923.

Tax hypocrisy of the Better Business Climate model

Recall that the fundamental idea of the Better Business Climate model was to get the government out of the economy, reduce its expenditures, and cut taxes. But under the model, businesses want *more* government support. They began demanding incentives to build new facilities. If a state or locality refused to hand over the extra tax incentives, subsidies, and government cash businesses wanted, they threatened to move to another state or country. This quickly led to a "war between the states" over which state would provide the biggest tax breaks.

As a result, states provide staggering amounts of money in tax giveaways to corporations – much more than they do in public pensions according to data published by Good Jobs First in 2014. Table 7.1 compares the amount of money selected states spend on corporate tax breaks with the total value of public pensions in those states. It's an illuminating comparison, since states are pleading poverty as they slash pensions for public employees. Clearly this is about priorities, since these state governments spend from 110

Table 7.1: State Tax Breaks/Subsidies Much More Costly than State Public Pensions			
	Annual Employer Normal Pension Costs	Annual Costs of corporate subsidies/tax breaks/ loopholes	Tax Giveaways as percent of Public Pensions
Arizona	$474,524,688	$522,108,211	110%
California	$6,822,294,460	$9,701,000,000	142%
Colorado	$179,560,282	$593,109,000	330%
Florida	$905,581,094	$3,810,902,291	421%
Illinois	$1,855,100,000	$2,400,796,000	129%
Louisiana	$348,471,694	$1,813,729,079	520%
Michigan	$586,592,328	$1,860,600,000	317%
Missouri	$427,300,226	$840,231,523	197%
Oklahoma	$221,501,696	$479,033,081	216%
Pennsylvania	$1,395,509,900	$3,888,000,000	279%

Source: Good Jobs First, "Putting State Pension Costs in Context," January 2014, http://www.taxjustice.net/cms/upload/pdf/Price_of_Offshore_Revisited_120722.pdf.

percent to 520 percent as much on corporate tax giveaways as they spend on public employee pensions.

The poor pay more than the rich in state and local taxes

Progressive taxes mean that the rich pay a higher percentage of their income in taxes than the poor. That was American tax policy from the New Deal until about 1980. A regressive tax means that the poor pay a higher percentage than the rich.

So what kind of tax system do we actually have today at the state and local level?

According to a January 2015 report by the Institute on Taxation and Economic Policy, the poor pay approximately *double the tax rate as the super rich* (see Chart 7.4). This means that state and local tax policies actually are accelerating runaway inequality. It's not surprising, given the influence the super-rich exert over the political process.

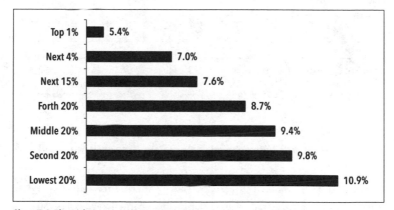

Chart 7.4: The Rich Pay Lower State Tax Rates
Source: Institute on Taxation and Economic Policy, *Who Pays: A Distributional Analysis of the Tax Systems in All Fifty States*, 2015, http://www.itep.org/whopays/executive_summary.php.

Impact on government services

As rich people and large corporations shoulder less and less of the tax burden, government services shrink, and we have fewer government employees to provide these needed services. Chart 7.5 shows the dramatic drop in government employees as a ratio of the total population. Note how the share of public workers (including military personnel) plunged as the Better Business Climate model set in during the early 1980s and plunged again after the Wall Street crash.

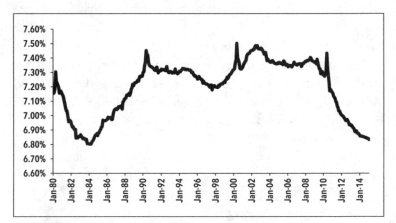

Chart 7.5: Government Jobs as Percent of the U.S. Population*
*Civilian, noninstitutional population
Source: Author's calculations from Bureau of Labor Statistics, Employment, Hours and Earnings from the Current Employment Statistics Survey, http://data.bls.gov/pdq/querytool.jsp?survey=ce.

No taxation without representation: Revolutionary potential?

We're in a whale of a tax mess. Runaway inequality will starve the government of funds as the tax burden shifts from corporations and the wealthy to the rest of us. Government services will decline as the rich evade their taxes and use their money to insulate themselves from the fallout of disintegrating public services.

In the past, we might have rectified the situation at the ballot box: We'd vote in candidates who supported fairer tax policies. But that's no easy task at a time when the wealthy so dominate the political process.

Deteriorating government services, tax avoidance by the rich, and unresponsive elected officials form a combustible mix. But it's far from clear what kind of explosion might result. Hopefully, we'll create a new movement to replace the Better Business Climate model altogether and tame runaway inequality. If not, it is likely that inequality will just keep on growing for now, as struggling taxpayers call for even deeper tax cuts.

The Trump Administration, with the full support of the Republican-dominated Congress, passed a new tax bill at the close of 2017 that is certain to accelerate runaway inequality. Those earning from $40,000 to $50,000 per year are expected to see a tax cut of $120 per year while millionaires will gain at least $25,000 per year according to the *Wall Street Journal*.[6]

In addition, the corporate tax rate was cut from 35 percent to 21 percent. Supposedly this will lure back corporate profits held overseas and lead to more U.S. investment and jobs. However, we know what is likely to happen based on the tax holiday given to corporations in 2004, during which more than $200 billion in corporate profits were repatriated to the U.S. Instead of investing in new plant, equipment and jobs, "a $1 increase in repatriations was associated with a $0.60-$0.92 increase in shareholder payouts," according to a study conducted by professors from University of Chicago, Harvard University and M.I.T.[7]

6   Joint Committee on Taxation, "A Distribution of Returns by the Size of the Tax Change for the 'Tax Cuts and Jobs Act,'" November 27, 2017, in *Wall Street Journal*, https: https://www.wsj.com/public/resources/documents/JCT-distribution-of-tax-returns-D-17-54.pdf.

7   "Watch What I Do, Not What I Say: The Unintended Consequences of the Homeland Investment Act," https://papers.ssrn.com/sol3/papers.cfm?abstract_id=1337206##.

Discussion Questions:

1. Do you think cutting taxes improves our standard of living? Why or why not?

2. Do you think the tax system is fair? Why or why not?

3. Why do we have the lowest tax rates among developed nations?

4. How do the wealthy go about evading taxes?

How Wall Street Occupies America: Rising Debt and Runaway Inequality

Increasing debt and runaway inequality go hand in hand. That's because debt, at compound interest rates, can transfer huge sums of money from the borrower to the lender, giving the lender enormous leverage.

Borrow a little today and, in time, you could be destitute. To get a feel for how debt accumulates, imagine that you borrowed just one nickel at 5 percent interest when Christ was born. You would now owe the tidy sum of $225,438,991,066,856,000,000,000,000,00 0,000, 000,000,000 – more money than ever existed in the history of the world. Which is another way to say that creditors – like the captains of high finance – wield huge economic power.

In our society we've handed that power to private financial corporations, and they've done a masterful job of pushing us into debt peonage. Our homes, schools, roads, bridges, highways, utilities, corporations and virtually every product and good produced and sold depend on debt. By some estimates as much as 30 cents of every dollar we spend goes to cover interest on the debt accrued to make what we buy. (For example, of the $7.1 trillion private enterprises earned in 2016, 35.4 percent went to interest payments.[1])

Since our banking system is in private hands, every rise in debt level accelerates runaway inequality. So one key to controlling runaway inequality is reining in high finance.

Instead, as a society we have loosened the reins. For nearly a half century between the New Deal and the 1970s, when Wall Street

---

1   Author's calculations based on U.S. Bureau of Economic Analysis, "Sources and Uses of Private Enterprise Income," August 3, 2017.

was tightly controlled, debt levels for consumers, companies and government were low. After finance was deregulated (circa 1980), private *and* public debt exploded – and, as we've seen, wages stalled, taxes on the rich fell and inequality soared.

Financialism transforms the modern corporation

Until about 1980, corporations ran up very little debt (see Chart 8.1). Their earnings were more than sufficient to cover their investments in new plant and equipment, research and development and increased wages and benefits for workers. This "retain and reinvest" corporate ethos was encouraged by the strict regulations governing high finance during that era. Banks were limited in size, geography and function. Speculation was kept to a minimum. So was the buying and selling of corporations by what we now call private equity firms and hedge funds.

But after 1980, these controls were radically reversed by an unholy alliance of academics, financial elites and pro-Wall Street politicians. And as finance became more and more deregulated, corporate debt grew and grew.

If that borrowed money had been reinvested in workers and products, it would have helped corporations and their employees prosper. But the new financial engineers weren't interested in "retaining and reinvesting." Instead, they wanted to "downsize and distribute." They often used the new debt to buy up corporations. And, as we've seen, these newly acquired, debt-saddled corporations were forced to use their revenues to pay off the debt. CEOs also used revenues of the companies they acquired to buy up shares so they could boost the stock price and enrich themselves.

To pay back their mounting loans, corporations squeezed their own workers. They downsized, moved abroad, cut wages and benefits and replaced full-time workers with temps. CEOs became financial engineers looking to make money through debt, leaving their

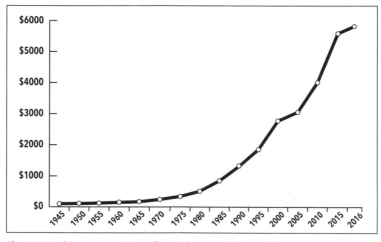

Chart 8.1: Total Corporate Debt (Non-financial sector in billions of U.S. dollars)
Source: Federal Reserve Bank of St. Louis, "Nonfinancial Corporate Business; Debt Securities; Liability, Level," http://research.
stlouisfed.org/fred2/series/NCBDB1A027N#.

companies and workers to foot the bill. And so, corporate capitalism morphed into financial strip-mining.

The invention of the indebted consumer

Throughout recorded history, societies have tried to mediate
the lender-borrower relationship with rules aimed at restricting
the power of creditors. In fact, the first known written laws, the
Hammurabi Codes (1780 BCE), set maximum interest rates on
various transactions.[2] To ensure stability, most civilizations also
evolved powerful customs and informal moral codes to discourage
personal debt. For most of American history, being in debt was
considered unwholesome, the province of gamblers, gangsters and
failing businesses.

But our righteous attitudes about debt eventually collided with
the demands of mass production. The ever growing cornucopia of

---

2   James M. Ackerman, "Interest Rates and the Law: A History of Usury,"
Arizona State Law Journal, Vol. 61 (1981).

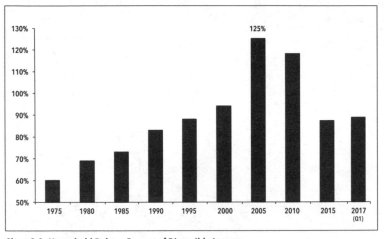

Chart 8.2: Household Debt as Percent of Disposible Income
Source: Bureau of Economic Analysis, National Income and Product Accounts tables, http://bea.gov//national/nipaweb/DownSS2.a.

goods produced by modern capitalist enterprises also required the mass production of "consumers" to buy the flood of goods. (Hence the advent of mass advertising.) Starting in the 1920s, consumers were urged to buy on credit, pumping up demand to match the enormous new supply of goods. And then during the New Deal, government-backed mortgages encouraged consumers to borrow money to buy homes.

Despite all this, however, household debt was extremely modest until that fateful period of deregulation. Before 1990, when the last vestiges of financial control evaporated, the average consumer's household debt was about 60 percent of disposable income (that is, income we can spend after we pay our taxes). But after modern financial engineering invaded the housing and credit card markets, household debt soared to nearly 125 percent of household income. (Sadly, this includes tens of billions of dollars of fraudulent mortgage loans, according to the FBI.)[3]

The more households paid to service their growing debt, the more money flowed into the financial sector. Rising inequality followed.

---

3   Federal Bureau of Investigation, "Mortgage Fraud Report 2010," http://www .fbi.gov/stats-services/publications/mortgage-fraud-2010.

Debt peonage for students

Student debt became the next territory for Wall Street to occupy. Once again, this required upending past practices that had actually worked pretty well. From WWII through the mid-1970s, young people typically didn't go into deep debt to pay for college. In fact public higher education was virtually free, first through the GI Bill of Rights and then through robust state education systems. California and New York provided tuition-free higher education. As Chart 8.3 shows, until the late 1980s, student loan debt was minimal. But as money for the public sector dried up (largely due to tax evasion by the rich, assisted by Wall Street, discussed in Chapter 7), public financial support for higher education lagged behind tuition costs. Wall Street filled the breach and student debt mushroomed.

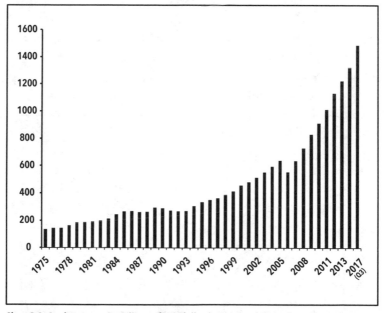

Chart 8.3: Student Loans (In Billions of U.S. dollars)
Note: Data on student loans not available before 2006. Data before 2006 is for "Other Consumer Credit" and includes student loans.
Source: Federal Reserve, Statistical Release, "Financial Accounts of the United States, Historical Tables," Table L.222, various years, available at: http://www.federalreserve.gov/releases/z1/current/annuals/a2005-2014.pdf.

Government debt is bad for whom?

Finally we turn to government debt, always a topic of ideological fervor. But no matter where you stand on the role of government and how it should be financed, we should acknowledge one basic fact: No matter what the era, the wealthy would rather lend the government money than pay taxes. The reason is simple: they stand to make more money in return. In contrast, if we finance the government not by borrowing money from the wealthy, but by taxing them, the returns to the rich are nil. (Unless, of course, we want to consider the huge benefits we all get from living in a well-functioning country with an educated workforce . . .)

This is even more true today, since the interest on government debt instruments is often tax-deductible. So the rich benefit doubly by lending money to the government (and having the rest of us pay them back through our taxes): They not only collect good interest on their loans, they can often deduct that interest from their taxes.

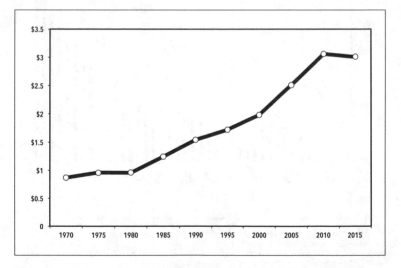

Chart 8.4: State and Local Government Debt (Adjusted for inflation in trillions of 2015 dollars)

Sources: U.S. Bureau of the Census, "State and Local Government Finances," http://www.census.gov/govs/local/; and *Statistical Abstract of the United States*, various issues, "State and Local Government Finances."

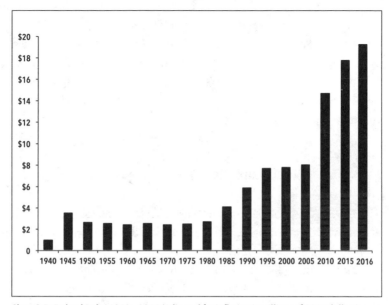

Chart 8.5: Federal Debt, 1940 - 2016 (Adjusted for inflation in trillions of 2015 dollars)
Source: Author's calculations based on Office of Management and Budget, Historical Tables, https://www.whitehouse.gov/omb/budget/Historicals/.

So, as financial interests and the wealthy increase their power over the economy and politics, we have seen federal, state and local government debt rise as well.

Again, this is quite a departure from the post-WWII period when Wall Street was tightly controlled. During that era, taxes on the rich were high and public debt levels were low. But after the deregulation of Wall Street, public debt mushroomed – just like corporate, household and student debt.

Chart 8.4 shows the steep rise of state and local debt. Note how it jumps up after 1980. Chart 8.5 shows how national debt also jumped after 1980.

Financial strip-mining of state and local government

State and local governments, starved for funds, must look to Wall Street to finance roads, schools and other infrastructure (except in

North Dakota, which has its own public state bank). These loans often leave taxpayers on the hook for enormous fees that fatten Wall Street financiers while undermining state and local finances.

How does this work? Here's a case study from Los Angeles. Similar reports could be written on nearly every major city in the country.

How Wall Street impoverishes Los Angeles

The city of Los Angeles paid at least $204 million in fees to Wall Street in 2013, according to the report, "No Small Fees: LA Spends More on Wall Street than Our Streets."[4] The study, issued by a coalition of unions and community organizations, shows that due to revenue losses from the Great Recession, Los Angeles "all but stopped repairing sidewalks, clearing alleys and installing speed bumps. It stopped inspecting sewers, resulting in twice the number of sewer overflows."

Remarkably, Los Angeles spends at least $51 million more on Wall Street fees than it does on the city's entire budget for the Bureau of Street Services.

The researchers caution that the $204 million figure likely underestimates the true amount, since current disclosure rules don't require the city to publicly disclose deals with private equity companies and hedge funds. Also, because the city doesn't list all these fees in one centralized report, gathering this data requires reviewing hundreds of documents. As one of the report's researchers stated,

> This is the first time an accounting of fees has been exposed for a specific public entity, and we don't think we have captured it all. So if you do this for every public

---

4   Fix LA Coalition, "No Small Fees: LA Spends More on Wall St. Than Our Streets," August 2014, http://fixla.org/wp-content/uploads/2014/07/No-Small-Fees-A-Report-by-the-Fix-LA-Coalition-2014-08-05.pdf.

entity, cities, counties, school districts, states, and universities, transportation agencies and other public entities, we could be looking at an astounding amount of money for education and community services money sucked out of the system.

The coalition offers the following pragmatic reforms to address this huge misallocation of government revenues:

- **Provide Full Transparency:** Each year, Los Angeles, not this grass-roots research coalition, should tally up and publish in one report all the fees it pays to financial firms.
- **Bargain:** The city has over $100 billion in cash, liquid assets and debts held with financial companies. That gives Los Angeles enormous leverage to bargain for lower fees. Unless there is illegal collusion among these private financial institutions (which is possible), competition for Los Angeles' $100 billion should drive fees down.
- **Sue Negligent Financial Firms:** Los Angeles, like hundreds of other state and local governments, bought interest rate swaps from Wall Street before 2008 to lower their interest rate payments on public debt.[5] But after Wall Street gambled our economy into the ground, interest rates collapsed and these swaps turned into bad bets for cities like Los Angeles, and, low and behold, big winners for Wall Street. More amazing still, these same contracts were pegged to the LIBOR interest rate benchmark, which we now know was illegally manipulated by the biggest global banks. So Los Angeles also has grounds to sue financial institutions for peddling predatory swaps

---

5   For more on these complex interest rate swaps, see Ellen Brown, "Wall Street Confidence Trick: How Interest Rate Swaps Are Bankrupting Local Governments," March 20, 2012, http://www.webofdebt.com/articles/interestrateswap.php.

in the first place and for manipulating the LIBOR rates. Simple justice demands that Wall Street not be permitted to profit as a result of an economic crash it caused, and as a result of illegal rate rigging.

Wall Street's Catch-22

The report begs the question: Why do cities and states go to Wall Street for financing in the first place? The answer is circular. They need to raise private capital through Wall Street because state and local tax bases are shrinking, and funds are limited. But the tax base is shrinking because of Wall Street's financial strip-mining of the economy. In effect, Wall Street creates the economic conditions that force cities and states to become its prey.

Heading towards debt peonage?

We are still beholden to Wall Street financiers, even after they nearly destroyed our economy and even after we paid trillions to bail them out. By 2006, 40 percent – more than $1 trillion – of all U.S. corporate profits went to Wall Street – up from 7 percent in 1980. Wall Street helped hide over $21 trillion in offshore tax havens. The system is relying – still – on Wall Street, and, more specifically, on the four banks (JP Morgan Chase, Bank of America, Wells Fargo, and Citigroup) that dominate the entire financial system. These oligopolists have made it clear to all: they are far, far too big to fail, jail, or curtail.

What will happen when this debt pyramid comes tumbling down again? As financial expert Ellen Brown points out, after the next crash we'll probably see a new kind of bailout.[6] It's called a "bail-in"

---

6   Ellen Brown, "Banking Union Time Bomb: Eurocrats Authorize Bailouts AND Bail-Ins," March 29, 2014, http://ellenbrown.com/2014/03/29/banking-union -time-bomb-eurocrats-authorize-bailouts-and-bail-ins/.

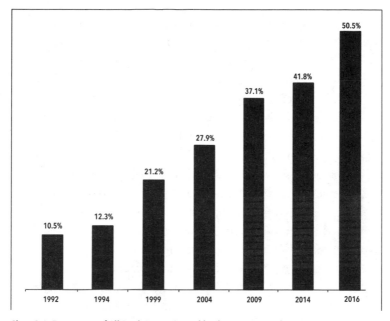

Chart 8.6: Percentage of All Bank Assets Owned by the Top Four Banks
Source: Calculations by author from FDIC Statistics on Depository Institutions for each year found at https://www2.fdic.gov/sdi/main.asp.

and it already has been adopted by European planners. Instead of giving billions to the banks, the government will ask the banks to take it from their depositors – namely us.

Escaping from debtors' prison?

With ever rising public and private debt, we seem trapped. After all, a cornerstone of civilization is that debts must be repaid. (Bankruptcy, the other option, isn't a question for countries like ours that can print their own money.) As the economy grows, federal debt as a percent of the entire federal budget will likely decline – and has been, as of this writing. But households aren't so lucky: with personal incomes stalled, families may be struggling with debt indefinitely. But there is another way out.

It starts with recognizing that the root of the problem isn't just the quantity of debt, but who controls and profits by it. Private banks don't have to be masters of the economic universe. Instead, we could model our financial system on public banks, like the Bank of North Dakota (which we will investigate further in Chapter 20). If we had 50 state banks, instead of just one, we could limit the income-distorting power of rising debt. *And* our public treasury would be replenished. In North Dakota, the state bank returned record profits nine years in a row, with $94 million flowing into the state coffers in 2013. This public bank supports infrastructure projects. It insists that when it lends money to businesses, jobs must be created in North Dakota. It helps ease the burdens of student loans . . . and it doesn't gamble in financial markets.

And then there's the part that Wall Street *really* detests: The CEO of the Bank of North Dakota makes *per year* what a top Wall Street banker makes per *hour*! Horrors! Imagine: public bankers willing to work for $335,000 a year instead of $20 million.

We are learning painfully each and every day what an uphill slog it is to reregulate Wall Street. Despite the horrific shock of the financial collapse, we've only been able to enact the most tepid of reforms. We fine banks over and over for every financial sin imaginable – money laundering for gangsters and rogue states, ripping off servicemen and women by financing payday loan sharks, colluding to fix interest rates, insider trading, controlling commodity markets, and illegal financial gambling. Yet the same executives and the same institutions stay in place, unscathed, not even embarrassed, as people shrug and conclude that apparently the crimes they have committed are just the normal cost of doing business.

But what if we transformed every discussion about debt into a debate about creating public banks to replace Wall Street's financial stranglehold?

Discussion Questions:

1. What's the relationship between the stalling of wages and the rise of consumer debt?

2. Why do we have so much student debt?

3. Why do state and local governments go to Wall Street for loans?

4. What will it take to get the country out from under the massive debt burden it faces?

Incarceration Nation

As public debt rises, the Better Business Climate model requires ever deepening cuts in social spending. As we saw in Chapter 3, government spending on non-military items dropped after 1980. Although there was a spurt of spending on the stimulus and bailouts after the Wall Street crash, now government social spending is falling yet again.

But the Better Business Climate model has spared one area of government social spending from the axe. In fact, spending in this area has accelerated like never before in all of American history: prisons.

As Chart 9.1 shows, our prison population began soaring precisely at the moment when the government adopted the Better Business Climate model. In fact, it soared to such heights that eleven states now spend more on corrections than they do on education.[1]

Is this just a coincidence, or is incarceration somehow entwined with Better Business Climate policies? Why would these policies lead to a colossal rise in our prison population?

We're number one in prisoners

By every measure the U.S. leads the world in prisoners, with 2.2 million people in jail and more than 4.7 million on parole. No nation tops that – not China with 1.7 million, not Russia with

---

1   Michael Mitchell and Michael Leachman, "Changing Priorities: State Criminal Justice Reforms and Investments in Education," Center for Budget and Policy Priorities, October 28, 2014, http://www.cbpp.org/cms/?fa=view&id=4220.

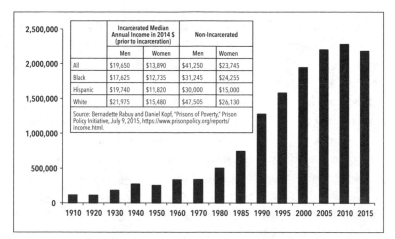

	Incarcerated Median Annual Income in 2014 $ (prior to incarceration)		Non-Incarcerated	
	Men	Women	Men	Women
All	$19,650	$13,890	$41,250	$23,745
Black	$17,625	$12,735	$31,245	$24,255
Hispanic	$19,740	$11,820	$30,000	$15,000
White	$21,975	$15,480	$47,505	$26,130

Source: Bernadette Rabuy and Daniel Kopf, "Prisons of Poverty," Prison Policy Initiative, July 9, 2015, https://www.prisonpolicy.org/reports/income.html.

Chart 9.1: Number of Persons in Jails and Prisons in the United States, 1910–2015
Sources: Bureau of Justice Statistics, "Correctional Populations of the United States," various years; and U.S. Bureau of the Census, *Statistical Abstract of the United States*, various years.

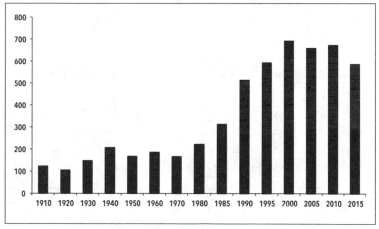

Chart 9.2: Number of Federal and State Prisoners per 100,000 Residents, 1923–2015
Sources: Bureau of Justice Statistics, Prisoners Series, various years, available at: http://www.bjs.gov/; population from Bureau of the Census.

670,000.[2] Chart 9.1 shows the dramatic rise of the state and federal prisoner population as well as local jail inmates since the Better Business Climate model took hold.

2   International Centre for Prison Studies, "Highest to Lowest – Prison Population Total," http://www.prisonstudies.org/highest-to-lowest/prison-population-total?field_region_taxonomy_tid=All.

We not only have the highest number of prisoners, we have the highest percentage of people in prison or jail. In the U.S., 593 of every 100,000 people were in prison or jail in 2015. Cuba has 510 per 100,000 people in prison, Russia has 467, and Iran has 290.

Black and Latino Americans have been especially hard hit: they form over 39 percent of the prison population. One in every three black men is expected to serve time during their lives (at least under our current criminal justice system).[3] Approximately half of all inmates are there for violating drug prohibition laws.[4] And of course, it is the poor who represent the overwhelming majority of those behind bars, with median income about half that of those not incarcerated. (See Chart 9.1.)

How is it that America, supposedly the beacon of freedom and democracy for the rest of the world, has more prisoners than any police state?

Did we suddenly become a crime-ridden country in 1980?

Those who study the question say that four factors explain the dramatic rise in U.S. incarceration: 1) overt racism; 2) Nixon's ill-fated War on Drugs; 3) punitive laws like New York State Governor Nelson Rockefeller's "three strikes" legislation; and 4) the 1984 Sentencing Reform Act, which forced judges to issue harsh minimum sentences.

But these explanations don't tell the whole story. After all, racism was much more virulent earlier in American history. Until the civil rights movement, blacks were routinely denied their most basic civil rights. And yet the prison population was stable (and low, compared to now) through the 1940s, 1950s, and the turbulent 1960s.

---

3   Heather C. West, "Prison Inmates at Midyear 2009 – Statistical Tables," Bureau of Justice Statistics, June 23, 2010, http://www.bjs.gov/index.cfm?ty=pbdetail &iid=2200.

4   U.S. Department of Justice, Bureau of Justice Statistics, *Prisoners in 2009*, December 2010, p. 30, Table 16c; p. 33, Table 18, http://bjs.ojp.usdoj.gov/content/pub/pdf/p09.pdf.

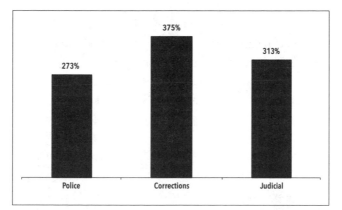

Chart 9.3: Percent Growth in Criminal Justice Expenditures, 1982 – 2012 (Adjusted for inflation)
Source: Author's calculations based on Bureau of Justice Statistics, "Justice Expenditures and Employment," various years, http://www.bjs.gov/index.cfm?ty=tp&tid=5.

Why are these Draconian laws so rigorously enforced? Why have we seen such a dramatic rise in criminal justice expenditures for police, courts and prisons? (See Chart 9.3.) And why are so many people engaging in underground job activities that put them at risk of imprisonment? The four explanations above don't answer these questions.

Deja vu all over again?

In this book, we have cast our eyes on many charts that suggest that something major happened around 1980. In fact, many of these charts have a similar shape: they all have a steeply rising hump on the right side, after 1980. We've already seen that all these things changed dramatically beginning around 1980:

- Wage increases no longer rise along with productivity. (Chapter 2, Chart 2.1)
- The CEO-worker wage gap takes off. (Chapter 2, Charts 2.2 and 2.3)
- Wall Street incomes shoot up while non-financial incomes stall. (Chapter 3, Chart 3.8)

- Wall Street profits skyrocket. (Chapter 4, Chart 4.5)
- The income gap between the super-rich and the rest of us widens rapidly. (Chapter 5, Chart 5.3)
- Taxes on the super-rich plunge. (Chapter 3, Chart 3.1)
- Corporate debt, consumer debt, student debt, and government debt all leap upward. (Chapter 8, Chart 8.1, 8.2, 8.3 and 8.4)
- The prison population explodes. (Chapter 9, Chart 9.1)

How do these trends fit together?

Unleashing Wall Street destroys manufacturing, older urban areas and America's standard of living

As we know, at the end of the 1970s, conservative economists persuaded U.S. leaders to experiment with a new kind of shock therapy aimed at ending stagflation (the crushing combination of high unemployment and high inflation): We would simultaneously deregulate Wall Street, cut social services to the bone, and slash taxes on the wealthy. This, in theory, would spur new entrepreneurial activity that would eventually trickle down to the rest of us.

Entrepreneurial activity did increase (on Wall Street, anyway), but with disastrous results for middle- and low-income workers. Rather than create new jobs and industries that would promote shared prosperity, the newly invigorated Wall Street instead began to financially strip-mine American manufacturing. Their main goal never was to produce tangible goods and services, but rather to make more money from money.

As we saw in Chapter 8, Wall Street's core American product is debt. Wall Street profits depend on loading up the country with it, and then collecting fees and compound interest on their loans.

Among the big debtors: state and local governments. And these are especially important to the incarceration story.

To review the story so far: After deregulation, waves of financial corporate raiders (now politely called managers of private equity firms and activist hedge funds) swooped in to suck the cash flow from healthy manufacturing facilities. They did this by buying up companies, loading them up with debt, and then cutting expenses to pay back the loans and enrich themselves.

Under this "downsize and distribute" policy, the raiders cut R&D, snatched pension funds, and slashed wages and benefits, decimating good-paying jobs in the U.S. and shipping many of them abroad. Nearly half of the raided companies failed, and in a few short years, America's heartland turned into the Rust Belt.[5] As Chart 4.4 in Chapter 4 shows, better paying manufacturing jobs declined.

But Wall Street prospered like never before: Its profits rose to account for 43 percent of all domestic corporate profits by 2002,[6] up from an average of about 12 percent from 1947 to 1980.

Impact of the Better Business Climate model on lower income Americans

The catastrophic collapse in manufacturing jobs was particularly tragic for African Americans. They had seen their standard of living rise during postwar years as they found higher paying, often unionized industrial jobs. But thanks to Wall Street raids, millions of these industrial jobs disappeared. There were still some jobs to be found in the service sector, but they paid about half of what manufacturing once paid.

The more fortunate Black and Latino men and women found work in the public sector, which was often unionized and paid a livable wage. But many more people had to take jobs in fast food

---

5   Most research indicates that M & A activity has an overall success rate of about 50 percent – basically a coin toss. Robert Sher, "Why Half of All M & A Deals Fail and What You Can Do About It," *Forbes*, March 19, 2012, http://www.forbes.com/sites/forbesleadershipforum/2012/03/19/why-half-of-all-ma-deals-fail-and-what-you-can-do-about-it/.

6   Author's calculations based on Bureau of Economic Affairs, National Income and Product Accounts Tables, Table 6.16, "Corporate Profits by Industry," available at: http://bea.gov//national/nipaweb/DownSS2.asp.

chains, box stores, warehouses, and in the lower ranks of the health care system. Overall, the Better Business Climate model brought soaring unemployment rates for young people, especially young people of color.

Many of the workers hit by these blows – people of all racial and ethnic backgrounds – found themselves in desperate straits, and some were forced to rely on the underground economy to survive.

The Ferguson scam: Using the courts to raise revenues from the poor for local government

It is a known fact that our judicial system discriminates against black and brown residents. The Sentencing Project reports that:[7]

- Young, black and Latino males (especially if unemployed) are subject to particularly harsh sentencing compared to other offender populations; ·
- Black and Latino defendants are disadvantaged compared to whites with regard to legal-process related factors such as the "trial penalty," sentence reductions for substantial assistance, criminal history, pretrial detention, and type of attorney;
- Black defendants convicted of harming white victims suffer harsher penalties than blacks who commit crimes against other blacks or white defendants who harm whites;
- Black and Latino defendants tend to be sentenced more severely than comparably situated white defendants for less serious crimes, especially drug and property crimes.

7   Tushar Kansal, "Racial Disparity in Sentencing: A Review of the Literature," The Sentencing Project, January 2005, http://www.sentencingproject.org/doc/publications/rd_sentencing_review.pdf.

Similarly, the American Civil Liberties Union finds that "Black people are 3.7 times more likely to be arrested for marijuana possession than white people despite comparable usage rates."[8]

Why are people of color targets for increased arrests and incarceration? Normally the explanation is simply racism. But the Justice Department report on the events in Ferguson, Missouri show the invisible hand of the Better Business Climate model hard at work. As stagnant wages and tax cuts for the rich squeeze state and local governments for funds, those jurisdictions look for new ways to raise money. One answer is to squeeze the poor through increasing the number of arrests and fines. Why? Because the poor have fewer resources with which to fight back. As the Justice Department report puts it:

> Ferguson has allowed its focus on revenue generation to fundamentally compromise the role of Ferguson's municipal court. The municipal court does not act as a neutral arbiter of the law or a check on unlawful police conduct. Instead, the court primarily uses its judicial authority as the means to compel the payment of fines and fees that advance the City's financial interests. This has led to court practices that violate the Fourteenth Amendment's due process and equal protection requirements. The court's practices also impose unnecessary harm, overwhelmingly on African-American individuals, and run counter to public safety. [9]

---

8   American Civil Liberties Union, "Groundbreaking Analysis Finds Marijuana Arrests Comprise Nearly Half of All Drug Arrests," Press Release, ACLU, June 4, 2013, https://www.aclu.org/criminal-law-reform/new-aclu-report-finds-overwhelming -racial-bias-marijuana-arrests.

9   U.S. Department of Justice, Civil Rights Division, "Investigation of the Ferguson Police Department," U.S. D.O.J., Civil Rights Division, March 4, 2015, http://www.justice.gov/sites/default/files/opa/press-releases/attachments/2015/03/04/ ferguson_police_department_report.pdf.

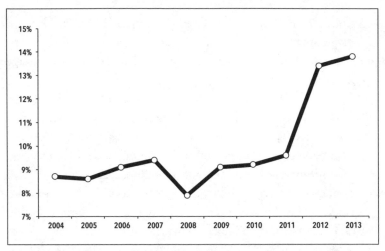

Chart 9.4: Percent of Ferguson, MO Revenues from Fines and Forfeitures, 2004 – 2013
Source: City of Ferguson, Missouri, "Comprehensive Annual Financial Report for the Year Ended June 30, 2013," http://www.
fergusoncity.com/470/Comprehensive-Annual-Financial-Report.

Amazingly, Ferguson amped up its revenue collection after the
Wall Street crash decimated the economy as Chart 9.4 clearly
shows.[10]

And it's not just Ferguson. We know for certain that the rest of
St. Louis county is playing the same game. As the *Washington Post*
reports:

> Some of the towns in St. Louis County can derive 40
> percent or more of their annual revenue from the petty
> fines and fees collected by their municipal courts. A
> majority of these fines are for traffic offenses, but they
> can also include fines for fare-hopping on MetroLink
> (St. Louis's light rail system), loud music and other noise
> ordinance violations, zoning violations for uncut grass
> or unkempt property, violations of occupancy permit
> restrictions, trespassing, wearing "saggy pants," busi-

---

10   Mike Maciag, "Skyrocketing Court Fines Are Major Revenue Generator for
Ferguson," *Governing the States and Localities*, August 22, 2014, http://www.governing.
com/topics/public-justice-safety/gov-ferguson-missouri-court-fines-budget.html.

ness license violations and vague infractions such as "disturbing the peace" or "affray" that give police officers a great deal of discretion to look for other violations. In a white paper released last month, the ArchCity Defenders found a large group of people outside the courthouse in Bel-Ridge who had been fined for not subscribing to the town's only approved garbage collection service. They hadn't been fined for having trash on their property, only for not paying for the only legal method the town had designated for disposing of trash.[11]

We also know that Missouri's Attorney General in 2014 sued 13 municipalities for relying too heavily on traffic fines to fund local government. Four of the municipalities received 30 percent or more of revenues from traffic fines and the rest did not provide the legally-required information to determine the percentage.[12]

The extent of this discriminatory revenue-raising across the country is currently unknown. But it is certain to extend far beyond the wide Missouri.

Financial strip-mining and gentrification

Financial strip-mining not only destroys middle-income manufacturing jobs, it destroys affordable housing by encouraging gentrification.

The rise of high-income financiers (along with banks eager to loan to them) creates upward pressure on housing prices in cities

11   Radley Balko, "How Municipalities in St. Louis County, Mo., Profit from Poverty," *The Washington Post*, September 3, 2014, http://www.washingtonpost.com/news/the-watch/wp/2014/09/03/how-st-louis-county-missouri-profits-from-poverty/.

12   "Missouri Sues St. Louis Suburb for Funding Government through Traffic Fines," *AllGov*, December 31, 2014, http://www.allgov.com/news/where-is-the-money-going/missouri-sues-st-louis-suburbs-for-funding-government-through-traffic-fines-141231?news=855232; and "Koster's Lawsuit against 13 St. Louis County Municipalities," http://www.stltoday.com/koster-s-lawsuit-against-st-louis-county-municipalities/pdf_c7d11bb7-c7e9-5867-9859-449c94629a1f.html.

that cater to elites like New York, Chicago, and San Francisco. Real estate development is lucrative in areas where land values are rising rapidly. Inevitably, lower-income residents are squeezed out, and their homes are turned into fashionable townhouses, coops, and condos for the wealthy. (Typically, the young adult children of the well-to-do unconsciously serve as the forward troops for gentrification as they flock into the cheaper neighborhoods of big cities.)

Gentrification and the "Broken Windows" theory of crime prevention

The commingling of the affluent and those living on the margins of the underground economy in gentrifying neighborhoods is explosive. Higher-income residents call for more protection and a halt to "crime in the streets."

Urban police departments, led by New York, began adopting the "Broken Windows" theory of crime prevention in the 1980s. The idea was that by targeting minor infractions (like drinking on the street, loitering, pan-handling, or selling loose cigarettes), police can prevent a slide to bigger crimes. The metaphor is that a neighborhood with no broken windows gives the community and its residents a more positive image, making it safer and less conducive to crime. It's a highly debatable theory. But it has unquestionably led to more arrests.

Inevitably, the combination of gentrification on one side, and joblessness and poverty on the other leads to more police patrols and arrests – including "stop and frisk" programs that disproportionately target people of color. The prison population surges.

In short, financial interests working to transform poorer neighborhoods into desirable real estate for the newly minted elites have an interest in ridding the neighborhood of the troublesome poor. Jail becomes the new home for many.

Downward pressure on the pubic sector

The housing bubble and bust hit low-income neighborhoods hard. Regions that were already struggling, including the Rust Belt, were decimated by the Wall Street crash. Joblessness spiked (again) and business and worker tax revenues fell. This led to more cuts in the public employee jobs that so many displaced manufacturing workers had relied on. Public sector services also got chopped.

Detroit became the poster child for ravaged American cities everywhere: First corporate raiders and private equity firms squeezed the life out of manufacturing all over Michigan. Then the Wall Street crash destroyed more jobs and undermined the tax base. And that led to urban bankruptcy and even more public sector job loss.

The Better Business Climate model's dirty little secret: Jail is America's jobs program

What will happen to all our unemployed people, given the massive shortage of jobs? What will happen to people trapped in neighborhoods crammed with foreclosed homes? Where are the job programs for the millions who need them?

In theory, the Better Business Climate model was going to lead to a boom that would create jobs for all those willing and able to work.

In practice, financial strip-mining did just the opposite. It caused decent jobs to evaporate, forcing cash-strapped cities to lay off public employees. Policing costs rose, squeezing the budget for social services and education. You had to be blind not to notice that those on the bottom were in serious trouble.

To cover for this abject failure of the Better Business Climate model, its supporters developed a novel jobs program that is now de-facto government policy: *Put the dislocated, the unemployed, the "surplus" youth in jail.*

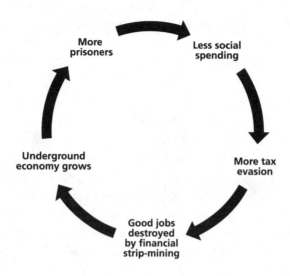

If incarcerating the poor turned America into the biggest police state in the world (and it did), so be it.

This is a remarkable shift in America's approach to joblessness. From the New Deal to the 1980s, the government had a strategy for dealing with enormous structural unemployment and poverty: it created jobs. Now, it puts the jobless in prison.

The Prison-industrial complex

The rapidly expanding prison sector warehouses millions of low-income people. But it also creates new jobs and profit opportunities.

As we know, the Better Business Climate model calls for privatizing public services. The idea is that privatizing generates new businesses and profits and it reduces the size of government. Plus, supporters claim that privately run businesses are always more efficient than the government.

Clearly, the growing prison population creates enormous privatization profit opportunities.

The first private prison opened in Tennessee in 1984. As of

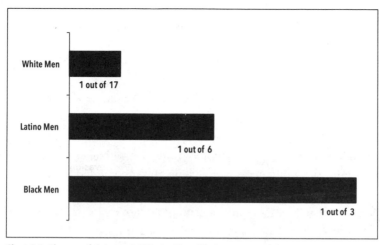

Chart 9.5: Chances of Going to Jail During Your Lifetime
Source: Report of the Sentencing Project to the United Nations Human Rights Committee Regarding Racial Disparities in the United States Criminal Justice System, August 2013, http://www.sentencingproject.org/doc/publications/rd_ICCPR%20Race%20and%20 Justice%20Shadow%20Report.pdf.

2016, U.S. Department of Justice statistics show that there were 128,323 state and federal prisoners housed in privately owned prisons in the U.S., constituting 8.5 percent of the overall U.S. prison population.[13]

Correctional, police, and judicial jobs at all levels of government have also grown dramatically since the early '80s, nearly doubling from 1.3 million in 1982 to 2.4 million in 2012.[14]

The prison guard unions and the private prison corporations (along with their Wall Street backers) have a vested interest in expanding the private prison system. Unfortunately for poor people, this requires rounding up more prisoners.

13   E. Ann Carson, "U.S. Department of Justice: Prisoners in 2016," U.S. Department of Justice, Bureau of Justice Statistics, January 2018, http://www.bjs.gov/ content/pub/pdf/p16.pdf.
14   Bureau of Justice Statistics, "Justice Expenditures and Employment Extracts, 2012–Preliminary," http://www.bjs.gov/index.cfm?ty=pbdetail&iid=5239.

Incarceration's color coding

The prison statistics describe an America stratified by skin color, as Chart 9.5 makes painfully clear. How do we account for that?

In this chapter we provide part of the answer: the financial strip-mining of our economy had an extremely negative impact on older urban areas where many people of color live. It also reduced the number of manufacturing jobs and then public employee jobs that minorities rely upon to move up the income ladder. In addition, statistics show that people of color are more often targeted for arrest, arrested for more minor crimes, and given longer sentences.

But lurking in the background is perhaps the most difficult question that America faces, and that we turn to in the next chapter: After all these years, why are people of color still overrepresented at the bottom of the income ladder?

Discussion Questions:

1. In your opinion what are the main causes for why the U.S. has the largest prison population in the world?

2. Why do local police departments want to extract so many fines from local residents of color?

3. In your opinion, what is the relationship between gentrification and the rise of our prison population?

4. Do you agree or disagree with the statement that prison has become America's new employment policy for the poor? Why or why not?

CHAPTER 10

The Color-coding of Wealth in America

Wealth and poverty

Another way to slice inequality is by skin color. And the numbers are not hard to find: 22 percent of all those classified as African-Americans live below the poverty line.[1] The figure is 19 percent for those labeled as Hispanic but only 10 percent for those labeled as white.[2]

We often focus on income when we're examining inequality. But in many ways, wealth accumulation is even more important than income because if you have any, you can pass it on to your family. You can help the next generation go to college or get a down-payment for a home. It's the key to moving entire generations out of poverty.

The wealth gap between white Americans and Americans we classify as Black or Hispanic is enormous. In 2016, if you were a typical white American, right in the middle of the wealth distribution, you had a net worth (assets minus debts) of $171,000. But if you were African-American, your median wealth was only $17,600. If you were Hispanic, it was $20,700.[3]

What if you are African-American and have earned a college

---

1   The poverty line is established by the U.S. Census Bureau using costs of goods consumed by a typical household, based on size of household and adjusted for inflation. For more information, see U.S. Census Bureau, "History of the Poverty Measure," http://www.census.gov/hhes/www/poverty/about/history/index.html.

2   U.S. Census Bureau, "Income and Poverty in the United States: 2016," http://census.gov.

3   Lisa Dettling, et al., "Recent Trends in Weealth-holding by Race and Ethnicity: Evidence from the Survey of Consumer Finances," Federal Reserve, September 27, 2017, https://www.federalreserve.gov/econres/notes/feds-notes/recent-trends-in-wealth-holding-by-race-and-ethnicity-evidence-from-the-survey-of-consumer-finances-20170927.htm.

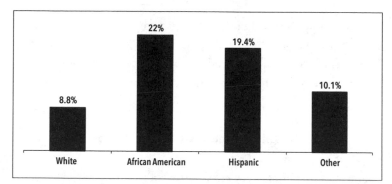

Chart 10.1: Poverty by Group, 2016
Source: U.S. Census Bureau, "Income and Poverty in the United States: 2016," http://census.gov.

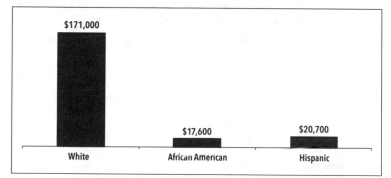

Chart 10.2: Median Wealth by Group, 2016
Lisa Dettling, et al., "Recent Trends in Weealth-holding by Race and Ethnicity: Evidence from the Survey of Consumer Finances," Federal Reserve, September 27, 2017, https://www.federalreserve.gov/econres/notes/feds-notes/recent-trends-in-wealth-holding-by-race-and-ethnicity-evidence-from-the-survey-of-consumer-finances-20170927.htm.

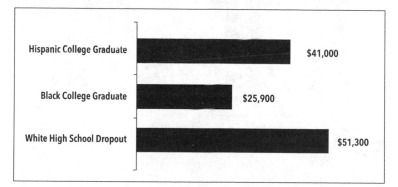

Chart 10.3: White High School Dropouts Have More Wealth than Black and Hispanic College Graduates
Source: Federal Reserve Data calculated by Matt Brunig, blog, http://www.demos.org/blog/9/23/14/white-high-school-dropouts-have-more-wealth-black-and-hispanic-college-graduates.

degree? Surely that will change the picture of extreme inequality, right? No, not much. Remarkably, as Chart 10.3 shows, the median Black and brown college graduate has accumulated less wealth than a white high school drop-out.

The primary sources of worker wealth

For most of us, our primary asset is our home. If we have any wealth at all, it's because we've bought a home at some point in our working lives and it has appreciated in value as we've paid down the mortgage. As we can see from Chart 10.4, African-Americans and Latinos are much less likely to own their homes than whites.

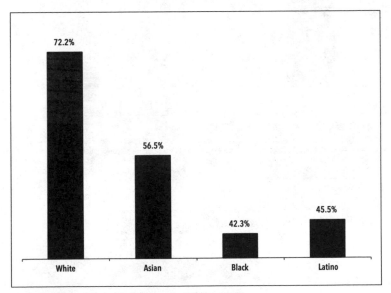

Chart 10.4: Home Ownership by Group, 2nd Quarter, 2017
Source: U.S. Census Bureau, "Homeownership Rates by Race and Ethnicity of Householder: 1994 to present," www.census.gov/housing/hvs/data/histtabs.html.

Location, location, location

Housing in America is still highly segregated, though the housing divide has softened somewhat. Blacks remain the most segregated racial group; Hispanics are the second most segregated. Housing segregation is highest in the largest metropolitan areas like Atlanta, Baltimore, Chicago, Cleveland, Detroit, Houston, Los Angeles, New Orleans, New York, Philadelphia and Washington, DC.[4]

While there are some high-income predominately Black or Latino neighborhoods, most of the neighborhoods where people of color live are poor, with few amenities. Home values are low. And that of course helps drive down the average wealth Black and Latino families accumulate.

Here is a brutal fact of economic life: separate is not equal, especially when it comes to housing values.

Why so much segregation? Why such a large wealth gap?

The evidence is overwhelming: Historical discrimination AND ongoing discrimination are responsible for the huge racial wealth gap.

The impact of American slavery on our people and our society is incalculable. It was an especially brutal form of slavery: Rarely before had people been enslaved in perpetuity, with slavery carried over from parents to children to their children.

Of course the subjugation didn't end with the abolition of slavery. For thirty years after the Civil War, elite whites battled ferociously to regain control over their sources of cheap labor. Eventually, they did.

By 1900, Jim Crow segregation became the norm. Legislatures across the south passed laws that disenfranchised Blacks, and poor whites as well. One-party rule in the South sent racist congress members to Washington, and through the seniority system, they

---

4   N.A. Denton, "Segregation and Discrimination in Housing," in eds. Rachel G. Bratt, et al., A Right to Housing: Foundation for a New Social Agenda, Philadelphia: Temple University Press, 2006, pp. 61-81.

gained control of key committees. Through racist courts and lynchings, whites suppressed nearly all resistance.

The New Deal marked a key turning point for both Black and white working people. It established a minimum wage and maximum work hours, and helped people pay their mortgages. It was the landmark moment for working people to begin to accumulate a bit of wealth.

Unfortunately, racist Southern congressional leaders made sure that wage and hour laws did not (and still do not) cover agricultural and domestic labor – the two most common types of work in the South at that time. They also made certain that new housing laws that encouraged home ownership excluded Blacks. People of color were largely blocked from participating in the postwar home ownership boom.

During the widespread rise of the American suburbs after WWII, housing discrimination was America's official government policy, as practiced by the Federal Housing Administration (FHA). Since its inception in 1934 until reforms in 1968, the FHA provided loan guarantees that enabled working class Americans to buy homes – but only some. As one scholar writes:

> Between 1930 and 1950, three out of five homes purchased in the United States were financed by FHA, yet less than two percent of the FHA loans were made to non-white home buyers. The FHA thus became the first federal agency to openly counsel and support segregation.[5]

Black neighborhoods were "red-lined," meaning they were ineligible for mortgages. The FHA issued virtually no mortgages for blacks in the growing suburbs, even when they qualified.

---

5   Marc Seitles, "The Perpetuation of Residential Racial Segregation in America: Historical Discrimination, Modern Forms of Exclusion, and Inclusionary Remedies," *Journal of Land Use and Environmental Law*, Vol. 141 (1996), http://www.law.fsu.edu/journals/landuse/vol141/seit.htm.

The net result: almost all-black urban ghettos and all-white suburbs. Another result: Generations of Black families were robbed of the chance to accumulate wealth by owning homes.

Aren't we now a color-blind society?

It's true that housing and hiring discrimination are now illegal. But recent studies show that discrimination still surrounds us. Here are some startling results (compiled by Sendhil Mullainathan in the *New York Times*) from carefully constructed studies that show the depth and extent of racial discrimination in America:

- When doctors were shown patient histories and asked to make judgments about heart disease, they were much less likely to recommend cardiac catheterization (a helpful procedure) to Black patients – even when their medical files were statistically identical to those of white patients.[6]
- When whites and Blacks were sent to bargain for a used car, Blacks were offered initial prices roughly $700 higher, and they received far smaller concessions.[7]
- Several studies found that sending emails with stereo-typically Black names in response to apartment-rental ads on Craigslist elicited fewer responses than sending ones with white names.
- A regularly repeated study by the federal Department of Housing and Urban Development sent African-Americans and whites to look at apartments

---

6   Kevin A. Schulman, M.D, et al., "The Effect of Race and Sex on Physicians' Recommendations for Cardiac Catheterization," *New England Journal of Medicine*, Vol. 340, pp. 618-626 (February 25, 1999), http://www.nejm.org/doi/full/10.1056/NEJM199902253400806.

7   Ian Ayres and Peter Siegelman, "Race and Gender Discrimination in Bargaining for a New Car," *American Economic Review*, June 1995, http://islandia.law.yale.edu/ayres/Ayres%20Siegelman%20Race%20and%20Gender%20Discrimination%20In%20Bargaining%20%20for%20a%20New%20Car.pdf.

and found that African-Americans were shown fewer apartments to rent and houses for sale.

- White state legislators were found to be less likely to respond to constituents with African-American names. This was true of legislators in both political parties.[8]
- Emails sent to faculty members at universities, asking to talk about research opportunities, were more likely to get a reply if a stereotypically white name was used.
- Even eBay auctions are not immune. When iPods were auctioned on eBay, researchers randomly varied the skin color on the hand holding the iPod. A white hand holding the iPod received 21 percent more offers than a Black hand.[9]

Racism creates race, not the other way around.

Race is the product of discrimination, not biology. It is a classification used to preserve and build a hierarchy of power and wealth. Whenever and wherever people are categorized by "race," we can be sure that economic and political elites are profiting from that classification.

As W.E.B. Dubois so famously put it, "the Black man is a person who must ride 'Jim Crow' in Georgia." He is saying as starkly as possible that he is defined as a Black man by the political act of discriminating against him, not by any innate characteristics.

Today, Black men are defined by "stop and frisk" and by being hauled to the side of the road for "driving while Black." Black chil-

---

8 Daniel M. Butler and David E. Broockman, "Do Politicians Racially Discriminate Against Constituents? A Field Experiment on State Legislators," *American Journal of Political Science*, Vol. 55, No. 3, pp. 463 – 477 (July 2011), http://onlinelibrary.wiley.com/doi/10.1111/j.1540-5907.2011.00515.x/full.

9 Jennifer L. Doleac and Luke C.D. Stein, "The Visible Hand: Race and Online Market Outcomes," *The Economic Journal*, Vol. 123, No. 572, pp. F469 – F492 (November 2013), http://onlinelibrary.wiley.com/doi/10.1111/ecoj.12082/abstract.

dren today learn the definition of race when they enter schools that are dilapidated and run like prisons. Black means your neighborhood gets fewer services, has fewer good food markets, has more crime. Black means that it is hard as hell to get a decent-paying job in an economy that has so few.

The changing definition of race

In wasn't until the 1800s that the term "race" became widely used. In Europe, people often used the word "race" to refer to someone's nationality, a quality that supposedly was both biological and cultural. European Christians generally thought that the Jewish "race" differed from them biologically. America's definition of "race" in the early twentieth century included the "one drop of blood" rule.[10] If you had one African ancestor anywhere in your family tree, you were legally Black. (But curiously, having one drop of "white" blood didn't make you white. Why is white blood so much weaker?) The Nazis tolerated considerably more Jewish blood than the Southern racists did Black blood: You could have as many as two Jewish grandparents under the Nuremberg Laws and still avoid being classified as Jewish, as long as the other grandparents and parents were not Jewish.

These conceptions of race were part of a global battle for supremacy, popularized through the notion of "Social Darwinism." Social Darwinists borrowed the scientific concept of the "survival of the fittest" and tried to apply it to countries, peoples ("races"), and classes. Nazi "Aryans" claimed they occupied the pinnacle of the world order of races created naturally by evolution. Therefore, they deserved to rule. They also used their claim to evolutionary superiority to justify their campaign to "purify" the races by extermi-

---

10   Shari L. Dworkin, "Race, Sexuality, and the 'One Drop Rule': More Thoughts about Interracial Couples and Marriage," *Sexuality and Society*, October 18, 2009, http://thesocietypages.org/sexuality/2009/10/18/race-sexuality-and-the-one-drop-rule-more-thoughts-about-interracial-couples-and-marriage/.

nating the impure Jews, gypsies, and homosexuals. The Nazis were not alone in this kind of reasoning: the British thought their "race" deserved to rule too, which justified their global empire over the "lower races."

In America, slaveholders used "race" to resolve a fundamental contradiction between ideologies of democracy and slavery. The declaration that "all men are created equal" did not square well with the brutal facts of inter-generational bondage. Slave owners resolved this conceptual problem by claiming that Blacks were a subordinate race. The Southern system of elite wealth extraction (before and after emancipation) depended conceptually on the creation and recreation of a "race" to justify oppression. (For an excellent account of the origins of race in America, see Karen Fields and Barbara Fields, *Racecraft: The Soul of Inequality in American Life*, New York: Verso Books, 2014. And for a definitive debunking of the genetics of race, see Dorothy Roberts, *Fatal Invention: How Science, Politics, and Big Business Re-create Race in the Twenty-first Century*, New York: New Press, 2012.)

The Financial strip-mining of Blacks and Hispanics

Clearly, the inequality in wealth and home ownership between those considered white and those considered Black runs deep. The housing bust that began in 2008 both reflected and deepened that inequality.

The housing bubble was itself the product of runaway inequality. As the wealthy became richer and richer, they needed new investment opportunities – someplace to put all that excess money that was flowing to the top. Wall Street obliged by coming up with new housing investments based on high-interest rate sub-prime mortgages that especially targeted Black and Latino would-be buyers. These loans became all the rage as mortgage brokers and banks focused on duping these would-be buyers, capitalizing on their fears that they would have trouble finding conventional mortgages.

Here's how the *New York Times* put it:

> Pricing discrimination – illegally charging minority customers more for loans and other services than similarly qualified whites are charged – is a longstanding problem. It grew to outrageous proportions during the bubble years. Studies by consumer advocates found that large numbers of minority borrowers who were eligible for affordable, traditional loans were routinely steered toward ruinously priced subprime loans that they would never be able to repay.[11]

That was Wall Street's goal: find prey for sub-prime loans, then repackage the loans into high yield bonds for investors. If and when the victims could no longer pay – that is, when the bubble burst – the houses would be foreclosed and the victims discarded. Here's one example of how it was done:

> In 1996, the company, renamed Long Beach Mortgage Co., paid $4 million to settle a Justice Department lawsuit accusing it of gouging older, female and minority borrowers. Prosecutors accused it of allowing mortgage brokers and its employees to add a fee to these customers of as much as 12% of the loan amount.[12]

As a result of these shenanigans, Blacks and Hispanics suffered more after the housing bust than any other group. As Charts 10.5 and 10.6 sadly reveal, people of color have fallen even further behind since the Wall Street crash in 2007.

---

11 "Fair Lending and Accountability," *New York Times* editorial, September 7, 2011, http://www.nytimes.com/2011/09/08/opinion/fair-lending-and-accountability.html.

12 Mike Hudson and E. Scott Reckard, "Workers Say Lender Ran 'Boiler Rooms'," *Los Angeles Times*, February 4, 2005, http://www.latimes.com/business/la-fi-ameriquest4feb0405-story.html#page=3.

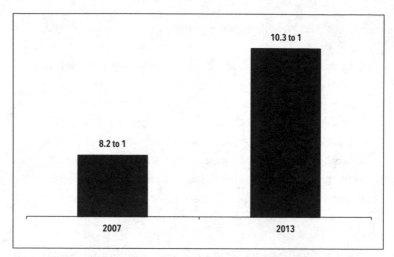

Chart 10.5: Rising Wealth Gap between Whites and Hispanics, 2007 – 2013
Source: Rajesh Kochhar and Richard Fry, "Wealth Inequality Has Widened Along Racial, Ethnic Lines Since End of Great Recession," Pew Research Center, December 12, 2014, http://www.pewresearch.org/fact-tank/2014/12/12/racial-wealth-gaps-great-recession/.

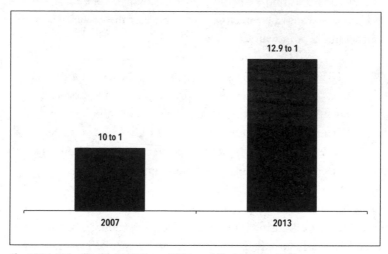

Chart 10.6: Rising Wealth Gap between Whites and Blacks, 2007 – 2013
Source: Rajesh Kochhar and Richard Fry, "Wealth Inequality Has Widened Along Racial, Ethnic Lines Since End of Great Recession," Pew Research Center, December 12, 2014, http://www.pewresearch.org/fact-tank/2014/12/12/racial-wealth-gaps-great-recession/.

Interconnectedness

The struggle to tame runaway inequality and the struggle to end racial discrimination must proceed together. Working people – Black, brown *and* white – are falling further and further behind as wealth increasingly accumulates in the hands of the few. But as always in American history, the hardest hit are those at the bottom.

Given the impact of discrimination on poverty, wealth, education, housing and incarceration, we must continue to demand fundamental justice and fairness for people of color. At the same time, we need to tame runaway inequality in our economy as a whole, or else everyone will fall further and further behind. Runaway inequality calls on us to remember and embrace an idea expressed by the International Workers of the World (IWW) back in the early 1900s as they struggled to overcome the differences between skilled and unskilled workers, recent and older immigrants, white and Black workers: "An injury to one is an injury to all."

Discussion Questions:

1. What is race?

2. Why do you think Blacks and Hispanics have so much less wealth than Anglo-Americans?

3. How does Wall Street's strip-mining of the economy impact race relations?

Immigration

Immigrants shaped, and continue to shape, the character of our country. As Chart 11.1 shows, immigrants have come to the U.S. in wave after wave. Immigrants formed the highest percentage of the population (14.7 percent) in the early 1900s, then dropped into the 1970s. Since then, immigration has been climbing again. Currently immigrants comprise 13.5 percent of our population.

How about the actual number of immigrants flowing into the country? For many years, the number ranged from about 10 million to 14 million. Then, around 1980, as in so many of our other charts, we see the number climb rapidly.

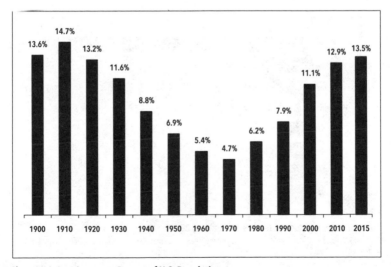

Chart 11.1: Immigrants as Percent of U.S. Population

Sources: Audrey Singer, "Contemporary Immigrant Gateways in Historical Perspective," *Daedalus*, Vol. 3, 2013, http://www.brookings.edu/~/media/research/files/articles/2013/09/05-immigrant-gateways-singer/singer-immigration-article-9513; and U.S. Census, "American Fact Finder," http://factfinder.census.gov.

Why has the number of immigrants taken off after 1980? Is rising immigration connected in some way with the Better Business Climate?

Where do immigrants come from?

In the colonial era, immigrants came mostly from England and Africa. Then came the families of the Irish laborers, the German craftsmen and the conscripted Chinese laborers to build our railroads, followed by the Italians, the East Europeans and Russians.

Many Latin Americans were already here when we annexed their land in Texas and the Southwest. In recent years, Hispanic immigrants again top the list as Chart 11.2 shows.

Immigration from Mexico rose rapidly, especially after 1970, according to Chart 11.3.

Why? What was going on in Mexico that spurred a rush of immigrants into the U.S.?

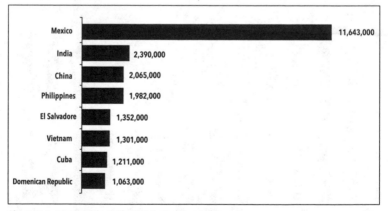

Chart 11.2: Immigration to the U.S. by Country, 2015
Source: U.S. Census Bureau data from Migration Policy Institute, http://migrationpolicy.org/programs/data-hub/us-immigration-trends#source.

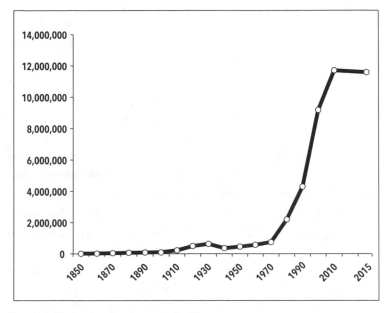

Chart 11.3: Mexican Born Immigrants in the U.S.

Source: U.S. Census Bureau data from Migration Policy Institute, http://migrationpolicy.org/programs/data-hub/charts/mexican-born-population-over-time.

The Better Business Climate model comes to Latin America

It would take dozens of books to do justice to the economic turmoil that has rocked Latin America since 1970. But, nearly all would note that the Better Business Climate model (known internationally as neo-liberalism and the Washington Consensus) invaded Latin American countries during this period. Why? U.S. leaders wanted to squelch what they viewed as creeping communism and socialism in the region.

In the 1960s, America was mired in a costly war in Vietnam. Meanwhile, Castro's Cuba defiantly offered Latin America an alternative model to what he called Yankee imperialism.

Latin American nations were moving towards more independence from Washington's control. Several created government-owned industries to control their natural resources and protect their countries from multinational corporations. They also adopted social policies and programs that provided support for working people and the poor. In Chile, Latin America's oldest democracy, Salvador Allende, a moderate socialist, was elected president in 1970.

This was simply too much to bear for President Nixon and his chief foreign policy advisor, Henry Kissinger. Fearing another Cuba, the United States engineered a CIA-led coup in 1973, and destroyed Chilean democracy. Allende and thousands of his followers were killed by the coup leaders allied with General Augusto Pinochet. Pinochet went on to rule Chile for the next 17 years. After consolidating his power through brutal violence, Pinochet brought in the architects of the Better Business Climate model from the University of Chicago to remake Chile's economy.

Pinochet and his American friends quickly privatized public industries, slashed social programs and support for the poor, and cut taxes, especially on the wealthy. They dismantled progressive unions and prohibited all political opposition. The elites favored by Pinochet became rich while poor and working people suffered.

Despite the violence and the violation of human rights and democratic norms, the architects of these economic policies deemed them a major success. In time, these policies came to be called the "Washington Consensus" – the blueprint for economic "reform" in any developing nation that wanted U.S. economic support.

To advance the U.S. geopolitical plan, Wall Street banks made enormous loans to Latin American countries during the 1970s (see Chart 11.4). The money, known as petrodollars, came from the vast profits earned by Middle East nations as they jacked up the price of oil in 1973 and 1979. These profits were deposited in Wall Street banks, and the banks then loaned the money freely to developing nations. Latin America became the prime destination for loan after loan because, as the chairman of Citibank, Walter Wriston, put it, "countries don't go bust." He meant that unlike a corporation, the people of a country always could be further squeezed to pay back the loans.

Mexico took on billions of dollars in loans, and in 1982 proved

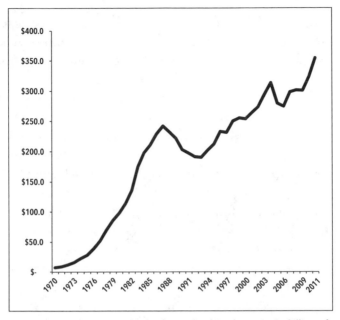

Chart 11.4: Increasing External Debt of Central and South America (In billions of U.S. dollars)

Source: Knoema, "External Long-term Debt of Developing Economies by Lending Source, Annual, 1970 – 2011," http://knoema.com/UNCTADLONGDEBT2013/external-long-term-debt-of-developing-economies-by-lending-source-annual-1970-2011.

Wriston wrong: Mexico's new neo-liberal economy couldn't repay the interest on its loans. This led to a massive debt crisis. The U.S. rushed in with a huge bailout for Mexico, hoping to save the American banking system from its predatory loans. In the wake of this crisis, Mexico was forced to further privatize public resources and further cut social programs. Millions of Mexicans lost their jobs or fell into deepening poverty. Crossing the border was looking better and better to impoverished Mexicans.

The North American Free Trade Agreement (NAFTA) upends Mexican farming

"Free trade" is a critical plank in the Better Business Climate model. As we know, the model aims to eliminate government regulations and taxes that inhibit business. That includes tariffs and other trade restrictions. Supposedly, the idea is to level the playing field so that all businesses have an equal chance of profiting. Of course, American multinationals are in a much better position to take advantage of this field than purely domestic companies. Among other things, multinationals can move jobs to the lowest wage areas of the world. Again, this is supposed to lead to more prosperity on both sides of the border.

NAFTA, which went into effect in 1994, broke the mold of previous trade agreements. This 900-page document didn't just cut tariffs and lift quotas on trade between the U.S, Mexico and Canada. It paved the way for corporations and investors by requiring each country to make its domestic laws conform to the agreement's terms, essentially overriding the power of democratically-elected representatives.

So why did NAFTA – and the Better Business Climate model in general – lead to more immigration to the U.S.? NAFTA left workers in all three countries defenseless against the decisions of profit-seeking corporations and investors. For instance, it allowed large, highly mechanized American farming conglomerates to move into Mexico, annihilating small-scale Mexican corn farmers who could not compete. Approximately 1.3 million Mexican farmers lost their jobs. Here's how one report put it:

> The majority of these farmers have limited education and cannot transfer their skills to the newly created jobs. Essentially, many of these people were "abandoned." In desperation, a great number of men emigrate to the U.S. in search of better jobs, increasing the number of female-headed households. Immigration increased from Mexico from approximately 350,000 per year in 1992 to approximately 500,000 per year in 2002 – 60 percent are undocumented. Data shows that they are coming from the rural agriculture sector. This can also be correlated to an increase of poverty in female-headed households as

they were left with limited job opportunities and households to run without a male bread-winner.[1]

So neo-liberalism, plus NAFTA, caused economic hardship for
the poor in Mexico, and this accounts for the dramatic rise in
immigration into the U.S.

Then came the War on Drugs, which further undermined living
conditions in Mexico.

How the War on Drugs pushes immigrants into the U.S.

Americans like their drugs, be it weed or whisky or Viagra. In this
we are only human, and as the history of the human race shows,
outlawing drugs never works. Prohibition didn't stop people from
drinking (and buying and selling) alcohol in the 1920s. And the
War on Drugs that began in 1970 hasn't stopped people from
getting high (or dealing). But the War on Drugs has had enormous
effects, including increased immigration.

- **Drug enforcement raised the profits of the drug cartels:**
  The U.S. Drug Enforcement Administration (DEA)
  and all the American courts and police that enforce
  the War on Drugs provide a massive price subsidy for
  those who peddle drugs. Enforcement raises the risk of
  growing, shipping and distributing drugs. But the more
  enforcement, the higher the profits for those who can
  survive in the drug business, including the Mexican
  drug cartels. This is economics 101 that even the most
  conservative economist knows full well.
- **Drug enforcement makes drug cartels grow:** Through the
  normal workings of the free market system, the most

---

1   Women's Edge Coalition, "NAFTA and the FTAA: Impact on Mexico's
Agriculture Sector," http://www.iatp.org/files/NAFTA_and_the_FTAA_Impact_on_
Mexicos_Agricultu.pdf.

efficient drug cartels will grow and wipe out the less efficient ones. But since these activities are illegal and people who engage in them run the risk of arrest and assaults by military forces, the cartels can survive only by resorting to more violence than their opponents – other cartels, the Mexican military, the Mexican government and the international arm of the DEA. In many areas of Mexico, the cartels grew so strong that they became the de facto government, having far more power than the local police.

Here's how PBS's *Frontline* put it:

> When the drug money ultimately makes its way into the foreign economy, it is used to pay the salaries of shippers and processors, as well as the bribes that supplement the incomes of government officials on both sides of the border. Whole regions of Mexico, Colombia and points in between have become dependent on the demand for drugs in the United States.
>
> Large scale drug organizations, such as the once powerful Cali cartel in Colombia or the Mexican Arellano Felix brothers, are said to resemble corporate organizations with division of labor and huge cash reserves designed to keep their operations moving smoothly.[2]

- **Drug cartels provide a path to upward mobility:** Given the dislocation caused by NAFTA and Mexico's embrace of neo-liberalism, many people have few options other than working in the drug trade and other areas of the underground economy. The drug cartels offer high-paid employment at a time when good jobs are hard to find.

---

2   Oriana Zill and Lowell Bergman, "Do the Math: Why the Illegal Drug Business Is Thriving," *Frontline*, PBS Channel Thirteen, http://www.pbs.org/wgbh/pages/frontline/shows/drugs/special/math.html.

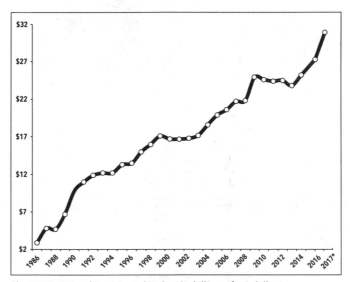

Chart 11.5: National Drug Control Budget (In billions of U.S. dollars)
Source: U.S. Office of the President, "National Drug Control Budget," various years, https://search.whitehouse.gov/
search?affiliate=wh&page=2&query=1985+u.s.+federal+drug+control+budget&utf8=%E2%9C%93
* budget request

- **Drug wars and drug enforcement lead to an exodus of Mexican citizens:** The violence needed to run a profitable cartel in the face of government- and DEA-supported crackdowns makes life extremely dangerous for the local population. Gun battles are frequent. Over 60,000 people have been killed from 2006 to 2012, according to the most recent data from Human Rights Watch.[3] As a result, tens of thousands of Mexican citizens prefer to flee across the border to relative safety. And if they can't do that, they hope to keep their children out of harm's way by shipping them to the U.S.

The net result: massive immigration to the United States. A tide of immigrants is the logical result of the twin policies of neo-liberalism and the War on Drugs.

---

3   Human Rights Watch, "Mexico's Disappeared: The Enduring Cost of a Crisis Ignored," HRW, 2013, http://www.hrw.org/sites/default/files/reports/mexico0213_ForUpload_0_0_0.pdf.

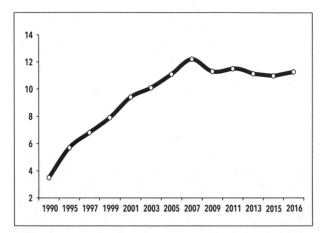

Chart 11.6: Number of Unauthorized Immigrants, 1990 – 2016 (Estimate in millions)

Source: Jeffrey S. Rassel and D'Vera Cohn, "As Mexican Share Declined, U.S. Unauthorized Immigrant Population Fell in 2015 Below Recession Level," Pew Research Center, April 25, 2017, http://www. pewresearch.org/fact-tank/2017/04/25/as-mexican-share-declined-u-s-unauthorized-immigrant-population-fell-in-2015-below-recession-level/.

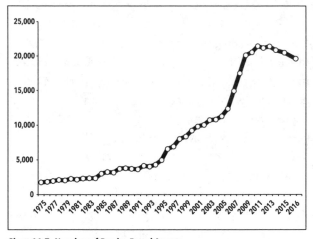

Chart 11.7: Number of Border Patrol Agents

Sources: U.S. Customs and Border Protection, "Border Patrol Agent Staffing by Fiscal Year," http://www.cbp. gov/sites/default/files/documents/BP%20Staffing%20FY1992-FY2014_0.pdf; and Syracuse University, Transactional Records Access Clearinghouse, http://trac.syr.edu/immigration/reports/143/.

In sum, these trends reinforce each other. The more we enforce drug prohibition (see Chart 11.5) the higher the risk premium for smuggling drugs into the U.S. Rising profits allow violent cartels to expand in Mexico, forcing more Mexicans to flee here without documentation (see Chart 11.6). To stem the tide, we spend more and more money on border patrol officers (see Chart 11.7).

Undocumented workers and runaway inequality

Of the 40 million immigrants in the U.S. today, approximately 12 million are undocumented.

Employers understand that undocumented workers live in constant fear of deportation (see Chart 11.8). This allows employers to hold these workers' wages and benefits to the absolute minimum. Employers can and often do disregard minimum wage laws and overtime regulations for workers who are undocumented. In all too many cases, employers simply refuse to pay at all. Yet this outright wage theft is extremely hard to prosecute, again because of the employees' fear of deportation.

Even the most anti-immigrant politicians understand that deporting all undocumented workers is impossible without turn-

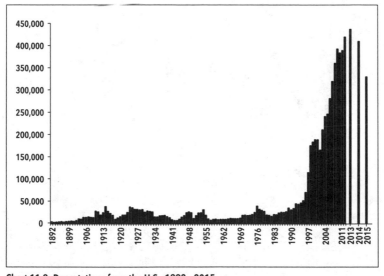

Chart 11.8: Deportations from the U.S., 1892 – 2015
Source: Homeland Security, *Yearbook of Immigration Statistics: 2015*, https://www.dhs.gov/yearbook-immigration-statistics-2015-enforcement-actions.

ing America into an even bigger police state. Enforcement at the Mexican border is increasingly costly, and yet it still hasn't stopped the flow of unauthorized immigrants. Providing immigrants with a path to citizenship is the logical and humane course of action. And it would lead to increased wages and benefits for these workers, upholding standards for us all.

Those who are troubled by unauthorized immigration should look closely at the data in this chapter. If the goal is to reduce the flow of immigrants to the U.S., then we need our own government to contribute to better – not worse – conditions in Mexico and other Latin American countries. We need to end the War on Drugs here and neo-liberalism in developing nations. As long as the DEA acts as the number one profit booster for drug cartels, victims will flee across the border. As long as neo-liberalism enriches the few at the expense of the many, Latin Americans will flee poverty with or without documentation.

Discussion Questions:

1. In your opinion, why was there so much immigration from Latin America to the United States?

2. What is the impact of the War on Drugs on immigration from Mexico?

3. In your opinion, what should be done about the 11 million undocumented immigrants in America today?

CHAPTER 12

Gender Equality, Family Life and Financial Strip-mining

Gender equality

Runaway inequality and financial strip-mining have spawned a super-elite of enormously wealthy CEOs, hedge fund and private equity managers and bankers. Almost none are women.

- Of the 1,000 CEOs listed by *Fortune*, only 51 (5 percent) are women.[1]
- Of the 400 wealthiest individuals listed by *Forbes*, 50 (12.5 percent) are women. And many of these are on the list because they're part of wealthy families. This includes four women from the Walton family (Wal-Mart), five women from the Pritzker family (Pritzker Group investment company), four women from the Johnson family (cleaning products), and five women from the Mars candy company.[2]
- Of the 25 top hedge fund moguls in 2015, none are women.[3]

---

1 Caroline Fairchild, "Women CEOs in the Fortune 1,000: By the Numbers," *Fortune.com*, July 8, 2014, http://fortune.com/2014/07/08/women-ceos-fortune -500-1000/.

2 "America's Richest Women," *Forbes*, October 17, 2017, https://www.forbes.com/ sites/angelauyeung/2017/10/17/richest-women-2017-forbes-400/.

3 "Highest Earning Hedge Fund Managers: 2016," *Forbes*, https://www.forbes. com/pictures/ghmf45mglj/22-nelson-peltz/#21a078c5539d.

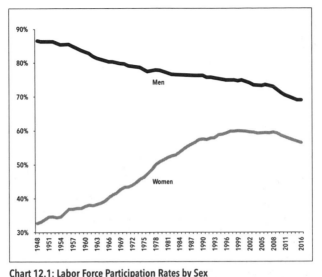

Chart 12.1: Labor Force Participation Rates by Sex
Source: Bureau of Labor Statistics, Labor Force Statistics from the Current Population Survey, http://data.bls.
gov/cps/cpsaat02.pdf.

- Of the top 50 "deal makers" listed by *Forbes* (mostly the heads of private equity firms), none are women.[4]

But, how has the Better Business Climate model affected the lives of regular women?

For one thing, it has probably pushed more women into the workforce to compensate for men's stagnating wages. Of course, the growing percentage of women in the workforce also reflects evolving gender roles and the rise of single or single parent households. For all these reasons, as Chart 12.1 shows, women have greatly increased their participation in the workforce since 1950.

At the same time, the gap between men's and women's wages has narrowed. The median wage of women working full time has risen from about 62 cents for every dollar in men's wages in 1979 to 82 cents per dollar in 2016. But unfortunately, as we can see from Chart 12.2, a

---

4   Ibid.

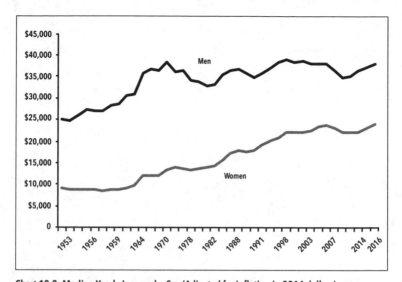

Chart 12.2: Median Yearly Income by Sex (Adjusted for inflation in 2014 dollars)
Source: U.S. Census Bureau, Historical Income Tables, Table P 5, http://www.census.gov/hhes/www/income/data/historical/people/.

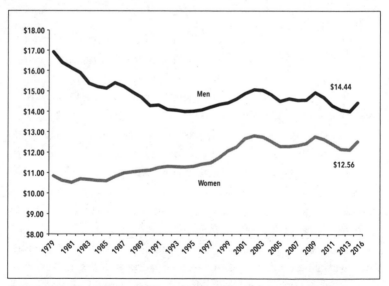

Chart 12.3: Median Hourly Earnings by Sex (Adjusted for inflation in 2013 dollars)
Source: Bureau of Labor Statistics, "Highlights of Women's Earnings in 2016," August 2017, http://www.bls.gov/opub/reports/womens-earnings/2016/pdf/home.pdf.

good deal of the gap closed because men's median wages stalled. (The wage gap for black women is 89 cents per dollar and for Hispanics it is 88 cents.)

Chart 12.3 (mapping median hourly wages) shows the pattern even more clearly: Men's wages have actually declined since the mid-1970s as financial strip-mining severed the tie between rising productivity and worker wages.

More revealing still, we can see that as runaway inequality accelerated over the last decade, wages for both men and women have followed the same track: Both flattened and now are declining. And progress toward closing the gender gap has stalled.

International comparisons

Every year, the World Economic Forum ranks gender inequality in 146 countries, using a range of measures. The U.S. looks okay in the ranking of women's "economic participation and opportunity": We're number 19. But we're 96 in political empowerment, and number 82 in health and survival. Combining the scores gives us a rank of 49 – putting us behind everyone from Iceland (number one) to Nicaragua and Rwanda.[5]

The countries with the most equal distributions of wealth – Iceland, Finland, and Norway – also were ranked one through three in gender equality.

Family life

One proven way to equalize pay for women is to adopt family-friendly work policies (like flexible hours) that make it easier for both men and women to raise children and take care of other

---

5   World Economic Forum, "The Global Gender Gap Report, 2017," http://www3. weforum.org/docs/WEF_GGGR_2017.pdf.

family members. Since women still do more of the childcare (and eldercare and housework) than men, they're more likely to be forced to abandon their jobs to take care of their families. Even their temporary absence from the workforce lowers their earning power over their lifetimes. So policies that allow them to stay at work and to share the burden of the work with their partners leads to higher pay overall.

Of course such policies have many benefits besides gender equality: They can enrich life for everyone.

Unfortunately, "family-friendly" policies don't square well with the Better Business Climate's anti-regulatory, anti-social program philosophy. As a result, the U.S. is close to last on the list of developed countries when it comes to family-friendly policies. So it appears that the country with the most inequality is also the country with the least support for women and families.

1) Family leave

Here's a remarkable and troubling fact: The International Labor Organization reports that among all the developed economies, only the United States does not pay maternity benefits.[6]

Chart 12.4 shows the amount of paid and unpaid leave for new parents (male or female) each country provides by law. We're dead last among developed nations. The ILO reports:

> Almost all OECD countries offer paid maternity leaves
> that last at least three months – which is not surprising
> given that both the ILO convention on maternity leave

---

6   Laura Addati, et al., *Maternity and Paternity at Work: Law and Practice Across the World*, Appendix II, "Key National Statutory Provisions on Maternity Leave, by Region, 2013," Geneva: International Labour Organization, 2014, http://www.ilo.org/wcmsp5/groups/public/---dgreports/---dcomm/---publ/documents/publication/wcms_242615.pdf.

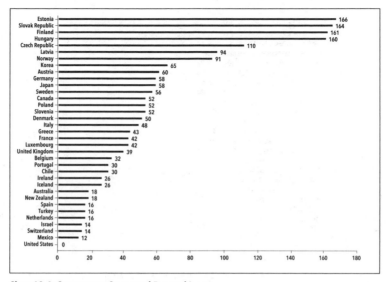

Chart 12.4: Government Supported Parental Leave

Source: 2011-2012 data based on International Labour Organisation, *Maternity and Paternity at Work: Law and Practice Across the World* (Geneva: International Labour Office, 2014), http://www.ilo.org/wcmsp5/groups/public/---dgreports/---dcomm/---publ/documents/publication/wcms_242615.pdf.

and the current EU directive on maternity leave stipulate that mothers should have access to at least 14 weeks of leave around childbirth – with the United States the only country to offer no statutory entitlement to paid leave on a national basis.

The report contrasts this lack with other countries:

In some countries entitlements to paid maternity leave extend to over six months. In the United Kingdom, for example, mothers can take up to nine months paid maternity leave.[7]

_____

7   Organisation for Economic Cooperation and Development, "OECD Family Database, Parental Leave Systems, 2016," http://www.oecd.org/els/soc/PF2_1_Parental_leave_systems.pdf.

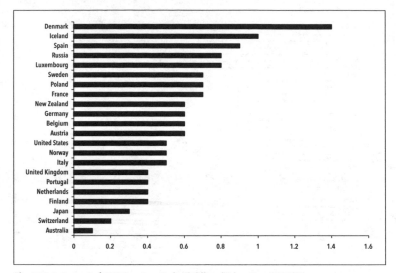

Chart 12.5: Percent of GDP Spent on Early Childhood Education, 2011/12
Source: OECD, *Education at a Glance 2014: OECD Indicators* (OECD Publishing, September 2014), http://dx.doi.org/10.1787/eag-2014-en.

2) Childcare

If you're affluent, you hire a nanny to care for the kids, allowing you and your spouse to hold down your lucrative jobs. If you're not so affluent, you're in trouble. Many families devote a huge percentage of their income to pay for childcare that would be free in other developed countries. Some families can't afford childcare, and one parent (usually the mother) who would often rather work is forced to stay home to care for the child, sacrificing her income and future earnings.

Research shows that high-quality childcare is one of the best investments we could possibly make in our children and the future. And yet, as a nation, we are well down on the list when it comes to early childhood education expenditures (see Chart 12.5).[8]

---

8 OECD, "How Do Early Childhood Education and Care (ECEC) Policies, Systems and Quality Vary Across OECD Countries?" *Educator Indicators in Focus*, February 2, 2013, http://www.oecd.org/education/skills-beyond-school/EDIF11.pdf.

Flexible work time

When workers are allowed to change their hours of work, change the number of hours they work, or work from home, they're better able to stay in the workforce as they take care of children and other family members. Once again, Denmark, Finland and Sweden lead the developed world in work flexibility, and because women still do more care-giving than men, these countries also have the best gender equality and the lowest overall income and wealth inequality.

Ensuring this kind of job flexibility requires regulating corporate practices, which Better Business Climate proponents frown upon. Therefore, as the OECD reports, the U.S. has low levels of work flexibility:

> [I]n the United States, 37% of employers with at least 50 employees allow most of their employees to vary the start and end of work periodically (Galinsky et al., 2008). Only 10% of employers grant it on a daily basis. Most of employees work in companies where flextime schemes are available only to a limited number of employees: generally those in more senior positions. Women are less likely than men to have access to flextime, but parents – including single mothers – are more likely to have access to workplace flexibility (Golden, 2001, 2006; McCrate, 2005).[9]

Work-life balance

Perhaps the best measure of how we treat families is the "Work-Life Balance index" created by the OECD. The OECD notes:

---

9   Heather Boushey, "Perspectives on Work/Family Balance and the Federal Equal Employment Opportunity Laws," Testimony to the Equal Opportunity Commission, Center for Economic and Policy Research, August 28, 2009, http:// www.cepr.net/publications/briefings/testimony/perspectives-work-family-opportunity.

Finding a suitable balance between work and daily living is a challenge that all workers face. Families are particularly affected. Some couples would like to have (more) children, but do not see how they could afford to stop working. Other parents are happy with the number of children in their family, but would like to work more. This is a challenge to governments because if parents cannot achieve their desired work/life balance, not only is their welfare lowered but so is development in the country.[10]

The workday for men is still very different than that of women. Women on average spend almost twice as much time on unpaid domestic work as men.

People spend one-tenth to one-fifth of their time on unpaid work.

The distribution of tasks within the family is still influenced by gender roles: men are more likely to spend more hours in paid work, while women spend longer hours in unpaid domestic work. While on average men in OECD countries spend 141 minutes per day doing unpaid work, women spend 273 minutes per day cooking, cleaning or caring.

The lower the numerical ranking on the work-balance index, the more likely that women and men can enjoy relative equality. Of the 38 countries surveyed, we ranked number 28.

Inequality, deregulation, gender equality

The story is getting clearer and clearer. The Better Business Climate model was supposed to bring us shared prosperity, but instead has delivered runaway inequality. The model prescribes

---

10   OECD, "Work-Life Balance," OECD Better Life Index, http://www.oecdbetter lifeindex.org/topics/work-life-balance/, accessed January 2017.

deregulating business and curbing government benefits including preventing regulations on paid sick leave, paid family leave, subsidized childcare, and flexible work time. And ever since the model was adopted, women's wages have stagnated and families have struggled with some of the most family-hostile policies in the developed world.

Gender equality and family-friendly policies will no doubt remain elusive until we put a halt to the financial strip-mining of our economy.

Discussion Questions:

1. Why are women virtually excluded from the top CEO and financial jobs?

2. How has the Better Business Climate model helped or hurt women's wages?

3. Why are we so far behind other nations when it comes to family life governmental policies?

CHAPTER 13

Everything Is Connected to Everything Else: Climate Change, Wall Street, and Runaway Inequality

Traditionally, we think of belching coal-fired plants, steel mills and other energy-intensive facilities as the main culprits in our pell-mell dash to environmental hell. Usually, we don't worry much about the environmental impact of the financial sector, which does most of its business electronically. In fact, several prominent financiers are garnering kudos for their big donations to environmental causes and their concern about global warming.[1]

But as we dig deeper, we are reminded that the late Barry Commoner, who helped found the modern environmental movement, was right: "Everything is connected to everything else."

What is the connection between runaway economic inequality, the rise of high finance and environmental disaster?

The rise of greenhouse gases

- Every one of the past 40 years has been warmer than the 20th century average.
- 2016 was the hottest year on record.
- The 12 warmest years on record have all occurred since 1998.[2]

---

1 Nicholas Confessore, "Financier Plans Big Ad Campaign on Climate Change," *New York Times*, February 17, 2014, http://www.nytimes.com/2014/02/18/us/politics/financier-plans-big-ad-campaign-on-environment.html?_r=0.
2 Union of Concerned Scientists, "Confronting the Realities of Climate Change: The Consequences of Global Warming Are Already Here," https://www.ucsusa.org/global-warming#.Wlt_qLkm5Ms.

In the United States in 2017 alone, there were 15 weather-related disasters that cost $1 billion or more each. And that doesn't include the latest wildfires in southern California. The total costs for extreme weather events in 2017 in the U.S. amounted to over $206 billion.[3]

And in the same year that President Trump pulled the U.S. out of the Paris climate accord, a government report released in November found that:

- [B]ased on extensive evidence…it is extremely likely that human activities, especially emissions of green-house gases, are the dominant cause of the observed warming since the mid-20th century.
- For the warming over the last century, there is no convincing alternative explanation supported by the extent of the observational evidence.[4]

But while the data on climate change is conclusive, a group of conservative politicians would like us to believe that humans are not the cause. (Apparently 56 percent of congressional Republicans say they deny or question the science on climate change.[5])

What is their evidence? The deniers claim that the scientific community is really still in doubt. But the scientific consensus about climate change is obvious. A survey of 2,259 peer-reviewed scientific articles about global warming authored by 9,136 scientists between November 2012 and December 2013, published in *Scientific American*, reveals that only ONE out of 2,259 articles argued that global warming was not caused by human-made pollution.[6] A

---

3   "'A Disproportionate Hit': 2017's Weather Disasters Are Among the Worst in U.S. History," *Time*, December 28, 2017, http://time.com/5081289/2017-weather-global-warming/; and Sara Shayanian, "2017 Set Record for U.S. Natural Disaster Costs — Over $300 Billion," UPI, January 8, 2018, https://www.upi.com/Top_News/US/2018/01/08/2017-set-record-for-US-natural-disaster-costs-over-300B/1791515432547/.].

4   "Highlights of the Findings of the U.S. Global Change Research Program Climate Science Special Report," November 2017, https://science2017.globalchange.gov/chapter/executive-summary/.

5   Tiffany Germain, "Here Are the 56 Percent of Congressional Republicans Who Deny Climate Change," Moyers and Company, February 3, 2015, http://billmoyers.com/2015/02/03/congress-climate-deniers/.

6   Ashutosh Jogalekar, "About That Consensus on Global Warming: 9136 Agree,

more recent study found that 97 percent of climate scientists and climate-related scientific articles agree that climate change is real and caused by human activity.[7]

And despite the deniers, the American public increasingly agrees that global warming is happening. In 2016, Yale University conducted a poll that found that 69 percent of Americans believe that global warming is happening and 70 percent trust the science on this.[8]

Some Americans do not trust scientists and many politicians either feel the same way or are catering to those voters. But in this book, we are driven by the facts as best as we can determine them. And the facts on climate change are painfully clear: The driving physical cause of global warming is the rise in the greenhouse gases that are emitted mostly by burning fossil fuels. CO_2 represents about 82 percent of all greenhouse gases.

Chart 13.1 tracks the rise in average global temperature and Chart 13.2 tracks rising CO_2 emissions since 1980. Scientists can measure these two numbers with great accuracy and they have concluded that rising CO_2 emissions are causing the Earth to heat up. The rise is the result of rapid industrial development all around the world, first in the U.S., Europe and other industrialized nations, and now in every developing nation.

The warmest year on record was 2016, making it the third year in a row to set the record. And 2017 was the second or third warmest year. The 13 warmest years on record have all occurred since 1998. The more heat in our atmosphere, the more violent and unstable our weather becomes. We see more and more droughts, storms, and floods. Scientists have clearly established that the polar ice caps are melting at an alarming rate, oceans are warming and becoming more acidic, and sea levels are rising. They warn that these changes

One Disagrees," *Scientific American,* January 10, 2014, http://blogs.scientificamerican.com/the-curious-wavefunction/2014/01/10/about-that-consensus-on-global-warming-9136-agree-one-disagrees/.

7   E.W. Maibach, et al., "Consensus on Consensus: A Synthesis of Consensus Estimates on Human-caused Global Warming," *Environmental Research Letters,* Vol. 11, 4 (April 13, 2016).

8   Jennifer Marlon, et al., "Yale Climate Opinion Maps – U..S. 2016," http://climatecommunication.yale.edu/visualizations-data/ycom-us-2016/?est=happening&type=value&geo=county.

will lead to food and water shortages, more rapid spread of disease, and political instability. They urge immediate action to dramatically decrease greenhouse gas emissions.

But why isn't each year warmer than the one before?

People who doubt the reality of climate change point to the variability in our weather. Clearly, not every day, week, or year is warmer or stormier than the last. That's because the weather is a vast, complicated system that fluctuates. So making a prediction involves probabilities.

Here's an example that may help those still questioning climate change. Imagine that you were rolling one die. Two sides of the die represent an above-average temperature; two sides represent average temperature, and two sides represent below average temperature. If you roll the die enough times you will get each result about one third of the time. That's the pattern we would see in the real world if it were not heating up – some years above average, some below and some average.

Now imagine that you change the die so that three of the six sides are above average, two are average and only one is below average. You roll that die and the odds are that at least half of the years will be above average. But you will also roll a few average years and still fewer below average years.

Greenhouse gases are changing the weather dice. The probability that a year will be warmer than average is rising and rising. That's where we are headed, even if it's not a steady march with each and every year hotter than the previous one.

Is Wall Street to blame?

In Charts 13.1 and 13.2, we can see that temperatures and CO_2 levels move up sharply starting around 1980. But this is NOT to say that runaway inequality and financial strip-mining are to blame

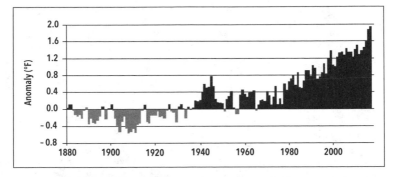

Chart 13.1: The Rise of Global Temperatures, 1880 – 2015 (Farenheit)
Source: Wuebbles, D.J., et al., "Our Globally Changing Climate," in Climate Science Special Report: Fourth National Climate Assessment, Volume I , U.S. Global Change Research Program, 2017, pp. 35-72, doi: 10.7930/J08S4N35.

for global warming. We cannot place the entire blame for climate change on Wall Street. The rapid rise of CO_2 emissions started after WWII, many years before the deregulation of finance.

The entire world depends heavily on our use of fossil fuels – coal, oil and natural gas. Climate scientists are now telling us we must keep the great majority of the remaining fossil fuels in the ground. It will be a hard habit to break, because for more than a century, we have spewed CO_2 and other greenhouse gases into the air without giving it a second thought. Those carbonized chickens are coming home to roost.

And they are coming home to roost with a vengeance for those at the middle and bottom of the income scale – the very same people who are hardest hit by the Better Business Climate model and financial strip-mining. Across the country and the world, the people most at risk from climate change are low-income and working people. This is one reason why so many people are now calling for "climate justice."

Low-income people can't afford to shield themselves from the floods and storms. Nor can they easily recover from the losses they suffer in catastrophes like Katrina or Sandy or Irma or Maria. They can't afford to pay the high food prices that result from the worsening drought now gripping the western states. They can't easily move somewhere else when the water dries up. Climate change only compounds the inequality created by the Better Business Climate model.

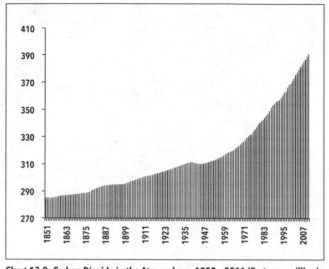

Chart 13.2: Carbon Dioxide in the Atmosphere, 1850 – 2011 (Parts per million)
Source: National Aeronautics and Space Administration, Goddard Institute for Space Studies, http://data.giss.nasa.
gov/modelforce/ghgases/Fig1A.ext.txt.

But far from helping us marshal our resources to address the climate change challenge, deregulated, high finance is busy extracting money from our wallets and sapping our government's power.

How financial strip mining contributes to environmental destruction

Let's roll back to Chapter 4, when we talked about Wall Street's shift, beginning in the late 1970s, from a strategy of "retain and reinvest" to "downsize and distribute."

As we know, since then, corporate raiders, private equity companies, and hedge funds have turned corporations into financial strip mines. They buy up companies, load them up with debt, extract fees and dividends and then use the earnings from the target company to pay off the debt. They also tie CEO compensation to the value of the company's stocks. This gives the CEO and other executives a big incentive to use company earnings to buy back stocks, increasing the value of stock options and enriching themselves.

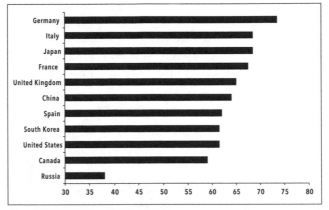

Chart 13.3: 2016 Energy Efficiency Ratings
Source: Kallaburi, et al., "2016 International Energy Efficiency Scorecard," American Council for an Energy-efficient Economy, 2016.

These tactics dramatically increased inequality. In 1965, the ratio of CEO to worker pay was 40 to one. Today it is almost 800 to one.

But this process also has dire consequences for worker health and safety and for the environment. As more and more money is siphoned out of a company, managers cut back on experienced workers and pollution controls. Meanwhile, the company moves to what workers call "breakdown maintenance" – nothing gets fixed until it breaks, leading both to more hazardous conditions for workers and more emissions. They postpone investment in the most modern, energy-saving equipment, sometimes indefinitely, as the cash flows up to the CEOs and out to the banks, hedge funds and private equity corporations. As a result, the U.S. lags far behind many other countries when it comes to environmental protection, even while we lead the world in financial sector power and profits.

Worker health and safety suffers along with the environment. As financiers and CEOs squeeze money out of their facilities, they trim or even eliminate health and safety training. They hire poorly trained subcontractors and temporary workers who are unfamiliar with health and safety rules.

Even as more and more of U.S. industry is shifted abroad, occupational fatality and injury rates are high in comparison to other major countries. For example, in the "Global Estimates of Occupational Accidents," we are ranked 20th of the 24 countries surveyed when it comes to both accident and fatality rates.

As we saw earlier, Yale University's Center for Environmental Law and Policy compiles an annual Environmental Performance Index that ranks 180 countries by health, air quality, water and sanitation, water resources, agriculture, forest and fishery management, biodiversity habitats, and climate/energy. In 2016, the U.S. ranks 26th overall. But in the all-important climate and energy category, we rank 44th.

These dire findings are confirmed by the American Council for an Energy Efficient Economy (ACEEE), which ranks the world's largest economies on an energy efficiency score card. We rank 9th out of the 11 economies listed in Chart 13.3.

Case study: The financial strip-mining of GM

Cars and trucks contribute about one-fifth of the U.S. emissions of carbon dioxide, the number one greenhouse gas.[9] So combating climate change requires that we develop a modern mass transit system that will dramatically reduce our dependence on cars. In addition, we need to quickly develop and manufacture more efficient cars. One would hope that GM, America's largest auto company, would be plowing as much money as possible into this new research.

Wall Street, however, has other ideas. A group of hedge funds led by Harry J. Wilson, a former Goldman Sachs manager who served on the Obama administration's auto industry task force, is buying up GM stock and pressing the company to move more money not to research, but to investors. According to the *New York Times*, on February 11, 2015, "Mr. Wilson put himself up for a seat on the G.M. board, as part of a campaign to persuade the company to buy

---

9 Union of Concerned Scientists, "Cars and Global Warming," http://www.ucs usa.org/our-work/clean-vehicles/car-emissions-and-global-warming#.VNuDBPnF9bI.

back at least $8 billion worth of shares by next year."[10] (On January 13, 2016, GM announced a $9 billion buyback!)

Why spend $8 billion to buy back stocks instead of investing more in new technology and other carbon reduction efforts? Because Wilson and his backers want to drive up the price of the stock to enrich themselves. As we saw in Chapter 4, when companies buy back shares they reduce the number of existing shares and so make each one more valuable. If you own millions of GM shares, the buy-back effort could be worth hundreds of millions of dollars to you.

Wilson is following the financial strip-mining tradition that began in earnest with deregulation 30 years ago. He is doing all he can to move $8 billion from GM to his group of investors – proving that these Wall Street investors have no interest in using their influence to stop climate change. They would much rather divert GM funds into their private coffers.

Tax avoidance by corporate America and the wealthy cripples our fight against climate change

It now appears that climate change will be the biggest challenge humanity has ever faced. We need to muster our resources to address it, both in the U.S. and in countries around the world.

Unfortunately, our resources are otherwise occupied. As we have seen, thanks in great part to the financial industry and the Better Business Climate model, our nation's wealth is nearly all tied up by the wealthy: The top 1 percent alone controls about 40 percent of the wealth. And high finance has done all in its power to keep that money to itself, resisting taxation and arguing that a small government is a good government. And then there's the direct siphoning of funds: The U.S. loses over $180 billion a year in tax revenues because Wall Street is parking U.S. corporate and individual money offshore.

---

10   Michael J. DeLaMerced and Bill Vlasic, "Hedge Fund-Backed Investor Puts Himself Up for G.M. Board," *New York Times*, February 10, 2015, http://dealbook. nytimes.com/2015/02/10/activist-investors-take-aim-at-g-m/?ref=todayspaper&_r=0.

Without that money, government is hard-pressed by weary taxpayers to come up with the funds necessary to fight climate change.

Wall Street greed changes attitudes towards climate change

When the economy nearly collapsed in 2008 due to Wall Street's greedy gambling spree, we lost nearly 8 million jobs in a matter of months, sending shockwaves throughout the workforce.

The shockwaves helped rob momentum from the climate justice movement. In fact, polls show that as the fear of losing one's job rose, the percent of people who thought climate change is caused by human activity declined and only began to recover by 2014 (see Chart 13.4).

Similarly, as job fear rises, concern for protecting jobs trumps protecting the environment (see Chart 13.5).

Chart 13.4: Percentage of People Believing Human Activity Is the Cause of Global Warming

Sources: Gallup, "A Steady 57% in U.S. Blame Humans for Global Warming," http://www.gallup.com/poll/167972/steady-blame-humans-globalwarming.aspx; and "Global Warming Concern at Three-decade High in U.S.," March 14, 2017, http://news.gallup.com/poll/206030/global-warming-concern-three-decade-high.aspx.

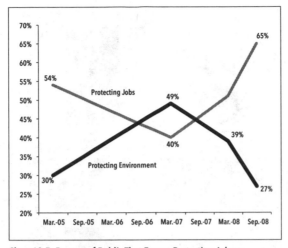

Chart 13.5: Percent of Public That Favors Protecting Jobs or Protecting the Environment

Source: Moore Information, "Protecting Jobs vs. Protecting the Environment: Poll," *Oregon Business Report*, November 19, 2008, http://oregonbusinessreport.com/2008/11/poll-protecting-jobs-vs-protecting-the-environment/.

Hispanics more supportive of action on climate change

A counter to these trends comes from the Hispanic community, the fastest growing group in the U.S.

A recent poll found that Latinos are more concerned about climate change than the rest of the population. Fifty-four percent of the Hispanic respondents in this poll said global warming was extremely important or very important to them. Only 37 percent of the "white" respondents said the same (see Chart 13.6).

When asked how much the government should do about global warming, 63 percent of Hispanic respondents said the U.S government should do a great deal or a lot, compared to only 49 percent for the non-Hispanic white respondents (see Chart 13.7).

The final question concerns whether or not to help poorer countries deal with the ravages of global warming. Here, by more than a two-to-one margin, Hispanics favored giving money to poor countries to reduce the damage that global warming may cause (see Chart 13.8).

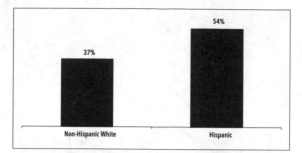

Chart 13.6: Global Warming Is Extremely Important to Me Personally

Source: Coral Davenport, "Climate Is Big Issue for Hispanics, and Personal," *New York Times*, February 9, 2015, http://www.nytimes.com/2015/02/10/us/politics/climate-change-is-of-growing-personal-concern-to-us-hispanics-poll-finds.html?_r=0.

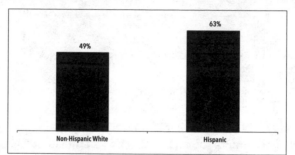

Chart 13.7: The U.S. Government Should Do a Great Deal, a Lot about Global Warming

Source: Coral Davenport, "Climate Is Big Issue for Hispanics, and Personal," *New York Times*, February 9, 2015, http://www.nytimes.com/2015/02/10/us/politics/climate-change-is-of-growing-personal-concern-to-us-hispanics-poll-finds.html?_r=0.

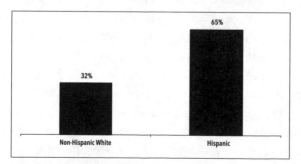

Chart 13.8: The United States Government Should Give Money to Poor Countries

Source: Coral Davenport, "Climate Is Big Issue for Hispanics, and Personal," *New York Times*, February 9, 2015, http://www.nytimes.com/2015/02/10/us/politics/climate-change-is-of-growing-personal-concern-to-us-hispanics-poll-finds.html?_r=0.

What do we make of these stark differences? First, many lower-income Hispanic people live in communities near sources of pollution and where they are likely to be hit hard by super storms like Katrina, Sandy, Irma, and Maria – storms that are expected to become more frequent as average global temperatures rise.

It may also be that Latinos from families that have immigrated relatively recently have ties to more agrarian Latin American countries that are suffering as a result of climate change.

Another poll of Latinos, this one by the Natural Resources Defense Council, also found very high levels of support for climate action. The poll asked respondents what motivated these strong feelings. What topped the list was a sense of responsibility for the future of their children and the generations to come. "It really embodies and embraces the American dream to have something, and to leave something better for next generations," said pollster Matt Barreto.[11]

However, Latinos' passion for addressing climate change is in direct conflict with the deregulatory policies of the Better Business Climate model and ongoing financial strip-mining.

Taking on climate change requires a movement that tackles runaway inequality and financial strip-mining.

The financial strip mining by Wall Street, financialized corporations and complicit politicians are the common root cause of so many of our most pressing problems:

- It is the root cause of ever growing inequality in income and in wealth.
- It is facilitating tax evasion.
- It is exacerbating poverty and homelessness.
- It contributes to the skin color divide and high infant mortality.

---

11   Katie Valentine, "For Latino Voters, Climate Change Is Almost as Important an Issue as Immigration," *Climate Progress*, January 23, 2014, http://thinkprogress.org/climate/2014/01/23/3198951/latinos-support-climate-action/.

- It produces the largest prison population in the world.
- It is undermining support for women, children and families.
- It is creating financial giants that are too big to fail and jail.
- It is helping to undermine democracy through money in politics.
- It is robbing us of the resources we need to combat climate change.

Barry Commoner always saw the systemic connections. He understood that the environmental movement needed to join with others to get to the heart of the problem – inequality and the rapacious corporations that foster it.

At the moment we have no such broader movement. Those of us who are politically active tend to be hunkered down in our particular issue. Some of us are environmentalists. Some of us are fighting racism. Some are working on programs to combat homelessness and poverty, and others are working on prison reform. Some are working to protect worker rights, strengthen our education system, or remove money from politics. All of this is needed, but few of us are working together.

We can't tackle any of these problems if corporations and wealthy elites continue to abscond with our money and our democracy. Immigrant groups, low wage workers, unions and environmental organizations need to take on Wall Street and runaway inequality, or all of us are certain to lose. This may be particularly difficult for those environmental organizations that rely on hedge fund moguls and other financial elites for funding.

But sooner or later the new reality will sink in. We are the most unequal nation in the developed world. We are lagging behind the rest of the world in addressing climate change. Our infrastructure is crumbling. Our public services are deteriorating and we haven't seen our real incomes grow in a generation. Hopefully, one day soon, we will realize that it's time for our many disparate groups to coalesce to take on the big boys.

Discussion Questions:

1. Do you believe that climate change is caused by human activity? If so, how important do you feel the issue is to you and your family? If not, what evidence do you rely upon?

2. In your opinion, what impacts, if any, does runaway inequality have on climate change?

3. Overall do you think climate change is more important an issue than runaway inequality? What are your reasons?

4. Are you worried that tackling climate change might cause job loss? If so, what should be done about that?

CHAPTER 14

Runaway Inequality and Democracy

The Better Business Climate model is stone silent about democracy. Its proponents apparently assume that as we cut regulations, social programs, and taxes, our political processes will lead to increased freedom. But logic would suggest that as the wealth gap grows and more money lands in the hands of the few, their political power will grow.

What are the facts about money and politics?

Cost of elections

Running and winning political office is costing more and more money. Chart 14.1 shows the dramatic rise in the cost of defeating a sitting member of the U.S. House of Representatives.

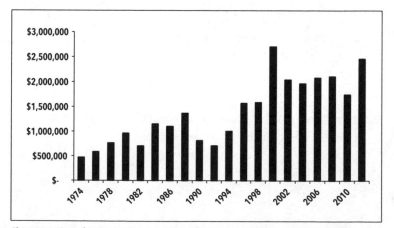

Chart 14.1: Cost of Beating a House Incumbant (Adjusted for inflation in 2012 dollars)

Source: Author's calculations based on Center for Responsive Politics, "The Dollars and Cents of Incumbency," OpenSecrets.org, http://www.opensecrets.org/bigpicture/cost.php.

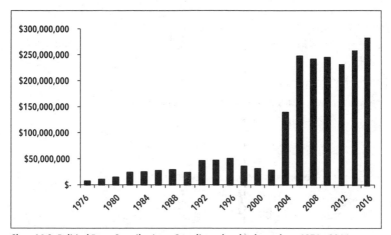

Chart 14.2: Political Party Contributions, Coordinated and Independent, 1976 – 2016
Source: Campaign Finance Institute, http://www.cfinst.org/pdf/vital/vitalstats_t12.pdf.

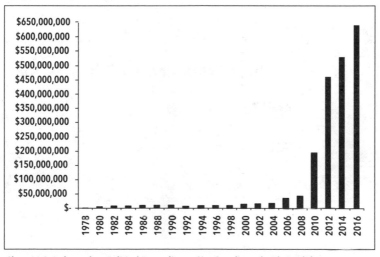

Chart 14.3: Independent Political Expenditures Not Coordinated with Candidate or Party
Source: Campaign Finance Institute, http://www.cfinst.org/data/pdf/VitalStats_t14.pdf.

But individual candidates are only the tip of the iceberg. Political parties also are raising much more money for elections than before. Note that political party contributions jumped beginning in the 2006 election cycle (see Chart 14.2), well before the Supreme Court's Citizens United decision in 2010, which prohibited the government from restricting independent political expenditures by a nonprofit corporation.

Next, we see another big jump (see Chart 14.3), this time in independent donations to elections that are not coordinated through parties. These contributions were uncapped by the Supreme Court in its Citizens United decision.

Money and Political Action Committees (PACs)

These committees allow for unlimited political donations as long as their activities are not directly coordinated by the campaign committees. Chart 14.4 is extremely revealing because it only counts donations of over $10,000. That means the entire column is filled with wealthy donors. Clearly their contributions dwarf all others.

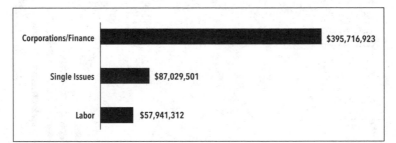

Chart 14.4: Political Action Committee Contributions, 2016
Source: Center for Responsive Politics data, http://www.opensecrets.org/overview/blio.php.

Lobbying

Corporations and the super-rich spend billions each year trying to shape legislation by lobbying members of Congress, the administration, and politicians at the local and state levels. This number also has risen rapidly, especially between 1998 and 2009 (see Chart 14.5).

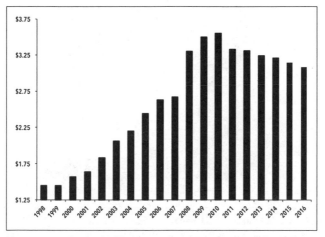

Chart 14.5: Total Federal Lobbying Spending, 1998 - 2016 (In billions of U.S. dollars)

Source: Center for Responsive Politics, "Lobbying Database," http://www.opensecrets.org/lobby/.

Millionaires in Congress

Another way to track the effects of runaway inequality on the political system is to see how many millionaires become members of Congress (and also how many Congress members become millionaires).

Because so many billionaires and millionaires are now pumping so much money into politics, these days you need to be rich to run for Congress. As a result, our political leaders have a very different wealth profile than the rest of us (see Chart 14.6).

Is this a new trend?

Yes. Just as the CEO/worker wage gap has been growing, so has the Congress/household wealth gap. Chart 14.7 looks at the median wealth of members of the U.S. House of Representatives in 1984 and 2009 and compares that with the median household wealth of our entire population. Clearly, Congress has become increasingly unattainable for people of moderate incomes. And so members of Congress are becoming more and more removed from the typical American.

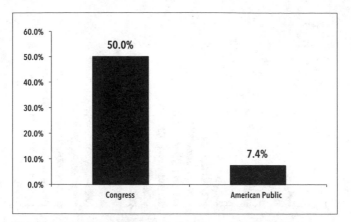

Chart 14.6: Percentage of Millionaires in Congress vs. American Public

Sources: Center for Responsive Politics, "Millionaires' Club: For the First Time Most Lawmakers Are Worth $1 Million Plus," January 9, 2014; and Spectrum Group, "Millionaire Households Back to Pre-recession Levels."

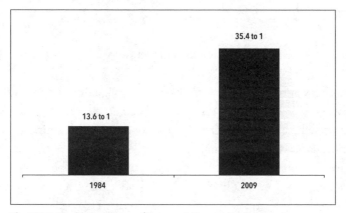

Chart 14.7: Wealth Gap: House of Representatives vs. Median American Household, 1984 and 2009

Source: Peter Whoriskey, "Growing Wealth Widens Distance Between Lawmakers and Constituents," *Washington Post*, December 26,2011, http://www.washingtonpost.com/business/economy/growing-wealth-widens-distance-between-lawmakers-and-constituents/2011/12/05/gIQAR7D6IP_story.html.

Whose interests does Congress represent?

Having rich people in Congress is only a problem if it allows the rich in general to twist policies in their favor. Is Congress voting against the interests of the majority of Americans? One way to check is to see if there's a gap between the policies they champion versus policies supported by the majority of Americans.

In a 2005 path-breaking study, Professor Larry Bartels of Princeton University analyzed the relationship between inequality and votes by U.S. Senate members. Professor Bartels divides the U.S. population into three groups – the affluent, the middle class, and the poor. Through polling, he uncovers the position of these three groups on important issues like the minimum wage, civil rights, government spending, and abortion. Then he looks to see which way the Senate voted. His conclusions are startling as well as troubling:

> I examine the differential responsiveness of U.S. senators to the preferences of wealthy, middle class, and poor constituents. My analysis includes broad summary measures of senators' voting behavior as well as specific votes on the minimum wage, civil rights, government spending, and abortion. In almost every instance, senators appear to be considerably more responsive to the opinions of affluent constituents than to the opinions of middle-class constituents, while the opinions of constituents in the bottom third of the income distribution have no apparent statistical effect on their senators' roll call votes. Disparities in representation are especially pronounced for Republican senators, who were more than twice as responsive as Democratic senators to the ideological views of affluent constituents.[1]

Simply put, Senate members, who themselves are affluent, cater to the affluent – the very people who fund their campaigns. This is one way runaway inequality shapes democracy.

Bartel's findings are confirmed in spades by Princeton Professor Martin Gilens and Professor Benjamin I. Page from Northwestern who reviewed 1,779 congressional votes in 2014. Their conclusion raises grave concerns about government by and for the people:

---

1 Larry M. Bartels, "Economic Inequality and Political Representation," Princeton University Woodrow Wilson School, 2005, https://www.princeton.edu/~bartels/economic.pdf.

[T]he American public actually have little influence over the policies our government adopts. Americans do enjoy many features central to democratic governance, such as regular elections, freedom of speech and association, and a widespread (if still contested) franchise. But we believe that if policymaking is dominated by powerful business organizations and a small number of affluent Americans, then America's claims to being a democratic society are seriously threatened.[2]

The revolving door

Former Congress members, former congressional staff and regulators can make a mint by moving into corporations and banks they once regulated or wrote legislation about. If you help out a particular industry when you're in Congress or a regulatory body, that industry will be eager to pay you richly for your services and inside information later on. Nobody needs to put this in writing – it's understood.

The flow also goes the other way. Bankers often move into government jobs where they can roll back legislation and regulations that slice into bank and corporate profits.

After taking much criticism on the role of bankers in government, the Federal Reserve researched the question and published a study that shows just how busy that revolving door is.[3] Note once again the shape of Chart 14.8, with the familiar slope that correlates with rising inequality after 1980.[4]

---

2   Martin Gilens and Benjamin I. Page, "Testing Theories of American Politics: Elites, Interest Groups, and Average Citizens," *Perspectives on Politics*, American Political Science Association, September 2014, Vol. 12, No. 3, http://scholar .princeton.edu/sites/default/files/mgilens/files/gilens_and_page_2014_-testing_ theories_of_american_politics.doc.pdf.

3   David Lucca, et al., "Worker Flows in Banking Regulation," Liberty Street Economics, Federal Reserve Bank of New York, January 5, 2015, http://libertystreeteconomics.newyorkfed.org/2015/01/worker-flows-in-banking-regulation.html#. VNvR6fnF9bJ.

4   For an excellent database on many types of revolving door arrangements see the Center for Responsive Politics, Open Secrets "Revolving Door," http://www. opensecrets.org/revolving/index.php.

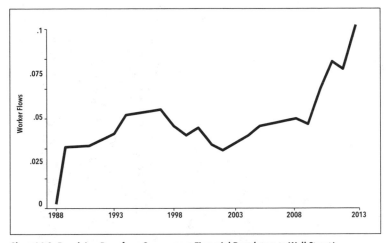

Chart 14.8: Revolving Door from Government Financial Regulators to Wall Street*

*Share of all workers who transition from the banking regulatory sector to the private sector.

Source: David Lucca, Amit Seru, Francesco Trebbi, "The Revolving Door and Worker Flows in Banking Regulation," August 11, 2014, http://www.voxeu.org/article/revolving-door-and-worker-flows-banking-regulation.

Too big to fail

Everyone now knows that when banks get too big, they become dangerous, because if they fail, they can take the whole financial system down with them. Everyone also knows that if they do fail, they'll be bailed out. The banks know this too, and it makes them reckless in their pursuit of profits. Economists call this a "moral hazard."

In the past, the U.S. government addressed this problem by breaking up large monopolies and oligopolies to promote more competition. Some argue that breaking up large banks would make the financial system less prone to enormous meltdowns.

But because the largest financial entities have such enormous political power, nobody is breaking up the banks – or nationalizing them. In fact, as Chart 14.9 shows, since deregulation the nation's four largest banks have grown and grown. Their size dipped a bit during the crash, but now is rising again to new heights. Neither party has the nerve to stand in the way as financial power becomes concentrated like never before.

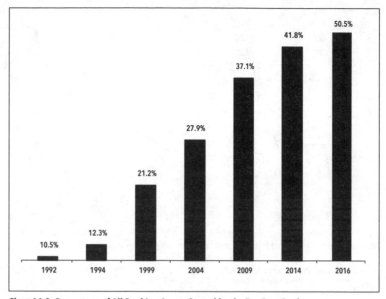

Chart 14.9: Percentage of All Banking Assets Owned by the Top Four Banks
Source: Author's calculations based on Federal Deposit Insurance Corporation Statistics on Depository Institutions for each year, https://www2.fdic.gov/sdi/main.asp.

Too big to jail

Perhaps the biggest sign of democratic failure is that the government has been unwilling to prosecute any bankers at all for the mountain of financial crimes they committed. While millions of lower-income Americans are being packed into prison, bankers are immune. When the government catches a bank doing something illegal, it prosecutes the institution, not the individuals involved. Nobody even has to pay a fine: that's covered by the bank out of their illicit profits.

Here's a story that illustrates justice for Wall Street versus justice for the poor:

London-based HSBC is one of largest, most profitable banks in the world. The American division of HSBC is regulated by the Federal Reserve. The Department of Justice determined that some of HSBC's super-profits resulted directly from massive money laundering on behalf of Mexican drug cartels. This was no mom-and-pop operation. It wasn't a few rogue bank officials skimming some bucks on the side. No, this was a main event: "at least $881 billion in drug proceeds" were laundered through the U.S. financial system, according to the DOJ. The department also cited HSBC for "willful flouting of U.S. sanctions laws and regulations [that] resulted in the processing of hundreds of millions of dollars in... prohibited transactions" with rogue nations and even terrorist organizations.

The penalty for this blatant corruption? $1.9 billion. This comes to less than six weeks of HSBC's 2011 profits. What about criminal penalties? As the *New York Times* laments in an editorial, "Too Big to Indict":

> It is a dark day for the rule of law. Federal and state authorities have chosen not to indict HSBC, the London-based bank, on charges of vast and prolonged money laundering, for fear that criminal prosecution would topple the bank and, in the process, endanger the financial system. They also have not charged any top HSBC banker in the case, though it boggles the mind that a bank could launder money as HSBC did without anyone in a position of authority making culpable decisions.[5]

After the Savings and Loan crisis of the late 1980s, over 1,000 bankers were convicted of felonies. But today, after the crash of 2008 – a crisis seven times larger and involving even more felonious activity – the number of banker convictions to date is zero.

This fact alone makes it impossible to deny the impact of runaway inequality on political power. It's also impossible to deny that the growing power of the financial sector is leading to more and more runaway inequality.

---

5   "Too Big to Indict," *New York Times*, Editorial, December 11, 2012, http://www.nytimes.com/2012/12/12/opinion/hsbc-too-big-to-indict.html?_r=0.

Discussion Questions:

1. What are the impacts of runaway inequality on our democracy?

2. What evidence do we have to suggest that politicians act or do not act on behalf of the average voter?

3. What do you think needs to be done to remove the power of money from politics?

Military Keynesianism

From WWII until around 1980, the U.S. said its primary military goal was to protect the "free" world from Communist aggression – a term used to describe any geopolitical gains of the Soviet Union, China and other countries that leaned towards communism. This policy of communist "containment" led to two hot wars – the Korean War and the Vietnam War – and to many minor skirmishes, often organized and led by clandestine U.S. forces. (Technically the Korean War was a "police action:" President Truman never declared war, and the U.S. was officially acting on behalf of the United Nations.)

But U.S. foreign policy during this period had another stated goal: stimulating the economy. Policymakers believed that high levels of military spending could prevent another depression. It was obvious that WWII had pulled the U.S. out of the Great Depression by generating millions of jobs and pushing up wages. This pump-priming was named Keynesianism after the British economist John Maynard Keynes, who argued that government spending was the key to uplifting depressed economies.

President Truman's 1950 National Security Council Document 68 made this policy goal official:

> From the point of view of the economy as a whole, the program (of military build-up against the Soviet Union and China) might not result in a real decrease in the standard of living, for the economic effects of the program might be to increase the gross national product by more than the amount being absorbed for additional military and foreign assistance purposes. One of the most significant lessons of our World War II experience was that the American economy, when it operates at a level approaching full efficiency, can provide enormous resources for purposes other than civilian consump-

tion while simultaneously providing a high standard of living.[5]

This policy of military Keynesianism led to an unofficial partnership between the government, large corporations and labor unions. These groups worked together (more or less) to prosecute the Cold War. Large corporations accepted unionism. Government worked towards full employment. Both wages and profits grew.

But increasing militarization worried President Eisenhower, who referred to this growing partnership as the "military-industrial complex." In 1961 he warned:

In the councils of government, we must guard against the acquisition of unwarranted influence, whether sought or unsought, by the military-industrial complex. The potential for the disastrous rise of misplaced power exists and will persist.[6]

The famous general who led the Allies to victory in WWII was worried that this vast military-industrial complex would produce unneeded weapons and push the country towards unnecessary military engagements. He also worried that the complex would amass so much power that it would endanger democracy.

But U.S. interventionist military policies and the military-industrial complex marched on despite Eisenhower's warnings. After all, the U.S.'s domestic economic well-being depended on large military expenditures.

5   "NSC 68: United States Objectives and Programs for National Security (April 14, 1950), A Report to the President, Pursuant to the President's Directive of January 31, 1950," National Security Council, April 7, 1950, http://fas.org/irp/offdocs/nsc-hst/nsc-68.htm.

6   "Military-Industrial Complex Speech, Dwight D. Eisenhower, 1961," *Public Papers of the Presidents*, Dwight D. Eisenhower, 1960, pp. 1035–1040, http://coursesa.matrix.msu.edu/~hst306/documents/indust.html.

The Better Business Climate model goes to war

By 1980, these military pump-priming policies no longer seemed to work. In the 1960s, in part as a result of the Vietnam War, the U.S. economy overheated, leading to inflation. The oil embargos of the period further raised prices. The economy contracted, and for the first time both unemployment and inflation soared.

As we've discussed, government policymakers and their corporate allies turned to the Better Business Climate model (neo-liberalism) to rebuild profits and tame inflation. They no longer needed labor as a partner. They closed plants and dismantled unions.

Advocates of the Better Business Climate model now had to grapple with a major contradiction about military spending: How do you maintain a large military establishment that can protect U.S. interests around the world even as you reduce the size of government and lower taxes?

Not an easy trick, but the model had a clear answer: privatization. The U.S. needed to move military expenses and programs from the government payroll into private hands. Not only would this limit the size of government, it would increase profits in the private sector. And holding down labor costs would be a lot easier for contractors than for the government itself.

Furthermore, the U.S. could reduce troop numbers – and official casualty numbers – by hiring private contractors to do the fighting. With lower body counts, the American public might be more willing to put up with long, costly wars. It could put an end to the "Vietnam Syndrome" – Americans' reluctance to support more military adventures.

By the time of the Iraq and Afghanistan wars, the number of private contractors doing military work had grown enormously, as the U.S. Government Accountability Office acknowledged:

> In 2011, a Congressional investigation into contracting practices estimated that about 199,783 contractors were employed by the U.S. in Iraq and Afghanistan

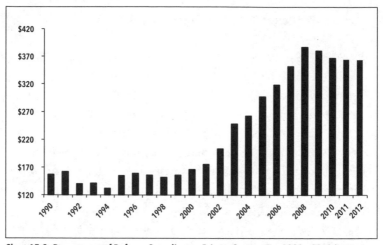

Chart 15.3: Department of Defense Spending on Private Contractors, 1990 – 2012 (In billions of U.S. dollars)

Sources: Center for Strategic and International Studies, "Defense Contract Trends," May 2011, http://csis.org/files/
publication/110506_CSIS_Defense_Contract_Trends-sm2.pdf; and Congressional Research Service, "Department of Defense Trends
in Overseas Contract Obligations," March 1, 2013, https://fas.org/sgp/crs/natsec/R41820.pdf.

in fiscal year 2010…. An estimate from the Government Accountability Office records a total of 262,681 contractors and assistance personnel employed by the Departments of Defense, State and USAID in Iraq and Afghanistan, 18% or 47,282 perform security functions.[7]

The author of the report uses these figures to calculate the amazing jump in contractors. He estimates that in the 1991 Gulf War, there was one contractor for every 50 deployed troops. Today the ratio is one or two contractors for each troop member. That's a fifty-fold increase in contractors.

Chart 15.3 shows the rapid rise in spending on private contractors.

This dramatic trend is further clarified in Chart 15.4. Note that there are more military contractors in Afghanistan than there are regular military personnel. It seems we now have two large armies, one public, one private.

---

7   Aaron Ettinger, "Neoliberalism and the Rise of the Private Military Industry," Queen's University Canadian Political Science Association, May 16-18, 2011, Waterloo, Ontario, http://www.cpsa-acsp.ca/papers-2011/Ettinger.pdf.

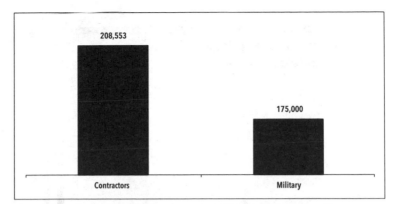

Chart 15.4: Deployment of Private Contractors and Military in Afghanistan and Iraq
Source: Defense Procurement and Acquisition Policy, "Contingency Contracting Throughout U.S. History," www.acq.osd.mil/dpap/pacc/cc/history.html.

Looking over the past two centuries, we can see that using large numbers of military contractors instead of troops is a relatively new practice (see Chart 15.5).

The danger of permanent war

Our nation now supports two overlapping military-industrial complexes. There's the traditional one that worried Eisenhower (large corporations and their profitable production of planes, ships, missiles, nuclear weapons, etc.). And now we have private contractors who make money by providing field services and security – functions formerly provided by the armed services.

The large private manufacturers of U.S. military hardware don't need nonstop war to maintain their profits, since there's always a reason, even in peacetime, to upgrade weapons technologies. But the private army of contractors must have wars, occupations and incursions to grow and survive.

It certainly seems that the private contractors are getting their profit needs met. We have been at war since shortly after 9/11. They've been sent to Iraq, and Afghanistan, and now ISIS is sending us back into Iraq and perhaps into Syria as well. And then

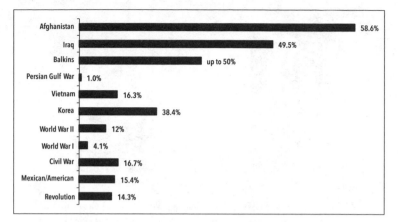

Chart 15.5: The Growing Use of Private Military Personnel (As share of total military personnel)

Source: Defense Procurement and Acquisition Policy, "Contingency Contracting Throughout U.S. History," www.acq.osd.mil/dpap/pacc/cc/history.html.

there's Yemen, and the Ukraine, which may require more military support and even troops. Almost every day you can hear political pundits and politicians calling for "boots on the ground" somewhere around the world, all in the name of "winning" the endless "War on Terror."

Of course no one has any idea what "winning" looks like. It's hard to see how a war against small, violent bands of true believers can end. But it's easy to see how private contractors can profit mightily from unending conflict.

What and who is responsible for this permanent war? The idea probably didn't originate with the private contractors. It probably came from our national security state – groups inside and outside government including the National Security Agency (which spies on communications), the CIA, the Defense Department, the State Department and the many think tanks and university centers that focus on foreign policy.

Although these agencies and their personnel have many disagreements, they did coalesce with very little dissent around the Bush administration's plan to turn 9/11 into the Iraq War. Collectively they wrongly claimed that 1) Iraq had weapons of mass destruction; and 2) Iraq supported Al-Qaeda and therefore was involved in the 9/11 attacks. In this, the leaders of the national security state blatantly lied to the American people and led us to wars in the Middle East that have proceeded for well over a decade.

The privatization of the military is part of this sleight of hand. Privatization allows our hawkish political and military leaders to hide how costly these wars really are. And if contractors are doing the fighting, we don't need a draft, which fueled mass upheaval during the Vietnam War.

If we want to halt runaway inequality, we need to capture the huge percentage of the U.S. budget now devoted to war and redirect it to address useful goals. This won't be easy, of course, since so many businesses are financially invested in our privatized war without end.

CHAPTER 15

Discussion Questions:

1. Why was President Eisenhower so concerned about what he called "the military industrial complex?"

2. Why do you believe we seem to be constantly engaged in wars?

3. What does it mean for the United States to rely so heavily on privatized military personnel and contractors?

CHAPTER 16

The Financial Strip-mining of Healthcare

We have the most complex and expensive healthcare system in the world. We have a system for soldiers and veterans, another on tribal reservations. We have Medicare for the elderly, Medicaid for the poor and CHIPs for children. Within these public programs are embedded scads of private programs, as the healthcare industry finds its profit-making niches. On top of all this, we now have the Affordable Healthcare Act (Obamacare), which extends subsidized health insurance to millions of citizens who previously had no coverage, largely by allocating public funds to help people pay for private insurance.

This hodgepodge system is costly and inadequate. As we saw in Chapter 6, the U.S. spends more on healthcare than any other developed nation both in absolute terms and as a percentage of our economy. What do we get for all that money? Poorer health outcomes. We lag behind in longevity, infant mortality and many other healthcare measures.

That's because our healthcare system is based on two rival and often warring healthcare financing and delivery systems. One system is public, paid for by tax dollars, and the other private, paid for by users (with and without government subsidies). These very different systems are based on entirely different philosophies that do not peacefully coexist. The privatized system is winning this battle, while most of us lose.

Our public healthcare system is based on the principle that healthcare should be a basic right for all residents. In Medicare and other federally funded health care programs, healthcare is paid for through general tax revenues and is financed by one government agency (called single-payer). The delivery of healthcare remains private through doctors, hospitals and other providers.

Most developed countries offer their people publicly funded universal healthcare, and this was the kind of system that both Presidents Roosevelt and Truman supported. However, lobbying by the American Medical Association and its allies kept it from passing. Portions of it came into being during Lyndon Johnson's presidency, including Medicare for senior citizens and Medicaid for the poor.

It seemed just a matter of time until the U.S.'s healthcare system evolved into a single-payer model like Medicare in Canada that would cover the entire population, not just seniors and the poor.

But of course, a different philosophy gained ground after 1980 as the Better Business Climate model took hold and drilled into our healthcare system.

Proponents of the Better Business Climate model not only forestalled efforts to achieve a single-payer system in the U.S., they undermined our existing public healthcare systems, opening up more and more pieces of it to private companies. Medicare includes a private drug plan and "Medicare Advantage" plans to cover other gaps. And beginning in the 1980s, states began receiving waivers that allowed them to use Medicaid money to cover their residents through private plans. This now comprises the bulk of Medicaid coverage. Through these holes in our public system and through Obamacare, private healthcare companies of all kinds are now doing better than ever, raking in billions of dollars in profits with public support.

As always, proponents of the Better Business Climate model were armed with plenty of arguments to support their push for privatization. They attacked the Medicare for All model as both socialistic and inefficient. "Free" healthcare would drive up prices, they argued, because consumers would overuse the system if they didn't have to pay for care themselves. If we all had "skin in the game," we would have to shop around for good healthcare bargains and wouldn't go to the doctor unless it was absolutely necessary.

Conservatives argued that the government should not make decisions about how much healthcare each of us needs. Instead, people should be free to choose as much or as little as they want, or none at all. Otherwise, the government would be coercing us and violating our fundamental freedoms.

They also maintained that healthcare could be delivered more efficiently through the private, for-profit market system. Private insurance companies would sell a variety of policies to match demand. The pharmaceutical companies would compete to produce the best drugs at the lowest prices, and hospitals and doctors would compete to provide the best care. Because consumers would be able to shop around, the market would deliver the best medical products for the lowest prices.

Once again, the theory of the Better Business Climate model doesn't describe the reality, especially when it comes to healthcare. Rather than deliver healthcare at lower cost with better results, it delivers more expensive healthcare with poorer results, leaving vulnerable patients with mountains of confusing paperwork and often frightening medical debt. But patient care isn't the main goal of our privatized healthcare system. The main goal is to enrich healthcare CEOs and Wall Street investors.

The privatized healthcare system contains three major arenas for financial strip-mining – private health insurance, hospitals and other health delivery companies, and the pharmaceutical industry.

Private health insurance

Insurance companies are a critical component of the financial sector. They are a vital part of Wall Street. In fact, the financial sector is called FIRE – finance, insurance and real estate. Insurance companies exist by collecting premiums, investing the proceeds, and then paying out claims that are less than the total value of the invested premiums.

The top ten health insurance and managed care executives average compensation in 2013 was $12,932,100 each.[1] The gap in compensation between healthcare company CEOs and the average nursing, psychiatric, and home health aide is 517 to one!

This money comes from pushing up premiums, deductibles, and co-pays as high as possible, while keeping healthcare delivery costs as low as possible. And as we all know, this often means delaying and denying even the most clear-cut claims. Private insurance companies are major beneficiaries of Obamacare, which mandates that everyone have some form of health insurance. Obamacare was essentially a deal between the government, the big health insurance companies and pharmaceutical companies that greatly enhanced the national market for health insurance. (In return, insurance companies face certain restrictions. For instance, they are no longer allowed to refuse coverage to people with prior medical conditions.)

As financial strip-mining has ripped through the private sector, we've seen a major shift away from employer-based healthcare. As we saw in Chapter 4, paying back Wall Street debt and using revenues for stock buy-backs leads to "lean and mean" production

---

1   For the ratios in this chapter, rankings based on "Fortune 500 Rankings, 2014," http://fortune.com/fortune500/; CEO compensation based on Proxy Statement Filings to the Securities and Exchange Commission, Edgar Database, http://www.sec.gov/edgar/searchedgar/companysearch.html; and from "2014 Equilar Top 200 Highest Paid CEO Rankings," http://www.equilar.com/in-the-news/2014-equilar-top-200-highest-paid-ceo-rankings; average salaries of nurses and nonsupervisory employees, from U.S. Department of Labor, Bureau of Labor Statistics, "May 2014 National Occupational Employment and Wage Estimates, United States," http://www.bls.gov/oes/current/oes_nat.htm#29-0000.

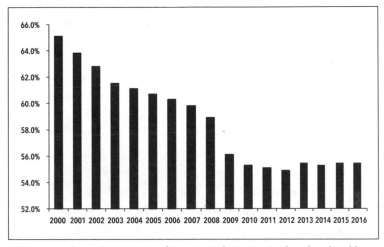

Chart 16.1. Decline in the Percentage of Americans Who Receive Employer-based Health Insurance, 2000 – 2016

Source: U.S. Census Bureau, Current Population Reports, P60-238, *Income, Poverty, and Health Insurance Coverage in the United States*, various years.

through cuts in wages, benefits (like healthcare coverage), and working conditions. Employer-based health insurance, as Chart 16.1 shows, is dwindling.

For-profit health insurance is extremely costly to both individuals and, increasingly, to taxpayers who subsidize private insurance companies through Obamacare, Medicare, Medicaid, and other "public" health programs. The complexity of the system, with its hundreds of private insurance companies, forces everyone who participates in it – including doctors, hospitals, insurance companies, and patients – to push lots of paper around and spend a lot of time on non-healthcare-related work. This is one reason why the traditional public part of Medicare allocates only 1 percent of total spending to overhead (according to a 2013 study in the *Journal of Health Politics, Policy and Law*),[2] while average overhead in the private health insurance industry is about 20 percent. (If you include the privatized part of Medicare, Medicare's overhead is 6 percent.)

---

2   Physicians for a National Health Program, "Setting the Record Straight on Medicare's Overhead Costs," February 20, 2013, http://www.pnhp.org/news/2013/february/setting-the-record-straight-on-medicare%E2%80%99s-overhead-costs.

As Dr. David Himmelstein and Dr. Stephanie Woolhandler, leading health cost researchers, write:

> [P]er capita annual insurance overhead costs have tripled since 2006, reaching $731. Switching to a single-payer system today could save more than $400 billion annually on bureaucracy.
>
> These savings would make it possible to provide universal coverage without copayments or deductibles and with no increase in health expenditures. In contrast, the Affordable Care Act has added another layer of bureaucracy – the health insurance exchanges – that cost $6 billion to get up and running, or $750 per new enrollee.
>
> Economics texts preach that markets breed efficiency, but the most market-oriented health systems are the least efficient. The transformation of American healthcare into a business has sharply increased transaction costs and rewarded entrepreneurs for financial games that add no value.[3]

The financial strip-mining of hospitals

Many for-profit and non-profit hospitals are designed to enrich their top executives and investors. Their income comes from government (payments through Medicare, Medicaid and other programs), private insurance, and out of patients' pockets. While many hospitals struggle to break even, the top tier for-profit chains are enormously profitable, according to reports they have to file with Medicare. These hospitals have sky-high operating revenues (profit margins as a percent of patient dollars). As *Forbes* reports:

---

3   David U. Himmelstein and Steffie Woolhandler, "High Administrative Costs: The Author's Reply," *Health Affairs Letter*, November 2014, Physicians for a National Health Program, http://www.pnhp.org/news/2014/november/the-high-administrative -costs-in-us-health-care.

. . . 24 hospitals in the country with over 200 beds make an operating margin of 25% or more. That kind of profit margin compares favorably to drug giants like Pfizer, who are often vilified for charging too much for their drugs. It easily beats the operating profit margin that General Electric reported last year.

The most profitable hospital in the country, 235-bed Flowers Medical Center in Dothan, Ala., recorded an incredible 53% operating margin. It is part of the big for-profit Community Health Systems chain in Brentwood, Tenn. Del Sol Medical Center in El Paso snared second place with an astronomical 45% operating margin. It's part of the big HCA chain, based in Nashville. Neither hospital returned calls asking for comment.[4]

The financial strip-mining takes place on many levels as hospitals try to maximize the fees they obtain from insurers, the government, and patients. Nurses are a major target. By forcing nurses to handle more and more patients, hospitals (and other providers like nursing homes and rehabilitation centers) can pump up their operating revenues and profits. This is precisely like the speed-up and stretch-out experienced by factory workers in companies that have been financially strip-mined by Wall Street.

The California Nurses Association/National Nurses United is effectively countering this trend through legislation that mandates safe staffing levels. After a campaign that showed how staffing levels impact patient health and mortality, California passed a law that mandates the staffing levels shown in Table 16.1.

4   David Whelan, "America's Most Profitable Hospitals," *Forbes.com*, August 31, 2010, http://www.forbes.com/2010/08/30/profitable-hospitals-hca-healthcare-business-mayo-clinic.html.

Table 16.1: California Safe-staffing Levels			
Type of Care	RN to Patients	Type of Care	RN to Patients
Intensive/Critical Care	1:2	Trauma Patients in the ER	1:1
Neo-natal Intensive Care	1:2	Step Down, Initial	1:4
Operating Room	1:1	Step Down, 2008	1:3
Post-anesthesia Recovery	1:2	Telemetry, Initial	1:5
Labor and Delivery	1:2	Telemetry, 2008	1:4
Antepartum	1:4	Medical/Surgical, Initial	1:6
Postpartum couplets	1:4	Medical/Surgical, 2008	1:5
Postpartum women only	1:6	Other Specialty Care, Initial	1:5
Pediatrics	1:4	Other Specialty Care, 2008	1:4
Emergency Room	1:4	Psychiatric	1:6
ICU Patients in the ER	1:2		

Source: National Nurses United, "RN Safe Staffing Ratios – Saving Lives," http://www.nationalnursesunited.org/site/entry/101-staffing.

The pharmaceutical financial prescription

Supposedly, the pharmaceutical industry's purpose is to discover and manufacture new drugs that alleviate pain, prevent diseases, and reduce their symptoms. But in fact, the primary goal of this industry is to enrich its CEOs and its major shareholders, usually hedge funds and private equity firms, that want higher short-term stock prices and dividends.

In 2013, the top 10 pharmaceutical CEOs received an average compensation of $17,586,700 each. Compared to the average pay of nursing, psychiatric, and home health aides, the pharmaceutical CEO/worker compensation gap is a bloated 703 to one.

Pharmaceutical companies make fantastic profits in the U.S., compared to other countries. That's partly because they have so far succeeded in keeping the U.S. government from using its bargaining power to reduce drug costs for American consumers. In other developed countries, the government negotiates lower prices

Table 16.2: U.S. versus Canadian Drug Prices				
	Quantity	U.S. Price	CanaRX	Canadian Discount
Nexium	84	$ 440.06	$ 207.40	53%
Singulair	84	$ 341.04	$ 130.40	62%
Advair Kiskus	180	$ 579.60	$ 237.40	59%
Lipitor 20 mg	90	$ 394.20	$ 136.40	65%
Lipitor 10 mg	90	$ 276.30	$ 114.40	59%
Plavix	84	$ 466.20	$ 213.40	54%
Spiriva	90	$ 562.50	$ 244.40	57%
Lipitor 40mg	90	$ 394.20	$ 199.40	49%
Celebrex	100	$ 367.00	$ 170.40	54%
Crestor	90	$ 357.30	$ 207.40	42%

Source: CanaRx, cited in Ann S. Kim, "Why Are Drugs from CanaRx Cheaper than Those in Maine?" *Portland Press Herald*, September 14, 2012, www.pressherald.com/2012/09/14/why-are-drugs-from-canarx-cheaper-than-those-in-maine__2012-09-15/.

for its consumers. For example, CanaRX, the Canadian national prescription drug program, uses its bargaining power to consistently obtain lower drug prices, as Table 16.2 shows.[5]

Even as the pharmaceutical companies are pumping up their drug prices, they're also cutting an expensive and in the short run less profitable aspect of their business: research and development. Astonishingly, Wall Street pressures pharmaceutical companies to cut back on R&D so that they have more money to buy back shares and boost their stock price to enrich the CEOs and major Wall Street investors.

For example, Amgen, a giant biotech firm based in southern California, agreed to cut 4,000 employees as part of a move to placate Wall Street hedge funds. According to the *Los Angeles Times*:

The job cuts were part of a sweeping set of financial maneuvers the company intended as a way to funnel

---

5   Ann S. Kim, "Why Are Drugs from CanaRx Cheaper than Those in Maine?" *Portland Press Herald*, September 14, 2012, http://www.pressherald.com/2012/09/14/why-are-drugs-from-canarx-cheaper-than-those-in-maine__2012-09-15/.

money back to Wall Street investors. The company also said it would buy back $2 billion in stock and increase its dividend 30%. It also made an ambitious promise of double-digit earnings growth for the next three years.[6]

While cutting R&D enriches Wall Street and CEOs in the short run, it will eventually harm our health. Here's how *Forbes* describes these cuts:

> Much of the news from the pharmaceutical industry over the past five years has been about scaling back R&D. Companies like Pfizer, AstraZeneca and Merck have done just that, much to the delight of Wall Street analysts who have been urging pharmaceutical companies to rethink reinvesting 17 – 20% of revenues into R&D and to scale this back to 10 – 14%. While such a decrease in spending can bring short-term returns with respect to higher financial returns, such policies have negative long-term consequences. Those companies that aggressively cut their R&D budgets will ultimately experience shrinking pipelines.
>
> More importantly, for patients, these cuts will lessen the chances of coming up with new medicines for diabetes, Alzheimer's disease, cancer, etc. Ironically, this is coming at a time when new insights into the cause of disease are occurring on a daily basis.
>
> Yet, as part of these cuts, major companies are getting out of research in key areas like antibacterials, depression, schizophrenia and AIDS.[7]

6   Dean Starkman and Andrew Khouri, "Amgen, Bowing to Hedge Fund Pressure, to Cut Up to 1,100 More Jobs," *Los Angeles Times*, October 28, 2014, http://www.latimes.com/business/la-fi-amgen-job-cuts-20141029-story.html#page=1.

7   John LaMattina, "Pharma R&D Cuts Hurting U.S. Competitive Standing," *Forbes.com*, January 3, 2014, http://www.forbes.com/sites/johnlamattina/2014/01/03/pharma-rd-cuts-hurting-u-s-competitive-standing/.

Winning the battle but losing the war?

The privatized insurance, hospital and pharmaceutical industries molded Obamacare into their own image. The Affordable Care Act increased the number of private insurance enrollees and outlawed the government from securing discounts from the pharmaceutical industry. Both industries have been making out like bandits ever since Obamacare was passed. Clearly, the financial strip-miners have won this battle.

But in the long run, all logic leads to single-payer healthcare systems like Canada's that will eliminate nearly all of the private health insurance industry and drastically curtail the price of prescription drugs. The cost and quality of care arguments for single-payer healthcare are overwhelming. (See Physicians for a National Health Program at www.pnhp.org and Labor Campaign for Single Payer www.laborforsinglepayer.org.)

By most measures, the best healthcare system in the world is in the UK, where both healthcare financing and healthcare delivery are public. (That makes it both a single-payer and single-healthcare provider system.) According to the Commonwealth Fund, the UK's system ranks number one globally. It's superior in both quality and efficiency, and yet is the least expensive system in the developed world, costing $3,405 per capita, compared to $8,508 in the U.S. and $4,522 in Canada. In healthcare, simplicity and a focus on health, not profits, matters.[8]

Standing in the way, of course, are the private healthcare establishment and the Wall Street strip-miners, both greedy for profits. But the American people still support single-payer even though few politicians dare to mention it for fear of being called "socialist."

More than five years after the single-payer system was scrapped from Obamacare policy debates, just over 50 percent of people say

---

8   Karen Davis, et al., "Mirror, Mirror on the Wall, 2014 Update: How the U.S. Health Care System Compares Internationally," A Report of the Commonwealth Fund, http://www.commonwealthfund.org/publications/fund-reports/2014/jun/mirror-mirror.

they still support the idea, including one-quarter of Republicans, according to a new poll.[9]

The single-payer option – also known as Medicare for all – would create a new, government-run insurance program to replace private coverage. The system, once backed by President Obama, became one of the biggest casualties of the divisive healthcare debates of 2009.[10]

We will be forced to choose between a healthcare system that covers us all from cradle to grave that actually saves us money, and a system designed to appease the financial strip-miners.

9   Sarah Ferris, "Majority Still Supports Single-payer Option, Poll Finds," *The Hill*, January 19, 2015, http://thehill.com/policy/healthcare/229959-majority-still-support-single-payer-option-poll-finds.
10   Ibid.

Discussion Questions:

1. What are your greatest concerns about your own health care coverage and about our system in general?

2. Do you think the government should use its bargaining power to negotiate lower pharmaceutical prices? Why or why not?

3. Do you think we should have a Medicare for All system (single-payer)? Why or why not?

CHAPTER 17

The Hedge Fund Attack
on Public Education

No one has benefited more from financial deregulation than hedge fund and private equity managers, the tiny elite at the apex of the financial pyramid. It is truly difficult to comprehend how much these financiers haul in.

Each year a handful of these guys make as much as a million dollars an *hour* through some barely legal and illegal investment schemes. The top 25 of them have so many billions of dollars that they can't possibly need to earn more. Yet they do. They live for the challenge, the fame, the competition. They strive to be number one on the "Forbes Rich List."

Although virtually all of their work is amoral at best, many of these hedge fund moguls claim to have a conscience. A significant number of them strongly believe that education must be "reformed" through increased privatization and competition. They use their money and the foundations they support to promote charter schools and to fight public school unions, which they view as the ultimate enemy.

For example, in the New York area, the Robin Hood Foundation, whose board is littered with hedge fund moguls, supports over 100 charter schools through grants to Achievement First, Democracy Prep, East Harlem Scholars Academy, Explore Schools, Inc., Harlem Village Academies, KIPP NYC, Inc., New York City Charter Schools Center, Success Academy Charter Schools, and Teach for America New York. In addition, some hedge fund board members give directly to particular charter schools.

The Bill and Melinda Gates Foundation says that it "has invested over $100 million in charter schools as part of its ongoing effort to raise graduation rates and give all students access to an array of high-quality educational options."[1] In 2014, Michael Bloomberg, the billionaire former NYC mayor, "poured more than $1.3 million into backing state and local candidates who share his vision for education reform," according to the website Politico:

> The biggest chunk of that, $500,000, supports former charter school executive Marshall Tuck in his race for California state superintendent. But Bloomberg is also a major factor in far less visible races. He gave $300,000 to Stand for Children, Arizona's political committee, which is supporting school board candidates in two districts along with two state legislators. Bloomberg also donated $250,000 to the California Charter School Association Advocates, which is heavily involved in school board races in Santa Clara County and West Contra Costa Unified School District in Richmond, CA. And Bloomberg gave $100,000 to a reform coalition backing two candidates in the Minneapolis school board race.[2]

But, why are billionaires so interested in the privatization of public schools?

If you ask them, it's pure altruism. Diane Ravitch, in her book *Reign of Error*, sums up the corporate school reform ideology:

---

1 "Investment to Accelerate Creation of Strong Charter Schools," Press Release, Bill and Malinda Gates Foundation, June 2003, http://www.gatesfoundation.org/Media-Center/Press-Releases/2003/06/Investing-in-HighQuality-Charter-Schools.

2 Catlin Emma, "Bloomberg Bets Big on Ed Reform," *Politico.com*, November 4, 2014, http://www.politico.com/morningeducation/1114/morningeducation15951.html.

We are the reformers. We have solutions. The public schools are failing. The public schools are in decline. The public schools don't work. The public schools are obsolete and broken. We want to innovate. We know how to fix schools. We know how to close the achievement gap. We are leading the civil rights movement of our era. We want a great teacher in every classroom. Class size doesn't matter. Teachers should be paid more if their students get higher scores. They should be fired if their students don't get higher scores. Teachers should have their seniority and tenure stripped from them because those things protect bad teachers. Bad teachers cause the achievement gap. Great teachers close the achievement gap. Teachers' unions are greedy and don't care about children.

People who draw attention to poverty are just making excuses for bad teachers and failing public schools. Those who don't agree with our strategies are defenders of the status quo. They have no solutions. We have solutions. We know what works. Testing works. Accountability works. Privately managed charter schools work. Closing schools with low test scores works. Paying bonuses to teachers to get higher scores works. Online instruction works. Replacing teachers with online instruction not only works but cuts costs while providing profits to edu-entrepreneurs who will spur further innovation.[3]

Unbelievably, it seems that this set of corporate billionaires (nearly all white males) think that they are the true leaders of a new civil rights movement that aims to give every poor child a chance at the American Dream. For example, Robert Reffkin, a Goldman Sachs vice president specializing in private equities, is

---

3   Diane Ravitch, "Public Education: Who Are the Corporate Reformers?" Moyers and Company, March 28, 2014, http://billmoyers.com/2014/03/28/public-education-who-are-the-corporate-reformers/.

deeply involved in charter schools. He calls charter schools "the civil rights struggle of my generation."[4]

Think for a moment about this self-serving, self-delusional inversion of history. The civil rights movement was built on the struggles of tens of thousands of Black activists who demanded justice. Many were beaten and killed in their fight for freedom. Now, in the era of runaway inequality, the ultra-privileged feel that their money makes them educational experts and entitles them to "lead" a money-driven battle against teachers' unions, without facing any personal risk or sacrifice. And they claim the mantle of Martin Luther King and other civil rights leaders as they do it.

The Better Business Climate model at work

The billionaires' delusional educational "reform" movement makes perfect sense when viewed through the prism of the Better Business Climate model. First, the Better Business Climate model's tax cuts for the rich and large corporations put the squeeze on public education. Then, here came the hedge fund billionaires to fund "reform" movements to privatize the schools.

The charter school and for-profit public school movement was a product of the era of rising inequality. In fact, there were no such schools until the early 1990s.

Millions of children, from preK to high school, have suffered from the ongoing attack on public education. One measure of this is class size. Research shows that reducing class size improves outcomes for children. Unfortunately, under the Better Business Climate model, class sizes have grown, especially over the past decade. Chart 17.1 shows how crowded New York City kindergarten classes have become.[5]

---

4   Nancy Hass, "Scholarly Investments," *New York Times*, December 4, 2009, http://www.nytimes.com/2009/12/06/fashion/06charter.html?pagewanted=all&_r=0.
5   Sam Dillon, "Tight Budgets Means Squeeze in Classrooms," *New York Times*, March 6, 2011, http://www.nytimes.com/2011/03/07/education/07classrooms.html?_r=0.

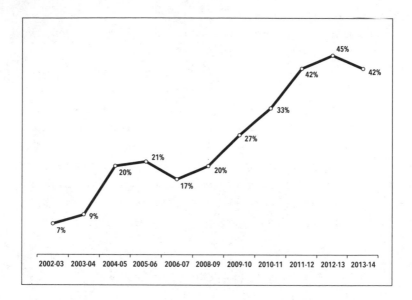

Chart 17.1: Percent of NYC Kindergarten Classes with 25 or More Students, 2002 – 2014
Source: Leonie Haimson, "Space Crunch in New York City Schools," Class Size Matters, based on IBO and DEO class size reports, classsizematters.org.

The hidden goal of the model is to destroy unions in the public sector, the country's last bastion of union strength. And teachers' unions are the biggest public sector unions of all. Smashing these unions has an added benefit for financial elites: It weakens the Democratic Party, which relies on public sector unions for dollars and campaign mobilization. Of course much of the Democratic Party is aligned with the financial industry. But sometimes the party fields candidates who refuse to cut public services and balk at tax cuts for the rich. Taking down teachers' unions helps Republicans, who never waver from the precepts of the Better Business Climate model.

Proponents of the Better Business Climate model argue that private companies always do a better job than the government. Therefore public schools should be privatized. Charter schools and for-profit public schools are better for society because competition and profit-seeking invite competition and creativity.

The Better Business Climate model portrays the hedge fund

moguls who are financing school privatization as "altruists." Let's look into that portrayal by following the money in this billionaire "civil rights" crusade.

Doing well by doing good?

Public education is a $632 billion industry (as of 2010-11) that creates many profit opportunities for wealthy investors, especially through charter and for-profit schools.

Through a tax break signed into law at the end of the Clinton administration, the wealthy can earn enormous sums by investing in charter schools. As the *Washington Post* reports,

> As a result of this change to the tax code, banks and equity funds that invest in charter schools in under-served areas can take advantage of a very generous tax credit. They are permitted to combine this tax credit with other tax breaks while they also collect interest on any money they lend out. According to one analyst, the credit allows them to double the money they invested in seven years. Another interesting side note is that foreign investors who put a minimum of $500,000 in charter school companies are eligible to purchase immi-gration visas for themselves and family members under a federal program called EB-5.[6]

Management companies and real estate firms also are hot on the trail of public money to run private schools. The trick is to get charter schools to pay exorbitant rents through self-dealing between the school, the financial managers and real estate firms. Here's how it plays out in Florida, according to the *Miami Herald*:

---

6   Valerie Strauss, "Why Hedge Funds Love Charter Schools," *Washington Post*, June 4, 2014, http://www.washingtonpost.com/blogs/answer-sheet/wp/2014/06/04/why-hedge-funds-love-charter-schools/.

Some schools have ceded almost total control of their staff and finances to for-profit management companies that decide how the schools' money is spent. The Life Skills Center of Miami-Dade County, for example, pays 97 percent of its income to a management company as a "continuing fee." And when the governing board of two affiliated schools in Hollywood tried to eject its managers, the company refused to turn over school money it held – and threatened to press criminal charges against any school officials who attempted to access the money.

Many management companies also control the land and buildings used by the schools – sometimes collecting more than 25 percent of a school's revenue in lease payments, in addition to management fees. The owners of Academica, the state's largest charter school operator, collect almost $19 million a year in lease payments on school properties they control in Miami-Dade and Broward counties, audit and property records show.[7]

The blinders of hypocrisy

The billionaires attending fundraising galas for their charter school "civil rights movement" are ever so proud of their contribution to society, especially to the downtrodden, who are blessed to attend these new schools. But in truth their contributions are but a pittance compared to the mighty tax break they are receiving (as discussed in Chapter 7). It's worth reviewing that tax break in the context of hedge fund philanthropy.

Hedge fund and private equity billionaires, the backbone of the charter school movement, are the lucky beneficiaries of an arcane tax rule called "carried interest." This rule allows them to claim

---

7   Scott Hiaasen and Kathleen McGrory, "Florida Charter Schools: Big Money, Little Oversight," *Miami Herald*, September 19, 2011, http://www.miamiherald.com/news/special-reports/cashing-in-on-kids/article1939199.html.

most of their income as capital gains, taxed at 20 percent (before deductions) instead of 39 percent (the top income tax rate). That 19 percentage point difference is an enormous tax loss for the rest of us and for our public educational system, since a growing percentage of education funding comes from the federal government.[8]

Here's a telling example. Six of the richest hedge fund managers in the world (all with close ties to the Robin Hood Foundation) received a total of $8 billion in income in 2013. The carried interest tax loophole gave these six people, the richest of the rich, a tax break of approximately $1,520,000,000 ($1.52 billion). How much is that? It's enough to provide New York with 30,000 entry-level teachers with Masters degrees!

Sadly these hedge fund titans did not choose to use their money that way. Instead, they kept most of their newly earned riches for themselves and donated a tiny fraction to charter schools. And then they caressed themselves for leading a new civil rights movement.

First, the hedge fund moguls collect their billions from the carried interest tax break (which they lobby incessantly to protect), thus starving our public schools. And then, they point to underfunded schools and claim that their charter schools are the answer to the problem that they themselves helped to create.

Hedge funds as the witting or unwitting agents of history

Whether the super-rich are destroying public schools out of personal greed, anti-union ideology, or pure-as-the-driven-snow altruism, the net result is the same: suffering children, families, and communities – and a big boost for runaway inequality. For all the hedge fund moguls' investments, charter schools on the whole show no better results than public schools. As one report put it, "A number of recent national studies have reached the same

---

8   "School Finance, Federal, State, and Local K-12 School Finance Overview," New America Foundation, http://febp.newamerica.net/background-analysis/school-finance.

conclusion: charter schools do not, on average, show greater levels of student achievement, typically measured by standardized test scores, than public schools, and may even perform worse."[9]

As privatized schools continue to enrich wealthy investors and management and real estate companies, the number of students at or near the poverty line keeps on rising. Public funds continue to dwindle as the wealthy keep on pulling down trillions through tax evasion.

The Better Business Climate model is what binds this all together. The hedge fund cheerleaders for charter schools are playing their historic role. Regardless of the words they mouth or even their very best intentions, their actions speak volumes: By what they do, they are undermining public services and enriching educational entre-preneurs who erroneously claim they will improve educational results through their profit-making enterprises. They are using loopholes to evade taxes that would otherwise build our public schools. They're using philanthropy to take over the very educational system that they are undermining.

Public education can only be protected and enhanced when we put an end to the Better Business Climate model and the runaway inequality it has unleashed.

---

9   "School Funding Reform across the Nation," Education Justice.org, http:// www.educationjustice.org/newsletters/nlej_iss21_art5_detail_CharterSchool Achievement.htm.

Discussion Questions:

1. Why do financial leaders support charter schools?

2. Do you think that charter schools will improve public education? Why or why not?

3. In your opinion, why are public schools and teachers under attack?

CHAPTER 18

Wall Street's Hidden Trade Tariff

America's good-paying, unionized, manufacturing jobs were once the envy of the world.

These are the jobs that provide a middle-class income. The ones that pay enough to let you buy a home and send your kid to college.

But these jobs are getting scarce (see Chart 18.1). They represent a declining percentage of all non-farm jobs, from 20.1 percent in 1980 to 8.5 percent in 2017.

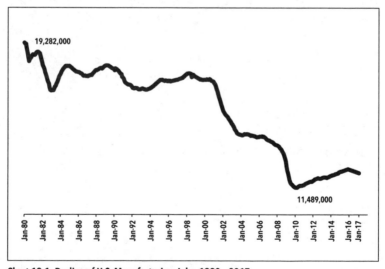

Chart 18.1: Decline of U.S. Manufacturing Jobs, 1980 – 2017
Source: Federal Reserve Bank of St. Louis, Federal Reserve Economic Data, http://research.stlouisfed.org/fred2.

Why are we losing these jobs?

The Better Business Climate people would say that unions priced manufacturing labor out of the international market. Union wages and benefits were too high here, so companies shipped their jobs abroad, where wages are in line with the global marketplace.

But this argument collapses when we compare the U.S. to Germany instead of China or Mexico. Germany's hourly manufacturing compensation costs ($45.79/hr) are far higher than the U.S.'s ($35.67).[1] And yet Germany still runs an enormous trade surplus ($285 billion in 2016) with the rest of the world.[2] In Germany, high-wage manufacturing is booming. But not here. So . . . why are employers blaming high U.S. wages and benefits for the loss of good manufacturing jobs here?

Some say the U.S. is losing these jobs because of unfair competition by foreign countries, especially China (and before that, Japan). They argue that China manipulates its currency rates in violation of global trading rules. This keeps the price of its products artificially low, which gives them a trade advantage. Because the U.S. imports so much more from China than it exports to China, we end up losing tens of thousands of manufacturing jobs.

While China may be manipulating its rates, Germany again provides a counter example. Germany, like the U.S., trades heavily with China. And yet its imports and exports to and from China are roughly in balance. Why doesn't China's supposed currency rate manipulation have the same effect on German manufacturing as it does on U.S. manufacturing?

---

1 U.S. Department of Labor, Bureau of Labor Statistics, "International Comparisons of Hourly Compensation Costs in Manufacturing, 2012," Chart 1, Hourly Compensation Costs in Manufacturing, US Dollars, 2012, http://www.bls.gov/fls/ichcc.htm#chart01.

2 "List of Sovereign States by Current Account Balance," Wikipedia from "Trade Profiles - Selection (maximum 10)," *World Trade Organisation*, WTO, http://www.en.wikipedia.org/wiki/List_of_sovereign_states_by_current_account_balance.

Free trade agreements

Mainstream economists argue that "free and open" markets benefit everyone. The idea is that when countries sign a treaty to lower tariffs, it lowers the price of products, increases overall production and efficiency – and leads to a better standard of living for workers in all the countries that signed the agreement.

However, the 1994 North American Free Trade Agreement (NAFTA) with Canada and Mexico cost the U.S. 700,000 jobs including many higher-wage manufacturing jobs, according to a study by the Economic Policy Institute (EPI). Workers who managed to hold onto their jobs weren't spared either, because employers used the threat of moving to Mexico to extract concessions or keep workers from unionizing at all. As EPI director Jeff Faux writes:

> As soon as NAFTA became law, corporate managers began telling their workers that their companies intended to move to Mexico unless the workers lowered the cost of their labor. In the midst of collective bargaining negotiations with unions, some companies would even start loading machinery into trucks that they said were bound for Mexico. The same threats were used to fight union organizing efforts. The message was: "If you vote in a union, we will move south of the border." With NAFTA, corporations also could more easily blackmail local governments into giving them tax reductions and other subsidies.[3]

And as we saw in Chapter 11, NAFTA also devastated Mexican farmers, which sent tens of thousands of people across our border in search of work.

Robert Reich, who was Secretary of Labor in the Clinton Administration, supported NAFTA at the time. But he now believes that

---

3   Jeff Faux, "NAFTA Impact on U.S. Workers," Economic Policy Institute, December, 9, 2013, http://www.epi.org/blog/naftas-impact-workers/.

free trade agreements, including the Trans Pacific Partnership (TPP), which President Obama supported, are really about transferring wealth to financial and corporate elites.

Reich argues that because tariffs already are so low, American consumers won't see a big drop in prices if the TPP is enacted. Instead, he says, this treaty is being negotiated in secret between government officials and corporate lobbyists to protect intellectual property and allow corporations to eliminate consumer, environmental and labor restrictions. As Reich puts it, these elites "want less protection of consumers, workers, small investors, and the environment, because these interfere with their profits. So they've been seeking trade rules that allow them to override these protections."[4]

His position recently was confirmed when someone leaked a provision from the secret TPP negotiations to the *New York Times*:

> Under the accord, still under negotiation but nearing completion, companies and investors would be empowered to challenge regulations, rules, government actions and court rulings – federal, state or local – before tribunals organized under the World Bank or the United Nations.[5]

It seems that the TPP is part of an effort by elites to establish a global financial/corporate governing process that can override democracy in the U.S. and other countries. Because treaties can supersede national laws, they can give corporations and financiers new powers that a democratic state would never grant. Some right-wingers have always worried that the United Nations would lead to a "new world government" that would replace sovereign states, including the U.S. They are looking in the wrong direction. These free trade agreements really are about robbing us of

---

4   Robert Reich, "Why the Trans-Pacific Partnership Agreement Is a Pending Disaster," Robertreich.org, January 5, 2015, http://robertreich.org/post/107257859130.

5   Jonathan Weisman, "Trans-Pacific Partnership Seen as Door for Foreign Suits against U.S.," *New York Times*, March 25, 2015, http://www.nytimes.com/2015/03/26/business/trans-pacific-partnership-seen-as-door-for-foreign-suits-against-us.html?_r=0.

our democratic rights and our sovereignty. The super-rich are using the mechanism of free trade agreements to trump environmental, consumer and labor laws they find objectionable. It's the elite path to deregulation even in a country that doesn't want to deregulate.

How Wall Street makes our economy uncompetitive

In 2016, the U.S. had a trade deficit with the rest of the world of $505 billion. About $347 billion of that came from the surplus of Chinese imports.

Imported goods are not a problem as long as we export a similar amount of goods and services to other countries. Imports should equal exports. But in the U.S., they don't. That's a clue that American goods cost more than those of other countries. Our products must be less competitive not just with products from low-wage areas like China, but also high-wage areas like Germany and the rest of northern Europe.

How can this be?

The answer, once again, is high finance. The more Wall Street loads up our economy with debt, the more uncompetitive it becomes. The trade deficit has little to do with our wages and benefits or even with Chinese currency manipulation. It's about Wall Street running wild.

As we saw in Chapter 8, our economy is packed with debt – student debt, consumer debt, corporate debt, and government debt. This debt is brought to us by the financial sector, which now dominates our economy. And it's undermining our competitive position in the global economy.

Compare Chart 18.2 on total U.S. public and private debt with Chart 18.1 above on the decline of manufacturing jobs. Notice that the steep rise in debt corresponds with the steep decline in manu-

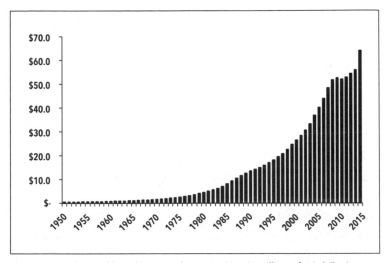

Chart 18.2: Total U.S. Public and Private Debt, 1950 – 2015 (In trillions of U.S. dollars)
Source: St. Louis Federal Reserve, Federal Reserve Economic Data, https://research.stlouisfed.org/fred2/series/TCMDO.

facturing jobs.

Are these two trends connected? If so, how and why?

Economist Michael Hudson provides piercing insight into how debt drives up the cost of living and the price of our products:

> [I]n America the easiest way to make money is not by "creating jobs" but by loading the economy down with debt, inflating asset prices on credit, privatizing natural monopolies and extracting economic rent in the form of higher access charges. None of this increases real output. But it does increase the cost of living and doing business.[6]

Nearly 30 cents of every dollar spent in the U.S. goes to interest payments. Meanwhile, the financial sector sees to it that much of this business goes untaxed: loans for buying and selling companies are tax-deductible. The financial industry buys and sells trillions of

---

6 Michael Hudson, "Trade and Payments Theory in a Financialized Economy," October 26, 2011, http://michael-hudson.com/2011/10/trade-theory-financialized/.

dollars of stocks, bonds and other financial products – but pays no sales tax on those transactions. What *is* taxed – heavily – is labor, through payroll and income taxes.

The net result is that the typical American spends much of his or her income on interest payments and taxes. This leads to a stagnant standard of living for the 99 percent – and to high-priced products.

Manufacturers are not just producing products for domestic and global consumption. In fact, their primary mission is to produce wealth for the financial sector, CEOs and wealthy investors. And to do that they have to make sure that the cost of their products is high enough to allow them to pay back all the loans they've taken out to buy and sell companies. Plus, of course, they need enough money from selling their products to buy back their stocks and pump up the CEO's stock options.

So China may keep its products cheap through currency manipulation. But the U.S. financial strip-miners are keeping U.S. prices artificially high by loading up our manufacturing companies and the rest of the economy with debt.

How does Germany do it?

Germany is a trading giant. It's the world's leading exporter of high-value manufactured goods. German manufacturing is like a Mercedes on steroids. How do they do it? How do the German manufacturers out-compete American companies – and withstand Chinese currency manipulation?

The answer has nothing to do with their level of technology. We have the same or better. It has nothing to do with the skills of their workers. We have the same or better. Both Germany and the U.S. are highly developed economies with knowledgeable workers and advanced technologies. Yet Germany has higher manufacturing wages, more manufacturing jobs relative to the size of their economy, and a trade surplus!

Again, Michael Hudson suggests a compelling answer: Germany

controls its financial system. We don't. It's that simple.

How does Germany keep its financial sector in check? It supports many public banks. It encourages renter coops to keep home prices and consumer debt down. It puts more controls on financial speculation. And it has a much smaller CEO-to-worker wage gap.

In the U.S., private sector debt is 192 percent of the size of the annual economy (GDP). That debt amounts to nearly twice the value of all the actual goods and services we produce in one year. In Germany, private sector debt totals only 77.2 percent of the German economy.[7]

All that extra U.S. debt comes at a steep price: We have to pay interest, and that cost has to be built into the price of our products. Since Germany's economy carries only half the debt load of the U.S., it can offer prices that are more competitive in the global marketplace.

Stand back again to look at the big picture. The American economy has become a cash cow for Wall Street and corporate CEOs, who get their outrageous incomes by siphoning wealth from American industry and from consumers. But someone has to pay for all the debt heaped on the private sector. That someone is the consumer/worker – here and around the world. The price of our products must reflect the cost of this enormous debt. We can blame this financial overhead for much of the size of our trade deficit and the loss of our good manufacturing jobs.

Once again all signs point to Wall Street and runaway inequality. If we want to revive manufacturing, we have to put the financial strip-miners out of business.

---

7   World Bank, "Domestic Credit to Private Sector (% of GDP)," World Bank Data, 2016, http://data.worldbank.org/indicator/FS.AST.PRVT.GD.ZS.

Discussion Questions:

1. Why has the U.S. lost so many manufacturing jobs?

2. What do you think is the impact of sky-high corporate and consumer debt on U.S. trade and manufacturing?

3. Why do you think that the U.S. runs such a large trade deficit with China, but Germany does not?

CHAPTER 19

The Wall Street Crash
Accelerates Inequality

When the stock market crashed in 1929 it ushered in the Great Depression, followed in 1933 by the New Deal. Most people understood that excessive Wall Street speculation and fraud had created a stock market bubble that led to the crash. They thought that if the super-rich had less gambling money, and if Wall Street were prohibited from operating financial casinos, we could avoid a repeat performance. We just needed to tightly regulate Wall Street and increase tax rates on the super-rich – two key elements of the New Deal.

The next three decades seemed to prove this theory right. The era saw next to no financial crashes in the U.S., and inequality levels plummeted (see Chart 1.4 in Chapter 1).

However, in the 1970s a new generation of policymakers turned their backs on the lessons of the New Deal, rejecting financial controls and high taxes on the super-rich. They ushered in the Better Business Climate model.

As New Dealers would have predicted, when the U.S. released Wall Street from regulations, economic inequality rose and financial instability returned. Crashes were back: There were 42 banking crises between 1970 and 2007, according to a study by the International Monetary Fund.[1]

The Savings and Loan crisis and subsequent bailout couldn't have happened without financial deregulation. Before deregulation, these banks (called thrifts) took in savings from the public

---

1   Luc Laeven and Fabian Valencia, "Systemic Banking Crises: A New Database," An IMF Working Paper, WP/08/224, November 2008, http://www.imf.org/external/pubs/ft/wp/2008/wp08224.pdf.

and used most of the money to finance mortgages. The interest rates the thrifts could offer to attract deposits were set by regulators, as were the kinds of mortgage products they could sell. The deposits were federally insured.

As inflation took off in the 1970s, the thrifts faced a mismatch between the low mortgage interest rates they received from mortgages they had issued in the past versus the rates they had to pay out to attract new savings deposits. Because of the fixed ceilings on interest rates, people were fleeing the banks and moving their money into other investments and uninsured money market funds where rates were much higher.

Of course the Better Business Climate model had a solution for this problem: deregulate the thrifts and let market forces do their magic. In 1980 and 1982 Congress passed two bills that gave the thrifts more freedom to raise interest rates and to expand their loans well beyond the mortgage market.[2]

At that point the free market did indeed work its magic. Thrifts embarked on a frenzied race to see who could raise interest rates the highest to attract deposits, and who could find the most lucrative (and risky) commercial investments. In their wild quest to capture the new money all this activity generated, an enormous number of thrifts took the next logical competitive step in an unregulated environment: they turned to crime. Many of the thrifts became fat piggy banks for bank owners and investors, who took full advantage of their federally insured deposits – they found ways to illegally pocket the money.

In short order, nearly a third of the more than 3,200 thrifts went bust. The government made 30,000 criminal referrals and 1,000 bankers were convicted of felony charges.[3] The bailout cost the U.S. treasury over $160 billion.

---

2   The two bills were the Depository Institution Deregulation and Monetary Control Act, 1980 and the Garn-St. Germain Depository Control Act, 1982.

3   Joshua Holland, "Hundreds of Wall Street Execs Went to Prison During the Last Fraud-Fueled Bank Crisis," Moyers and Company, September 17, 2013, http://billmoyers.com/2013/09/17/hundreds-of-wall-street-execs-went-to-prison-during-the-last-fraud-fueled-bank-crisis/.

Deregulation accelerates

You might think that the Savings and Loan debacle would have led policymakers to reinstitute New Deal controls. Instead, the opposite happened. Policymakers, many who came from Wall Street or were heading there, thought financial markets overall were extremely healthy and that less regulation could only improve the situation.

Wall Street vehemently argued that to keep up with large global banks in Europe and Asia, American financial institutions should be allowed to provide more kinds of financial products and services, including insurance, stock-brokering and investment banking. So the largest American banks used their rising wealth and political power to undo nearly all of the New Deal controls that had limited their size, scope and products.

Arguably, the two largest deregulation steps were the repeal of the Glass-Steagall Act (through passage of the Financial Services Modernization Act of 1999) and a law that prohibited the government from regulating new financial products (2000).

With the repeal of the New Deal Glass-Steagall Act, commercial banks with government insured deposits were allowed to branch out into riskier financial fields. They were free once again to engage in the kind of speculation that had caused the bubble and crash 70 years before. If the investment bank side of these new mega-banks gambled and lost, taxpayers were likely to find themselves on the hook.

But Better Business Climate zealots like Alan Greenspan, then head of the Federal Reserve, were certain this risk would be contained. After all, he argued, banks and investors were more sophisticated than before, and they monitored each other far more effectively than government regulators could do.

After rolling back Glass-Steagall, the Better Business Climate cheerleaders took one more bold step. This time, instead of deregulating, they pressed for a bill that would prohibit new regulations on the rapidly growing market for "derivatives." Derivatives are complex financial instruments that allow banks and wealthy investors to make bets worth trillions of dollars on such events as whether or not a company's bonds will fail. If these bets were considered insurance policies, which they obviously are, then they would be subject to regulations insuring that buyers and sellers had enough reserves to cover losses, just like any insurance company.

But that didn't sit well with the bankers. Requiring those reserves would cut into the profits of this rapidly growing financial market.

So in 2000, Congress passed and President Clinton signed the Commodities Futures Modernization Act, which protected the vast new mega-market of derivatives from government oversight. Again, the idea was that sophisticated investors could police themselves in this labyrinthine market for complex insurance bets.

These two laws represented a major and long-sought victory for the financial industry. As Bill Moyers, the veteran American journalist and commentator, put it:

> After 12 attempts in 25 years, Congress finally repeals Glass-Steagall, rewarding financial companies for more than 20 years and $300 million worth of lobbying efforts. Supporters hail the change as the long-overdue demise of a Depression-era relic.[4]

The bubble and bust

Financial bubbles and crashes are the natural outcome of the Better Business Climate model. The model puts enormous wealth in the hands of the few, but the few don't necessarily invest that wealth in productive enterprises. In fact, investors have such huge stockpiles of money, they can't find enough brick-and-mortar companies to invest in.

---

4   "The Long Demise of Glass-Steagall," *Frontline*, PBS, http://www.pbs.org/wgbh/pages/frontline/shows/wallstreet/weill/demise.html.

Deregulation now permits Wall Street investment firms to meet this high-end demand by creating new paper assets with high rates of return, supposedly at little risk.

So now we have all the ingredients needed for a bubble and bust: too much money in the hands of a few plus a deregulated Wall Street selling risky financial securities.

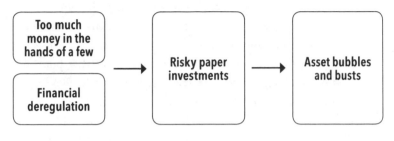

The housing bubble

In the years leading up to the 2008 crash, Wall Street turned the housing market into a vast casino that poured money into its coffers. Using all the latest "financial engineering" techniques, Wall Street developed a global financial assembly line that turned high-risk mortgages into AAA-rated securities that they sold all over the world. It was truly a remarkable feat that will forever show the phoniness of the Better Business Climate model.

It all happened in six relatively simple steps:

> **Step 1:** Find as many high-risk mortgages as possible. This involves encouraging banks to give mortgages to homebuyers who might not normally qualify for a mortgage and who are desperate enough to pay very high interest rates. Or, alternatively, manipulate homebuyers who actually would qualify for, or already have, a safe, cheaper conventional mortgage into switching to a riskier mortgage.

Step 2: Pressure mortgage originators to do anything and everything to gather up high-risk mortgages. This might include encouraging buyers to lie about their income, job status and anything else that would help close the deal. Offer homebuyers low "teaser" rates for two years, interest-only payments, lower-payments that tack on more principle in the future, and so on. Push those mortgages out by any means, including fraud.

Step 3: Sell the mortgages to Wall Street firms that put them into big mortgage-backed securities that Wall Street can chop up into smaller pieces and resell to investors.

Step 4: Create new financial assets that are nothing more than bets on these pools of mortgages, called synthetic collateralized debt obligations (CDOs). The bets don't have title to any of the mortgages, but they're paid off exactly as if they did. (If you want the details, see my book, *The Looting of America*.)

Step 5: Through market incentives (as in, "either you do what we want or we'll take our business elsewhere"), make sure the three rating agencies give these new bets good-as-gold AAA ratings.

Step 6: Make more money than you ever dreamed of.

In short, tons of rich people's money pours into the high-risk mortgage market, and tons more pours into covering bet upon bet on those very same mortgages.

In the lead-up to the 2008 crash, Wall Street took one more dangerous step in an attempt to protect itself: It took out insurance policies against defaults on many of its CDO securities – the derivatives that Congress had exempted from all regulations.

This created a remarkable upside-down pyramid of assets.

This assembly-line drove millions of people into the housing market, which sent housing prices skyrocketing like never before.

Buyers flocked in, because just about anyone could get a mortgage. The mortgage lenders told the buyers not to worry about those high interest rates, because in a few years they could refinance based on the ever increasing value of their homes.

Please look carefully at Chart 19.1 of U.S. housing prices going back to the 1800s. Note the magic performed on housing prices by Wall Street's financial engineering. This is what a bubble looks like.

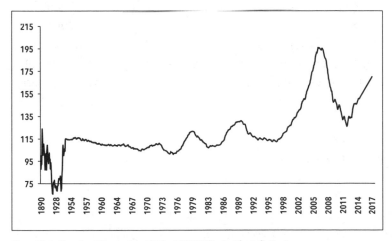

Chart 19.1: Housing Price Index, 1880 - 2017 (Adjusted for inflation)
Source: Robert Shiller, "On-line Data," http://www.econ.yale.edu/~shiller/data.htm.

The crash

Like all bubbles, everything looks great on the way up. Mortgages were issued, houses built and bought, mortgage bets made and insured, and Wall Street raked in the money all along the way.

But as soon as housing prices stopped rising, the entire upside down pyramid came crashing down.

- High-risk mortgage holders couldn't make their payments and couldn't sell their houses.
- The CDOs with AAA ratings were turned into junk bonds, causing major losses for investors and Wall Street banks.
- The insurance on the bets had to be paid off, which sent the nation's largest insurer, AIG, towards bankruptcy, along with the privatized federal housing corporations Fannie Mae and Freddie Mac.

In a matter of months the entire financial system froze. Money markets froze. Loans that covered payrolls froze. Credit lines companies needed for operations dried up. Bank financing froze. Insurance financing froze. Homeowners saw their home prices collapse, leaving them with mortgages worth more than the value of their homes. Eight million workers lost their jobs in a matter of months. The stock market crashed. It looked like 1929 all over again.

But there was one major difference: Wall Street knew it had grown too big to fail.

The bailout

The government scrambled for a plan that would keep the economy from falling into another Great Depression. They had several options:

- They could take over the insolvent banks and insurance companies as they would smaller insolvent banks. This would mean getting rid of the bad bets and loans from the bank's books, removing the corporate officers, and eventually selling the bank back to the public to cut the taxpayers' losses. This process would also wipe out the value of shares owned by private stockholders.
- They could take over failed banks and run them indefinitely as public utilities.
- They could reduce the principle owed by those homeowners who had mortgages worth more than the value of their homes. This would stimulate economic activity and alleviate much hardship for those who saw the value of their homes collapse due to Wall Street's reckless gambles.
- They could bail out the banks with trillions of dollars of loans and guarantees.

Given the revolving door between money and politics, and between Wall Street and government regulators, the first priority was to bail out Wall Street.

The numbers were staggering. This crisis was approximately seven times larger than the Savings and Loan debacle.

Both the Bush and Obama administrations threw money at Wall Street to try to halt the implosion. ProPublica.org reports that the government disbursed a total of $626 billion dollars in cash, divided up among the players shown in Chart 19.2.[5]

The government got all of its money back, plus a profit of $87.7 billion according to estimates by ProPublica.[6]

Author Nomi Prins, who spent ten years working on Wall Street, puts a higher value on the bailout. Her figures not only include the value of the loans the government made to Wall Street, but also the value of the many asset guarantees – insurance – that the

---

5   Paul Kiel and Dan Nguyen, "Bailout Tracker," *ProPublica*, October 31, 2017, http://projects.propublica.org/bailout/main/summary.
6   Ibid.

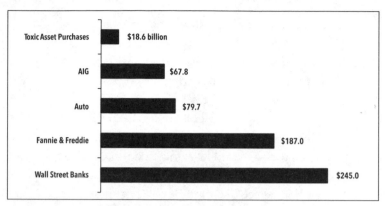

Chart 19.2: Bailout (In billions of U.S. dollars)
Source: Paul Kiel and Dan Nguyen, "Bailout Tracker," ProPublica, October 31, 2017, http://projects.propublica.org/bailout/main/summary.

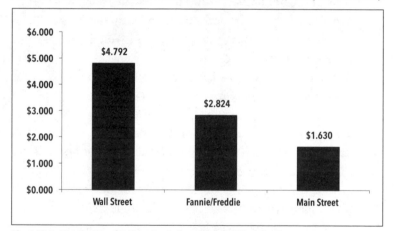

Chart 19.3: Distribution of Bailout Funds (In trillions of U.S. dollars)
Source: Nomi Prins and Krisztina Ugrin, "Bailout Tally Report," October 1, 2011, http://www.nomiprins.com/storage/bailouttallyoct 2011CLEAN%20NO%20FORMULAS.pdf.

government issued. That insurance also puts the taxpayer on the hook in the event of another crisis.

Prins estimates that the U.S. supplied a total of $9.2 trillion in bailout cash and guarantees.[7] Her summary chart (see Chart 19.3) shows that Wall Street received most of the money, followed by

---

7   Nomi Prins and Krisztina Ugrin, "Bailout Tally Report," *Nomprins.com*, October 1, 2011, http://www.nomiprins.com/storage/bailouttallyoct2011CLEAN%20 NO%20FORMULAS.pdf.

Fannie Mae and Freddie Mac. The smaller Main Street column includes the auto bailout and other programs to help the rest of the country.

The backdoor bailout

Saving the giant insurer AIG from total collapse was a big part of the bailout. AIG fell off the deep end because it provided insurance for billions upon billions of dollars in CDO derivatives and other financial products. Because these markets were unregulated, AIG didn't have to put aside any reserves in case they had to pay out. And since so many of these insured assets were wrongly rated as AAA, AIG figured they could take in the premiums without any risk at all. And then the risk appeared, big time.

But no worries: The government promised to provide over $170 billion in taxpayer cash to cover AIG's bad bets. After all, AIG was the key link in a great daisy chain of bets. It owed billions to all the major banks around the world (see Tables 19.1 and 19.2).

If AIG went bankrupt and couldn't pay up, many of these interconnected banks would have gone under as well. This was just the kind of chain reaction that happened during the Great Depression.

Table 19.1: Distribution of AIG Bailout Funds	
US	$ 43.5 billion
France	$19.1
Germany	$16.7
UK	$12.7
Switzerland	$5.4
Netherlands	$2.3
Canada	$1.1
Spain	$0.3
Denmark	$0.2
Total AIG debts owed	**$101.3 billion**

Source: Michael Mandel, "German and French Banks Got $36 Billion from AIG Bailout," *Bloomberg Business*, March 15, 2009, http://www.businessweek.com/the_thread/economicsunbound/archives/2009/03/german_and_fren.html.

Table 19.2: Top Recipients of Federal Bailout	
Goldman Sachs	$12.9 billion
States and Cities	$12
Merrill Lynch	$6.8
Bank of America	$5.2
Citigroup	$2.3
Wachovia	$1.5
Morgan Stanley	$1.2
AIG International Inc.	$0.6
JPMorgan	$0.4
Citadel	$0.2
Paloma Securities	$0.2
Regions Financial	$0.2
TOTAL AIG payments	**$43.5 billion**

Source: Michael Mandel, "German and French Banks Got $36 Billion from AIG Bailout," *Bloomberg Business*, March 15, 2009, http://www.businessweek.com/the_thread/economicsunbound/archives/2009/03/german_and_fren.html.

In real terms, the AIG bailout was a backdoor bailout of the Wall Street bets. As soon as AIG got the government money, it paid the biggest Wall Street banks 100 cents on the dollar. Why? Because those banks refused to take less and the government refused to force them to.

An evaluation of the bailout from its watchdog

Neil Barofsky was in charge of monitoring the government's $700 billion Troubled Asset Relief Program (TARP), which was supposed to resurrect the economy. Despite repeated promises to Congress that much of the TARP money would be used to assist troubled homeowners, Barofsky found that nearly all of it went to Wall Street. Here's his stinging assessment of what happened and why:

> So, for example, TARP was supposed to be used by the banks to restore lending, help pump that oxygen into

the lifeblood of the economy, and it just didn't happen. One of the reasons why it didn't happen is the money went to the banks with no strings attached, no conditions, no incentives, just essentially piles of money given to them without any instructions whatsoever and sort of this hope that somehow or other they use the money to achieve the policy goals of the administration. Of course, that never happened and you just look at the malaise the economy has been in the years ever since.[8]

Barofsky also was keenly aware of the revolving door and the power of money over regulators. He was told there was a great deal of money waiting for him if he stopped being so critical of Wall Street:

On the Washington side . . . you have the problems of regulators who often have incentives not to be really good regulators. The curse there again is partly the revolving door. I was told point blank in 2010 that if I didn't change the harshness of my tone on Wall Street, as well as on the administration, that I was going to be doing me and my family real harm because I wasn't going to have this job forever. If I wanted to get a job on Wall Street or advance within the administration, I needed to soften my tone. I was told that if I did soften my tone, very good things could potentially [follow].

The unequal recovery

The Better Business Climate model officially insists on no government interference. The model is all about freeing the market from

8 Jason Breslow, "Neil Barofsky on the Broken Promises of the Bank Bailouts," *Frontline*, August 12, 2012, http://www.pbs.org/wgbh/pages/frontline/business -economy-financial-crisis/money-power-wall-street/neil-barofsky-on-the-broken -promises-of-the-bank-bailouts/.

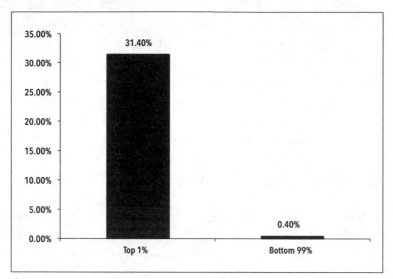

Chart 19.4: Income Growth During Recovery, 2009 – 2012
Source: Emmanuel Saez, "Striking It Richer," September 3, 2013, http://eml.berkeley.edu/~saez/saez-UStopincomes-2012.pdf.

all constraints and letting it work its magic. But history has rarely seen the level of interference government provided to bail out its biggest political investors – the giant Wall Street banks and investment companies.

This totally rips off the last tiny fig leaf covering the Better Business Climate model.

And yet the bailout was sold as a way to help all Americans. It was the only way we could halt the financial crisis and promote recovery, we were told.

While we did avert another Great Depression and a slow, halting recovery has begun, that recovery has not much benefited everyday Americans. Virtually all the economic gains of the recovery are going into the pockets of the super-rich. Because of runaway inequality and the power of the super-rich to direct economic policy, eight years after the recovery, we're still not seeing that famous trickle-down.

Between 2009 and 2012, the top 1 percent saw their incomes grow by over 31 percent, as Chart 19.4 shows. Meanwhile, the bottom 99 percent received almost no increase at all. Never before has a "recovery" enriched so few with so much, and provided so little to so many.

This is the raw power of runaway inequality. In 1929, the Wall Street crash led to stronger government regulation and higher taxation, and that then produced a much more equal distribution of wealth and income. Since the great crash of 2008, we are moving in the opposite direction: Runaway economic inequality is accelerating. The financial elites, who should have paid dearly for taking down the economy, have been rewarded instead.

How can we bring a semblance of fairness and justice to the American economy?

Discussion Questions:

1. What do you think were the most important causes of the 2008 crash?

2. Do you think the bank bailout was fair? Why or why not?

3. How has the current recovery impacted inequality?

4. What do you think we should do about the Wall Street banks?

PART FOUR

Solutions

CHAPTER 20

Public Banks Challenge Wall Street

Wall Street deregulation let the genie out of the bottle. Wall Street now dominates the economy. Corporations have been financialized and inequality is accelerating.

How do we regain control over out-of-control Wall Street?

In this chapter, we'll look at reforms that would bring a semblance of fairness and justice to our society.

Public banking

To stop the financial strip-mining of America, the root cause of runaway inequality, we must drastically change our banking system.

There is no shortage of proposals for taming Wall Street. Some advocate restoring the Glass-Steagall Act, which would prohibit regular federally insured commercial banks – the places where we put our money – from also being investment banks that speculate. Others advocate breaking up large banks into smaller private banks to increase competition. And still others say that we should have nationalized the large banks after the collapse, instead of bailing them out. Far better to have government own these big banks than private behemoths with a record of running roughshod over us.

An intriguing version of that last proposal is being played out right now in an unlikely place: North Dakota.

CHAPTER 20

Why is socialism doing so well in deep-red North Dakota?

North Dakota is the very definition of a red state. It voted 63 percent to 27 percent for Trump over Clinton. It has a Republican governor and Republicans dominate its state house and senate (119 Republicans, 22 Democrats). The state's Republican super-majority is so conservative that in March 2013 it passed the nation's most severe anti-abortion bills.[1]

But North Dakota also is red in another sense. It fully supports its state-owned Bank of North Dakota (BND), a socialist relic that exists nowhere else in America.

Why is financial socialism still alive in North Dakota? Why haven't North Dakotan free-market crusaders slain it? Because it works.

In 1919, the Non-Partisan League, a vibrant populist organization, won a majority in the North Dakota legislature and voted the bank into existence. The goal was to free the state's farmers from impoverishing debt dependence on the big banks in the Twin Cities, Chicago and New York. More than 90 years later, this state-owned bank is thriving, providing reasonably priced loans for community banks, businesses, consumers and students. It also delivers a handsome profit to its owners – the people of the state of North Dakota (all 700,000 of them). In 2013, the BND replenished the state's coffers to the tune of more than $94 million. "It is more profitable than Goldman Sachs Group Inc., has a better credit rating than J.P. Morgan Chase & Co. and hasn't seen profit growth drop since 2003," writes the *Wall Street Journal*.[2]

What if California, with its huge economy, decided to create *its*

---

1   Laura Bassett, "North Dakota Senate Passes Two Unprecedented Abortion Bans," *The Huffington Post*, March 15, 2013, http://www.huffingtonpost.com/2013/03/15/north-dakota-abortion_n_2885452.html.

2   Chester Dawson, "Shale Boom Helps North Dakota Bank Earn Returns Goldman Would Envy," *Wall Street Journal.com*, November 16, 2014, http://www.wsj.com/articles/shale-boom-helps-north-dakota-bank-earn-returns-goldman-would-envy-1416180862.

own bank? The state would be looking at an extra $4 billion a year in revenues that could fund education and infrastructure.

Some people say that BND's success is just the fortuitous outcome of the state's oil shale boom. But as financial writer Ellen Brown points out, the boom didn't start until 2010, long after the Bank of North Dakota's profit streak began.[3] No, it's not so easy to explain away this populist bank. It really works because it is a real bank and not a casino and because its aim is to address public needs, not enrich private owners.

Proposal: Let's create 49 more state banks to match the one in North Dakota. And give every large city its own bank as well. That's a way to directly challenge the financial power of Wall Street.

One of America's best kept secrets

What do our city and state governments do with the taxes and fees we pay them? They deposit these revenues in a bank. If you are not lucky enough to live in North Dakota, most of your taxes and fees end up in Wall Street too-big to-fail banks, because they're the only entities large enough to handle the load. Most of the nation's 7,000 community banks are too small to provide the array of cash management services that state and local governments require.

We're talking big bucks: at least $1 trillion of our local tax dollars find their way to Wall Street banks, according to Marc Armstrong, a consultant who advises government officials and labor unions about public banking.

So, not only are we, as taxpayers, on the hook for too-big-to-fail Wall Street banks, but also we are unknowingly handing our money over to these same banks every time we pay a sales tax or

---

3   Ellen Brown, "WSJ Reports: Bank of North Dakota Outperforms Wall Street," *Web of Debt*, http://ellenbrown.com/2014/11/19/wsj-reports-bank-of-north-dakota-outperforms-wall-street/.

property tax or buy a fishing license. In North Dakota, however, all that public revenue runs through its trusty public state bank, which reinvests the money in small businesses and public infrastructure via partnerships with 100 smaller community banks and financial institutions.

How the state bank creates jobs

Under our free enterprise system, banks are supposed to serve as intermediaries that turn our savings and checking deposits into productive loans to businesses and consumers, creating jobs in the process. But the BND, a state agency, goes one step further. Through its Partnership in Assisting Community Expansion, for example, it provides loans at below market interest rates to businesses if and only if those businesses create at least one job for every $100,000 loaned.

If instead of dropping $1 trillion dollars into Wall Street banks each year, we deposited that money in our 50 public state banks with programs like BND's, we could create up to 10 million new jobs, improving the lives of regular people.

No bailouts for the BND

Banking doesn't have to be a casino designed to enable bank traders and executives to make seven- and eight-figure salaries through reckless gambling.

As BND president Eric Hardmeyer said in a 2009 *Mother Jones* interview:

> We're a fairly conservative lot up here in the upper Midwest and we didn't do any subprime lending and we have the ability to get into the derivatives markets

and put on swaps and callers and caps and credit default swaps and just chose not to do it, really chose a Warren Buffett mentality – if we don't understand it, we're not going to jump into it. And so we've avoided all those pitfalls.[4]

As state government employees, BND executives have no incentive to gamble their way to enormous pay packages. As you can see, the top seven officers earn a good living,[5] but on Wall Street, these salaries would be considered chicken feed:

Eric Hardmeyer, President and CEO:	$335,316
Todd Steinwand:	$204,000
Tim Porter, Chief Administrative Officer:	$185,234
Kirby Evanger:	$178,448
Lori Leingang, Chief Administrative Officer:	$144,275
Joe Herslip, Chief Business Officer:	$141,527
Jeffrey Weiler:	#140,700

To put these incomes into perspective, in 2016, the top five Wall Street bankers averaged $19,986,081 each.[6] That's 60 times more than Mr. Hardmeyer earned as CEO of the BND.

In 2017, the top five hedge fund managers and traders averaged $1.13 billion in income each.[7] These are the people who raid corporations, load them up with debt, gamble on markets, and so on. For every one dollar the top five Bank of North Dakota executives earn for their worthwhile efforts, the top five hedge fund managers received an unbelievable $13,903.

4   Josh Harkinson, "How the Nation's Only State-Owned Bank Became the Envy of Wall Street," *Mother Jones.com*, March 27, 2009, http://www.motherjones.com/mojo/2009/03/how-nation%E2%80%99s-only-state-owned-bank-became-envy-wall-street.

5   Salaries as of 2017, provided to author by the Bank of North Dakota.

6   Compiled from "The New York Times/Equilar 200 Highest-Paid-CEO-Rankings," 2015.

7   "The Highest Earning Hedge Fund Managers and Trainers, 2017 Ratings," *Forbes.com*, http://www.forbes.com/hedge-fund-managers/.

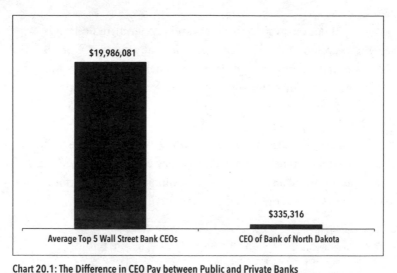

Chart 20.1: The Difference in CEO Pay between Public and Private Banks
Sources: Compiled from "The New York Times/Equilar 200 Highest-Paid-CEO-Rankings," 2017; and salaries provided to the author by the Bank of North Dakota.

In fact, those hedge fund moguls took home on average $543,269 *an hour.*[8] That means they got as much in one hour as Mr. Hardmeyer earned in 1.6 years!

Here's another interesting fact. The lowest paid, full-time employee at the BND earned $30,523 as of 2015. That makes the CEO/worker ratio at the BND about 8.6 to one, which is almost exactly what the American people want such ratios to be.

These contrasts completely undermine Wall Street's claim that it has to offer enormous pay packages to attract the best talent. North Dakota was able to find the talent to run one of the soundest banks in the country, while Wall Street's rich bankers almost crashed the whole economy. The BND is living proof that Wall Street's high pay rationale is a self-serving fabrication.

---

8   Figure based on a work year of 2,080 hours.

Wall Street is gunning for the Bank of North Dakota

As you can well imagine, financial elites would love to see this successful (socialist!) bank disappear. Its salary structure and local investments make a mockery of Wall Street's casino banking system. But the bigger threat is that this public banking concept could spread to other states. Already, about 20 state legislatures are exploring state banks. Collectively, more public banks would pose an enormous threat to the $1 trillion of state and local bank deposits that now run through Wall Street.

But elite financiers stand to lose even more than this. In the 49 states without a public bank, local governments desperate for loans to rebuild schools and finance other public infrastructure projects are forced to turn to Wall Street banks. These firms hook localities on expensive loan programs, such as capital appreciation bonds, that can end up costing local governments ten times the original loan. In addition, investment bankers and advisors make enormous fees by selling expensive, high-risk financial schemes to state and local governments.[9]

Sadly for Wall Street, such schemes are useless in North Dakota where the state bank provides the capital for a fraction of the long-term costs.

Free trade agreements: Wall Street's weapon of mass destruction

From Wall Street's perspective, the North Dakota bank must go, and must never be replicated. Wall Street's stealth weapon may be lodged within the latest Pacific Rim free-trade agreement, called the Trans-Pacific Partnership (TPP), which currently is being negotiated in secret.

---

9   Trey Bundy and Shane Shifflett, "School Districts Pay Dearly for Bonds," *SFGate*, January 31, 2013, http://www.sfgate.com/education/article/School-districts-pay-dearly-for-bonds-4237868.php.

We already know that Wall Street wants the trade deal to remove all tariff restrictions that would keep the U.S. financial service industry from doing business in countries including Brunei, Chile, Malaysia, Mexico, New Zealand, Peru, Singapore, and Vietnam. The biggest banks also want the treaty to eliminate "non-tariff" barriers, including regulations that create "unfair" competition with state-owned financial enterprises. Depending on the final language, such a measure could put the Bank of North Dakota out of business, since "foreign bankers could claim that the BND stops them from lending to commercial banks throughout the state," according to an analysis by Sam Knight in *Truthout*.[10] How perfect for Wall Street if a foreign bank could be a shill to knock out the BND.

The public bank movement

A small but highly dedicated group of financial writers, public finance experts and former bankers have formed the Public Bank Institute to spread the word. Working on a shoestring budget, its president, Ellen Brown (author of *Web of Debt*), and consultant Marc Armstrong, have become the Johnny Appleseeds of public banking, hopping from state to state to encourage legislatures and the postal labor unions to explore state-owned banks.

They point to the success other countries are having with public banking. In Germany, for example, approximately 40 percent of all banking assets are in public banks.[11] Switzerland also has a large, profitable public banking system.[12] Many countries, includ-

---

10   Sam Knight, "Corporate-backed Trans-Pacific Partnership Shrouded in Secrecy," *Truthout*, March 19, 2013, http://truth-out.org/news/item/15142-corporate-backed-trans-pacific-partnership-shrouded-in-secrecy.

11   *Felix Hüfner*, "The German Banking System: Lessons from the Financial Crisis," Economic Department Working Papers No.788, OECD, p.7, June 13, 2011, http://www.oecd.org/officialdocuments/publicdisplaydocumentpdf/?doclanguage=en&cote=eco/wkp(2010)44.

12   Ellen Brown, "Why Public Banks Outperform Private Banks: Unfair Competition or a Better Mousetrap?" Global Research, February 10, 2015, http://www.globalresearch.ca/why-public-banks-outperform-private-banks-unfair-competition-or-a-better-mousetrap/5430588.

ing Japan, China and Brazil, provide public banking at post offices – which could easily work here in the U.S..

The Better Business Climate model worships the false god of privatization of everything. But the large private banks that control so much of the economy exist only to make money for the super-rich. If we're going to protect the public interest from Wall Street's grip, we need to do more than pass new regulations that the wily bankers can manipulate and water down with clever lobbying. We need to build public institutions that serve the public interest – like the Bank of North Dakota.

Discussion Questions:

1. What do you think should be done about the big Wall Street banks?

2. Do you favor the establishment of more public banks like the Bank of North Dakota? Why or why not?

3. Would you favor bank executive pay on Wall Street to be similar to executive pay at the Bank of North Dakota? Why or why not?

CHAPTER 21

The Maximum Wage, Minimum Wage, Free Higher Education and Full Employment

What do we do about a CEO-worker wage gap that is 793 to one and climbing? Challenging Wall Street with public banks is certainly a good start. But we can do much more.

The people of Switzerland are engaged in a frontal assault on their wage gap. First, in March 2013, voters passed (by a 68 percent margin) a binding national referendum giving shareholders full power to set CEO pay. Even more stunningly, the referendum mandates that companies will "no longer be allowed to give bonuses to executives joining or leaving the business, or to executives when their company was taken over," according to the *New York Times*. "Violations could result in fines equal to up to six years of salary and a prison sentence of up to three years."[1]

In November 2013, Swiss activists put forth an even bolder national referendum called the 1:12 Initiative. It would have barred the CEOs of companies from earning more in one month than the lowest paid workers in their company earn in one year. This time the measure lost by a margin of 65 to 35. Nevertheless, the losing side captured nearly 1 million votes. According to *The Nation*:

> The 1:12 initiative was running dead even in the polls
> into October – until Swiss corporations unleashed a

---

1   Raphael Minder, "Swiss Voters Approve a Plan to Severely Limit Executive Compensation," *New York Times*, March 3, 2013, http://www.nytimes.com/2013/03/04/business/global/swiss-voters-tighten-countrys-limits-on-executive-pay.html?_r=0.

lushly financed fear-mongering ad blitz. If the 1:12 initiative passed, they argued, Swiss-based multinationals would shift their operations to friendlier locales, Switzerland's tax receipts would plummet and the nation's social safety net would tear into tatters.[2]

Is it possible that we too could start a 1:12 movement here in the U.S.?

Maximum wage options

1. Pay ratios

In Chapter 1 we saw that most Americans want a CEO-worker wage gap of from five to one to 12 to one with even strong Republicans supporting the 12 to one maximum gap just like the cap proposed in Switzerland.

In the U.S., we can estimate a 12 to one maximum corporate wage by using the current (2017) median weekly worker wage of $857 or $44,564 per year. (Median means that exactly half of American workers earn more and half earn less.)

So if a company's workers earned the median wage, CEOs, under our American 12-1 Initiative, could earn about $535,000 a year. However, if the company doubled the wage of its lowest paid workers, the CEO could earn just over $1 million.

It's key that the CEO figures we use include all forms of compensation: stock options, bonuses and retirement packages (golden parachutes), as well as salary. Because, as we noted in Chapter 4, CEO financial strip-miners now receive most of their compensation in stock options.

The charm of this ratio is that it rewards CEOs and companies that pay their workers well. The better the company pays its lowest-paid workers, the higher the CEO's compensation.

---

2   Sarah Anderson and Sam Pizzigati, "Swiss Activists: Let's Cap CEO Pay," *The Nation*, December 2, 2013, http://www.thenation.com/article/177424/swiss-activists-lets-cap-ceo-pay.

One knotty question: Who counts as an employee? Today, virtu-ally all large companies use a myriad of contractors, sub-contractors and sub-sub-contractors from all over the world, many of them paid a pittance. So, would Apple's CEO be forced to earn no more than 12 times the company's full-time employees? Or 12 times the pay of the company's extremely low-paid workers in China? Maybe the very necessity of determining the answer to this question would raise public awareness about the policies of global corporations like Apple.

The National Nurses United union took a first step toward limit-ing CEO pay in 2013. The union got over 100,000 signatures on a ballot initiative in Massachusetts that would have limited CEO pay in healthcare companies that get taxpayer money to no more than 100 times the pay of the company's lowest paid employees.

2. Maximum Wage
Another strategy to tame runaway CEO pay is to impose a simple wage cap like the one used in professional sports: that industry sets a new maximum salary for players each year, depending on the league's revenue. Professional football and hockey have such "hard" salary caps.

We could set our CEO salary cap each year using a formula based on the median wage. For example, the law could require that each year no CEO could receive more than 12 times American workers' median wage that year. So if our wages stall, so does CEO total pay. If our wages rise, then the cap would automatically rise by the same percentage.

3. High marginal tax rate on the wealthy
The most traditional way to reduce runaway inequality is to set a high marginal tax rate (for example, 91 percent on income over $200,000 – roughly $2 million in today's dollars – as was the case from 1946 to 1951). The wealthy person would only receive five cents on every dollar over, say, $2 million in total compensation.

This is roughly what the U.S. did during the New Deal and onward until 1980, the period when U.S. inequality was the lowest ever.

The upside of this approach to equalizing pay is that we know it can work – it's been done before. And the IRS could administer it easily.

The downside, as with all taxes, is loopholes, and the knack rich people have for stashing money in overseas tax havens. Those tax havens must end.

There is also an important ethical problem. When the government taxes the income of the wealthy after the income is in their account, it is considered "earned" income. This terminology legitimizes the idea that these wealthy people earned the money fair and square, and the government took some of it away. Can you hear the hue and cry about "redistribution"?

However, if there is a hard compensation cap or a ratio, then the money never "belongs" to the CEO in the first instance. Nothing is being taken away.

Financial speculation tax

A sizable portion of Wall Street's profits comes from the rapid buying and selling of all kinds of financial instruments – especially stocks, bonds, options, and derivatives. In the U.S., we are taxed when we buy most goods, but Wall Street is not taxed when it conducts its buying and selling, even though this business runs into the trillions of dollars.

Economists like the late James Tobin believe that taxing these transactions not only would produce needed government revenue, but also put the brakes on the rapid short-term buying and selling of financial assets, a practice that is both dangerous and damaging.

Unions, including the National Nurses United and the Chicago Teachers Union, are calling for such taxes both to tame Wall Street and to fund social programs and education. A small tax could generate as much as $350 billion a year in revenues. The nurses call it a Robin Hood Tax, and they have pushed the issue across the country, picking up many allies. On its website the union writes:

Among the array of groups which embrace and endorse this critical program – revenue over austerity, a Wall Street tax to pay back Main Street – are ACT UP Chapters from across the U.S., Voices of Community Activists and Leaders (VOCAL-NY), Health GAP and National Nurses United; AIDS foundations joined in; the American Medical Student Association listed itself, as did Community Voices Heard; Consumer Watchdog and the Gray Panthers joined up, as well as Greenpeace, Housing Works, the National Organization of Women and the Maine People's Alliance. Religious organizations bring strong support to Robin Hood, including Interfaith Worker Justice, the Maryknoll Office of Global Concern, the Sisters of Holy Cross – Congregation Justice Committee and National Advocacy Center of the Sisters of the Good Shepherd. Labor is standing firm behind the tax, with the Farm Labor Organizing Committee, the Coalition of Labor Union Women, the United Automobile Workers, Communication Workers of America and United Steelworkers. United Students Against Sweatshops is with Robin Hood, too. And more than 100 others – all have come together for Robin Hood and its concrete commitment to social and economic justice.[3]

A Robin Hood Tax would both cut Wall Street revenues and put serious downward pressure on enormous financier compensation packages.

Great Britain already has such a tax and the European Union is considering one (which the U.S. opposes). If we want to build a movement to contain Wall Street and rebuild our nation, we need that tax.

---

3 RobinhoodTax, "Solidarity Grows around HR 6411," Blog, *RobinhoodTax.org*, October 15, 2012, http://www.robinhoodtax.org/blog-entry/solidarity-grows -around-hr-6411.

Closing the "Carried Interest" loophole

This is a no-brainer. As we mentioned in Chapter 7, the richest of the rich – the people who run hedge funds and private equity firms – love the carried interest loophole, which lets them declare much of their income as capital gains, slicing their top tax rate from 39 percent to 20 percent. The top 25 hedge fund managers save about $4.8 billion a year through this loophole. Their loss would be our gain. Unfortunately, neither the Democrats nor the Republicans have an interest in eliminating it. We will need to build a movement of considerable proportions to get their attention. This tax loophole is a disgrace to our nation.

Raising the minimum wage and minimum benefits

Wage caps on the wealthy should be coupled with policies that enable people at the bottom of the wage ladder to climb up a few rungs. The CEO might have to take a pay cut, but that doesn't necessarily mean that workers will get a raise.

We need to raise the minimum wage for all workers to something like $15 to $20 an hour, and then index it to inflation so that it never falls so far behind again.

From 1938 to the late-1960s, the U.S. minimum wage rose steadily, as Chart 21.1 shows. This was, of course, the period of the least inequality in our country. After the Better Business Climate model took hold in 1980, the real value of the minimum wage dropped. To bring inequality back down again, we've got to give the minimum wage a big boost.

But won't raising the minimum wage kill jobs?

Students in Econ 101 courses all over the country have been hearing this argument for decades. It goes like this: As the minimum wage increases, employers will find it more profitable to replace workers with machines – e.g., lay off a dishwasher at a restaurant and bring in a new dishwashing machine.

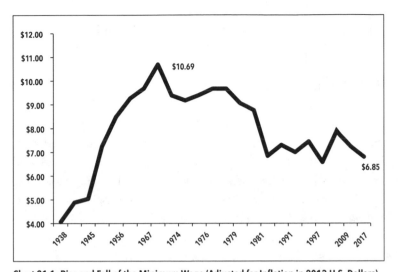

Chart 21.1: Rise and Fall of the Minimum Wage (Adjusted for Inflation in 2013 U.S. Dollars)
Source: Craig K. Elwell, "Inflation and the Real Minimum Wage, Congressional Research Service, January 8, 2014, https://www.fas. org/sgp/crs/misc/R42973.pdf, updated by author December 2017.

But studies have shown that raising the minimum wage has little or no impact on jobs.[4] In some cases, raising the wage may actually increase worker commitment to their job, leading to less turnover and absenteeism and higher productivity, increasing the employer's profits.

The minimum wage isn't just an economic question. It's a moral one. The minimum wage sets a minimum standard of decency for work in our society. A higher minimum wage says that we believe all workers should be able to support themselves and their families with dignity, even in the lowest-paid job categories. As a society we have to replace jobs that pay poverty wages with better-paying jobs that enhance workers' dignity. No full-time worker should ever have to rely on food stamps.

In recent years, militant campaigns to increase the minimum

---

4   John Schmitt, "Why Does the Minimum Wage Have No Discernible Effect on Employment?" Center for Economic Policy Research, February 2013, http://www. cepr.net/index.php/publications/reports/why-does-the-minimum-wage-have-no -discernible-effect-on-employment.

wage have lit up the country. Led by the successful effort to win a $15 per hour wage in SeaTac, Washington, Seattle and Los Angeles. Even conservative states like Arkansas, Nebraska, and South Dakota passed ballot referenda raising the minimum wage (by lesser amounts) in 2014.[5]

If we're going to bring dignity to work, we also need to pass laws making paid holidays, sick leave and maternity leave mandatory. As we saw in Chapter 6, every developed country in the world except ours provides mandatory paid time off for every worker. We should be demanding a minimum of four weeks paid vacation, 10 holidays, and at least six months paid family leave, as well as paid sick leave.

Campaigns to win paid and unpaid sick leave are gaining ground in communities across the country. Here's a 2014 summary:

> In 2006, San Francisco became the first locality in the nation to guarantee access to earned paid sick days. In 2008, the District of Columbia passed a paid sick days standard that included paid "safe" days for victims of domestic violence, sexual assault and stalking. In 2011, the Connecticut legislature became the first in the nation to pass a statewide paid sick days law and, in the same year, Seattle also passed a paid sick days law. In 2013, Portland, Ore., New York City and Jersey City, N.J., adopted paid sick days standards. Newark, N.J., followed in early 2014, followed by Eugene, Ore., San Diego, the state of California, and the New Jersey cities of Passaic, Paterson, East Orange and Irvington. In November 2014, paid sick days ballot measures passed in Massachusetts, Oakland, Calif., and the New Jersey cities of Montclair and Trenton. Altogether, more than two dozen states

---

5   Marianne Levine and Timothy Noah, "Minimum Wage Increase Wins in Four Red States," *Politico*, November 5, 2014, http://www.politico.com/story/2014/11/minimum-wage-increase-wins-in-four-red-states-112565.html. In May 2015 and March 2016, Los Angeles and New York, respectively, passed a $15/hr minimum wage.

and cities considered paid sick days proposals in the most recent legislative session.[6]

Free higher education

Providing more Americans with a quality education will produce more knowledgeable citizens and more productive workers. And yet young people are being squeezed out of college by ever-rising costs. Once again, we should follow the lead of other developed nations and eliminate tuition at all public colleges and universities. Revenue from the financial transaction tax mentioned above could more than cover the costs.

Not only would this greatly broaden access to higher education for low-income students,[7] it would eliminate the enormous student loans that now burden so many young people.

What's more, free higher education would lead to a building and hiring boom on college campuses, creating jobs that can't be shipped abroad.

Single payer healthcare

Runaway inequality is boosted by a system of health care that relies on the private insurance industry and that has no control over giant pharmaceutical companies. It is also the reason we rank first in costs but near the bottom in health outcomes as we saw in Chapter 7. There is no excuse for allowing these large corporate entities to place the enormous profits above our health needs. Our system

---

6   National Partnership, "State and Local Action on Paid Sick Days," May 2015, http://www.nationalpartnership.org/research-library/campaigns/psd/state-and-local-action-paid-sick-days.pdf.

7   A similar argument can be made for converting Obamacare into a single-payer system similar to those used in many other countries. See Physicians for a National Health Program (http://www.pnhp.org/) and Labor Campaign for Single-payer Healthcare (http://www.laborforsinglepayer.org/) for excellent descriptions of the advantages of such systems.

could become much less costly, cover everyone, and be more effective if we move to a system of Medicare for all, similar to the Canadian healthcare system. For excellent research, argumentation and mobilization, see Physicians for a National Health Program (www.pnhp.org) and Labor Campaign for Single Payer Healthcare (www.laborforsinglepayer.org).

Jobs

To tame runaway inequality, we need full employment. When employment levels are high, employers have to bid up wages to retain and attract employees. Besides, every society has a moral obligation to make sure that everyone who is able and willing to work can do so.

However, the private sector generally can't produce a sufficient number of jobs, even with enormous government stimulus programs like military spending. In fact, the real unemployment rate is much higher than what we hear each month in the news. The Bureau of Labor Statistics makes a regular tally not only of how many workers are officially looking for work and can't find it, but also those who work part time but want to work full time, and those who are "marginally attached" to the workforce (which means that at the moment they aren't looking for work, but have in the last 12 months, and still would like a job).

As Chart 21.2 shows, if you include this "hidden" unemployment (the Labor Department's "U6" measure) our level of unemployment is enormous. As of December 2017, after seven years of "recovery," it was still 8.0 percent. That's 13 million people who want full-time jobs but cannot find them.

Since the private sector can't produce enough jobs by itself, it is imperative that government expand the number of public employment jobs. Look around: there's plenty of work to be done – from rebuilding our crumbling infrastructure to early childhood education.

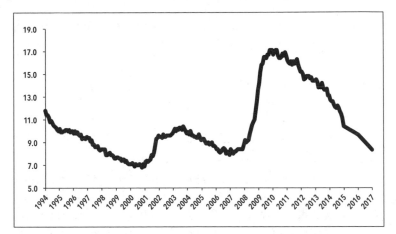

Chart 21.2: Real Unemployment Rate*

*The Bureau of Labor Statistics' U6 includes total unemployed, plus all persons marginally attached to the labor force, plus total employed part time for economic reasons, as a percent of the civilian labor force plus all persons marginally attached to the labor force.

Source: U.S. Bureau of Labor Statistics, "Alternative Measure of Labor Underutilization," http://data.bls.gov/cgi-bin/surveymost.

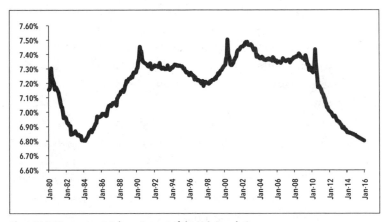

Chart 21.3: Government Jobs as Percent of the U.S. Population

Source: Federal Reserve Bank of St. Louis, Federal Reserve Economic Division, http://research.stlouisfed.org/fred2.

Unfortunately, the Better Business Climate model still has us heading in exactly the opposite direction. Instead of creating more government jobs to counter the enormous spike in unemployment after the Wall Street crash, we actually cut government jobs. That kept unemployment rates excessively high – which, in turn, held wages down, exacerbating runaway inequality.

Just Transition for communities, jobs and the environment

Under the laissez-faire policies of the Better Business Climate model, making the transition to sustainable energy will be extremely painful for coal, oil, and gas industry workers – and for their communities.

For example, the city of Tonawanda in upstate New York depends on the Huntley coal-fired power plant, which supplies millions of dollars in payments in lieu of taxes to support area schools. When production at the plant slowed recently because of a drop in the price of rival fuels, the city had to lay off 140 public sector workers. When the plant shuts down entirely in the next few years, 75 power-plant workers – and another 134 public sector workers – are slated to lose their jobs.

The Better Business Climate model has no answer to this kind of dislocation. It would let "free market" forces determine all future development, leaving it to workers to find new jobs and the community to find new revenues. But a local environmental justice group, the Clean Air Coalition, is calling for a "Just Transition" plan that will allow the workers to stay employed by helping them through public financial support to transition into sustainable industries.

Just Transition efforts like this are needed across the country. But they'll only succeed if we're able to build a powerful movement that tackles runaway inequality.

Writ large the problem is this: Moving to a sustainable economy will require phasing out carbon-intensive facilities that workers and communities depend on. That might seem like a small price to pay to combat climate change. But it's not a small price at all for the families and communities affected: Why should they have to shoulder so much of the burden for a benefit we all share? Why should their children's schools be forced to cut their budgets or even shut down when tax revenues collapse? Why should public and private sector workers give up their jobs for the sake of the common good? Without a program to address this problem, the transition away from fossil fuels is certain to exacerbate runaway inequality – and face vigorous opposition from people at risk of losing their jobs and communities.

The late Tony Mazzocchi (1926-2002), a labor and environmental leader, said dislocated workers and their communities should be made whole through investments from a national Just Transition fund. He argued that workers who are laid off in the transition to a new economy should get at least four years of wages and benefits plus tuition to the school of their choice – much like the benefits that three million returning WWII vets received under the GI Bill of Rights. Mazzocchi argued that this Just Transition fund should also provide revenues to local communities to prevent further layoffs and public service cutbacks.

How would we pay for such a fund? There are many ways. The money could come from a small share of the financial transaction tax we discussed previously. Or it could come from a small tax on fossil fuels. Mazzocchi rightly argued that the richest country on Earth could easily afford such a transition fund, once we come to understand that it is both just and necessary.

Racial justice

As we saw in Chapter 10, racial discrimination is built into the basic economic and social structures of our nation. It would take many more books to provide the detailed prescription for all we must do to eliminate these injustices from every aspect of society – from education to health care, from home ownership to finance, from employment to criminal justice. But the broad themes are clear. Police violence and harassment against people of color must stop, and the police must be transformed from an occupying army to a protective partner in the community. Housing and school segregation must finally end through major investments in public education and homes. Prison must no longer serve to warehouse the unemployed and dispossessed abandoned by our financial and corporate elites. Instead, we need to create decent paying jobs for all those willing and able to work.

Addressing racial injustice and ending runaway inequality demands that we reinvest hundreds of billions of dollars in our human and physical infrastructure. And those billions must come from those who have strip-mined our economy and evaded taxes by hiding their wealth overseas.

Massive economic investment in all of our people, especially the most vulnerable, will not end discrimination all by itself. But it is a critical step, and it requires a unified movement to conquer runaway inequality.

And then some

We could take on runaway inequality many other ways as well. Strong pollution controls could not only protect us from the ravages of global warming but also protect low-income communities from excessive chemical exposures.

Ending the "war on drugs" and mandatory prison sentencing would enable hundreds of thousands of people to return to productive work and address a grievous injustice that criminalizes many young men for the color of their skin.

Fully enforcing laws to protect gay, lesbian and transgender people from all forms of discrimination and halting skin color and gender discrimination, especially in employment and law enforcement, would help close the wage and wealth gaps for people in those categories.

All of these struggles can contribute to our effort to tackle the primary driver of runaway inequality: the financial strip-mining of America. To truly enhance freedom, justice and a sustainable environment for all, we have got to tame high finance.

Next we'll turn to a vital player in halting runaway inequality: labor unions.

Discussion Questions:

1. In your opinion, what is the most important policy that needs to be enacted in order to tackle runaway inequality?

2. Would you be in favor of a campaign that pushed for a mandatory 12 to one CEO to worker pay cap? Why or why not?

3. What do you think should be done to prevent the hiding of trillions of dollars in off-shore accounts?

When Unions Decline,
Inequality Soars and We All Lose

Runaway economic inequality is closely linked to the precipitous decline of labor unions in the United States. To understand why, let's review two critical charts from previous chapters.

The first (Chart 22.1) shows the rise and decline of union membership in the private sector from the depths of the Great Depression to today. Clearly unions represented a major slice of the workforce from the mid-1930s to the early 1980s. By 1953, more than one out of three private sector workers were union members. That means that in many parts of the country, nearly every family included at least one union member.

Through the late 1950s and 1960s, the percentage of workers who were in unions declined, but the absolute number continued to increase, peaking at nearly 21 million members in 1979. Much of this increase came from an influx of public sector workers during the 1960s and 1970s.

After that, labor's slide got steeper: the percent of workers in unions fell by half between the mid-1970s and the early 1990s. In 2017, only about 6.5 percent of private sector workers were in unions. If we include public employees, it's 10.7 percent.

Compare this chart to Chart 22.2, which traces the share of income that goes to the top 1 percent. Notice that it's basically the inverse of the unionization chart. When unions were the strongest, inequality was the lowest.

In 1928, the top 1 percent hauled off 23.94 percent of all U.S. income. As unions grew, the income share for the richest 1 percent dropped to less than 10 percent. But when unions declined, the

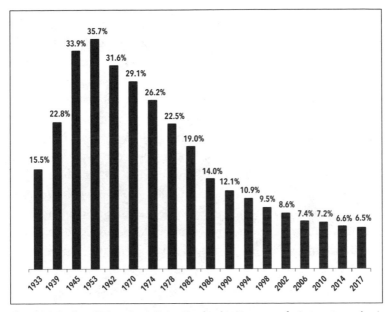

Chart 22.1: Decline of Private Sector Union Membership (As percent of private sector workers)
Sources: Data from 1933 – 1982 from Leo Troy and Neil Sheflin, *U.S. Union Sourcebook* (West Orange, NJ: IRDIS, 1985); Data for 1986 – 2017 from Bureau of Labor Statistics, "Union Affiliation of Employed Wage and Salary Workers," various years.

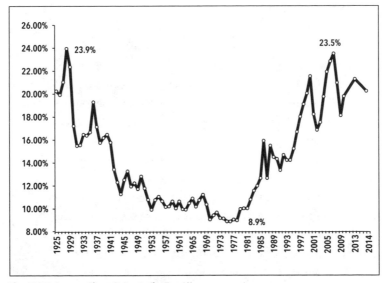

Chart 22.2: Income Share Going to the Top 1%
Sources: Emmanuel Saez and Thomas Piketty, "Income Inequality in the United States, 1913-1998," *Quarterly Journal of Economics*, Vol.118, No. 1, 2003 (Tables and Figures Updated to 2010), http://eml.berkeley.edu/~saez/; and "World Wealth and Income Database, "http:/widworld/data/.

richest 1 percent went back to grabbing a high percentage of the total U.S. income. In fact, their share shot back up to 1928 levels and is climbing again.

The relationship between these two charts isn't coincidental: Wealth inequality and unionization levels are intertwined. When unions are strong, they bargain for and win higher wages and benefits. And that has a ripple effect, since many non-union firms then try to keep workers from unionizing by raising *their* wages and benefits too. Meanwhile, these strengthened unions have more political clout, enabling them to push for and win legislation that benefits middle- and low-income people (like unemployment benefits, minimum wage, progressive taxation, Medicare, Medicaid, and Social Security). The result: a more balanced income distribution.

What happened to unions?

That's a question that has generated some heated discussion over the years. Theories abound. They include:

- The decline of unionism started when unions started cooperating with the government "anti-red" efforts during the McCarthy era. When unions ousted their radical members, they shot themselves in the foot because these radicals were their most effective organizers and officials.
- Unions spent far too much time and resources working with the government to prosecute the Cold War abroad. While they were helping to build anti-communist unions overseas, corporations were undermining unions at home.
- The merger of the AFL and the CIO in 1955 ended the organizing competition between them, leading to a drop in organizing. Also, the CIO's more militant culture was subsumed in the merger.

- Unions alienated the baby boomer generation by supporting the Vietnam War. Young progressive anti-war activists who in other eras would have been drawn to the labor movement were instead alienated from it.
- Unions became too bureaucratic and undemocratic, and some became corrupt. Union leaders crushed internal progressive democratic insurgents, which further weakened unions.
- Unions haven't learned how to deploy successful community organizing techniques to recruit new union members.
- Unions haven't kept up with globalization by linking with labor in other countries.

While many of these theories point to real flaws in post-WWII unionism, they only hint at the core underlying problem: Unions and the rest of us are on the losing side of a gigantic class war – a war that we have to recognize, discuss and address if unions are to grow again.

Revenge of the elites

The top 1 percent and their political allies understand that unions are uniquely suited to challenging the power of financial and political elites. For that reason, elites have launched a deliberate, sustained and merciless assault on unions (all in the name of efficient deregulation, of course). This includes weakening labor laws so severely that it has become almost impossible for unions to organize new members.

Employees who try to unionize can be easily fired, and challenging this in court can take years. Even when unions are certified as the official bargaining agent, employers can resist the bargaining process, again for years.

The anti-union attack, which first focused on private sector

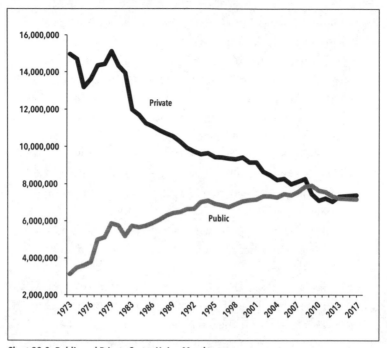

Chart 22.3: Public and Private Sector Union Members

Source: Barr T. Hirsch and David A. Macpherson, "Union Membership and Coverage Database from the CPS," Unionstats.com, http://www.unionstats.com/.

unions, has spread to public sector unions. When unionization rates were high in the private sector, public sector unions could use those wages and benefits as a benchmark for their own bargaining. But now that private sector unionization rates are so low, most of these workers earn less than public employees. Political demagogues use this as a lever to further drive down wages. They ask taxpayers: "Why should you be paying for public sector wages and benefits that are better than what you get yourself?"

Conservative governors love to use this vulnerability to cripple public sector unions, especially teachers' unions, which generally back Democrats.

The conservative attack is working. As Chart 22.3 shows, private sector union membership is declining in numbers (and as a percentage of private sector workers) while public sector union membership is relatively stable, but declining as a percentage of all public sector workers.

Anti-unionism is spreading fast. Governor Scott Walker of Wisconsin has built his entire political career on attacking public and private sector unions. In 2011 he led a fearsome battle to undermine public sector unions, especially the teachers' unions. He succeeded in enacting legislation that not only cut pension and health insurance benefits, but eviscerated core union functions. Wisconsin's anti-union law, called Act 10:

- limited collective bargaining contracts to one year
- limited all raises to the cost of living unless otherwise approved by a referendum
- forced unions to win an election every year to be recertified
- eliminated automatic dues check-off
- allowed any member of the bargaining unit to opt out of joining the union and opt out of paying dues.

Walker exempted police and fire unions from Act 10's restrictions on collective bargaining. In Wisconsin, these unions generally support Republicans.

Walker's "reforms" have reportedly reduced public sector union membership in Wisconsin by half.[1]

As Walker geared up for a presidential run in March 2015, he took aim at private sector unions as well. He and the Republican-dominated legislature passed a bill that would create an "open shop," allowing private sector union members to opt out of paying dues.

Unions and their allies have mounted huge protests against Walker and his legislation.

---

1   Monica Davey and Mitch Smith, "Scott Walker Is Set to Deliver New Blow to Labor in Wisconsin," *New York Times*, February 25, 2015, http://www.nytimes.com/2015/02/26/us/politics/walker-is-set-to-deliver-new-blow-to-labor-and-bolster-credentials.html?_r=0.

But Walker is proud and confident of his assault on unions. He says that his courage in fighting unions at home proves that he has the guts to take on "Islamic terrorists" (a disturbing parallel to draw):

> I want a commander in chief who will do everything in their power to ensure that the threat from radical Islamic terrorists does not wash up on American soil. We will have someone who leads and ultimately will send a message not only that we will protect American soil but do not, do not, take this upon freedom-loving people anywhere else in the world. We need a leader with that kind of confidence. If I can take on 100,000 protesters, I can do the same across the world.[2]

Walker is not alone. In state after state, conservative governors are repealing laws that protect unions. They are especially targeting "agency shop" rules that require all members of a bargaining unit to pay dues to the union once it is elected and certified.

The goal is clear – zero percent unionization.

But conservatives and elites have already reached another key goal: the virtual elimination of mass strikes. Let's again look at the amazing decline of strike activity since the Better Business Climate model came into being (see Chart 22.4).

Remarkably, as weakened as unions are, conservative politicians still find it politically profitable to use them as scapegoats. They still point to unions to explain why average Americans aren't feeling the benefits of the Better Business Climate model. It's unclear whether conservatives can keep on profiting from this lie as runaway inequality spreads.

Union leaders, of course, have been pressuring Congress for years

---

2   Valerie Strauss, "Yes, Scott Walker Really Did Link Terrorists with Protesting Teachers and Other Unionists," *Washington Post*, February 27, 2015, http://www.washingtonpost.com/blogs/answer-sheet/wp/2015/02/27/yes-scott-walker-really -did-link-terrorists-with-protesting-teachers-and-other-unionists/.

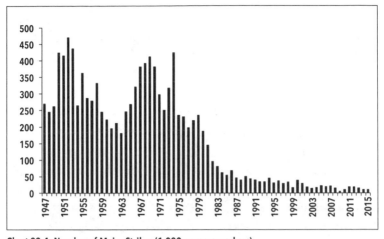

Chart 22.4: Number of Major Strikes (1,000 or more workers)
Source: Bureau of Labor Statistics, "Work Stoppages Involving 1,000 or More Workers, 1947 - 2016," http://www.bls.gov/news.
release/wkstp.t01.htm.

to reform labor law. In fact, they were dead certain they could pass the Employee Free Choice Act (a bill that would greatly facilitate union organizing) from 2008 to 2010, when the Democrats controlled the White House and Congress. It didn't even come up for a vote. (Nevertheless, nearly all union leaders continue to be entirely devoted to the Democrats, and fear the idea of independent politics, especially the creation of a new political party.)

What is to be done?

Despite this gloomy account, the country today is alive with worker activity. Right now, hundreds of small worker centers all over the country are helping unorganized immigrant workers confront workplace issues – and organize for other causes as well. These proto-unions, staffed by young activists, are full of hope.

Some major unions are deeply engaged in community organizing, trying to build large coalitions to fight for worker rights, a higher minimum wage, and unionization. Nearly every union is also fighting to prevent state governments from destroying public sector unions and passing right-to-work laws. And of course, unions continue to invest in organizing, and some drives, especially in health care and building services, have been quite successful.

Yet, the overall decline of unions continues unabated.

Do Americans still support unions?

Union organizers like to say that working people overwhelmingly want to join unions, but can't because of anti-labor laws and practices. What do the polls say about this?

It is true that a majority of Americans approve of unions. But as Chart 22.5 shows, unions' approval rating has dropped from its historic highs in the 1950s, in concert with the decline of unionization.[3] But the ratings are still high enough – and appear to be on the rise – to suggest that scapegoating unions should not be a winning strategy.

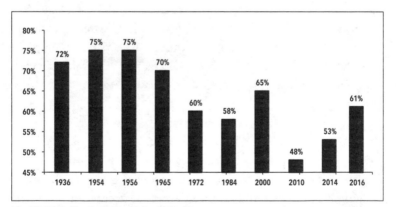

Chart 22.5: Do You Approve of Labor Unions?

Sources: Jeffrey M. Jones, "Americans Approve of Unions," Gallup, http://www.gallup.com/poll/175556/americans-approve-unions-support-right-work.aspx; and Art Swift, "Labor Union Approval Best since 2003, at 61%," Gallup.com, http://news.gallup.com/poll/217331/labor-union-approval-best-2003.aspx.

---

3   Jeffery M. Jones, "Americans Approve of Unions but Support 'Right to Work'," Gallup.com, http://www.gallup.com/poll/175556/americans-approve-unions-support-right-work.aspx; and Art Swift, "Labor Union Approval Best since 2003, at 61%," Gallup.com, http://news.gallup.com/poll/217331/labor-union-approval-best-2003.aspx.

When do unions grow?

Working people flocked to unions during the New Deal. After years of pent-up anger about management abuses, working conditions, and low wages, workers wanted the protection and dignity provided by unions. But what leads to such an upsurge?

One day soon?

Many unions are betting that soon workers will flock to them again. Unions have invested millions of dollars in recent years in organizing drives at Wal-Mart, the country's largest employer, and at fast-food companies, hoping for a major breakthrough. But as anyone familiar with the process knows, organizing low-income workers is excruciatingly difficult. It's hard to get large numbers of these already burdened workers involved in organizing. It's harder still to keep them involved, especially in industries with high turnover. And it is hardest of all to get a union election and contract. Nevertheless these organizing drives continue in many creative ways, making a major breakthrough indeed possible.

Community unionism by and for immigrants

Immigrant workers have always been a potent organizing force. It was immigrants who organized many of the first U.S. unions, including the needle trades at the turn of the twentieth century. As many as half the members of the Congress of Industrial Organizations (CIO) were foreign-born during its early years in the 1930s. And it may be immigrants who lead a labor revival today.

Hispanic workers, both legal and unauthorized, desperately need organizations to protect their rights at work and in the community. That's why over 200 worker centers have sprouted up around the country.

But it's an open question whether worker centers will develop into traditional unions. First, recent immigrants often work in industries (like construction) that are especially hard to organize, in part because they are layered with contractors and sub-contractors. Second, worker centers often depend on private foundation money rather than membership dues, and it's not clear how long foundation money will continue to flow, especially as unions become more involved. Finally, it's not entirely clear that all unions are ready to give undocumented workers the support they need to become citizens.

Some argue that it will take a new kind of unionism – community unionism – to reach new immigrants and other vulnerable workers. Unions and worker centers can and have collaborated on community-based fights to win a $15 per hour minimum wage, to prevent wage theft, to provide immigrant drivers' licenses, and to prevent discrimination in housing and employment. But these campaigns require unions to invest heavily without the prospect of a quick return in union dues. Unions also have to accept that worker centers and new immigrants themselves will probably be the ones to lead any new community union that this joint effort produces.

Given the enormity of the problems we've explored in this book, we know that labor unions and worker centers need to be part of a wider effort if they are to succeed: a mass movement for economic justice aimed at halting runaway inequality.

Unions and social movements

Unions grow during tumultuous eras when many social movements are shaking the country to its core. The union upsurge in the 1930s rose side by side with thousands of unemployment councils, tenant organizations, and popular campaigns that attacked the disparities of wealth and poverty. These movements had many leaders and heroes, known and unknown. Among those we know:

Louisiana populist Huey Long, until his assassination in 1935, led a national movement to redistribute wealth from the rich to the poor. In California, Upton Sinclair helped build a mass movement that demanded and nearly won stipends for every California citizen over the age of 50. And FDR followed this fervor with his own New Deal policies, which had been advocated by overlapping mass movements for years, including bargaining rights for unions and a plethora of programs to support working people like Social Security. This was the context for the massive growth of unions through the CIO.

Unions (public unions, in this case) also grew rapidly during another era of mass upheaval – the tumultuous 1960s and 1970s. Again, this was a time when movement after movement shook the established ways. The anti-war, women's and civil rights movements provided enormous energy that helped fuel the rapid rise of public employee unions.

It's going to take another mass social movement to revive unions and tame runaway inequality. How to get there is the subject of our next and final chapter.

Discussion Questions:

1. Do you think that union growth is necessary for taming runaway inequality? Why or why not?

2. In your opinion, why have unions declined over the last 30 years?

3. What do you think needs to be done to promote union growth in America?

4. Should unions continue to provide support for the Democratic Party? Why or why not?

CHAPTER 23

An Open Letter to
New Movement Organizers

Thank you for committing to build a new coherent national mass movement for economic, social and environmental justice.

Be prepared. The one-percenters will come after you. They will try to divide, to discredit and even destroy. Your courage and careful organizing will be tested again and again. But you may be surprised by the response you get. People are waiting for something defiant. We all want to join a movement that helps spread the word, that fights for structural change, that links us together, that multiplies our efforts, that keeps us hopeful.

Runaway inequality is accelerating and no one is organizing a movement to stop it. Except you. Let's hope it's not beyond the grasp of our imagination, even though nothing like it has been built in America for a long, long time.

We need you and your efforts badly, because there is nothing in the economic universe that will automatically rescue us. There is no pendulum, no invisible political force that "naturally" will swing back towards economic fairness. Neither climate change nor racial discrimination is going to heal itself. Either we wage a large-scale battle for economic, social and environmental justice, or we will witness the continued deterioration of the world we inhabit. The arc of capitalism does not bend towards justice. We must bend it.

The limits of silo organizing

Your movement will build on the activist terrain inhabited by thousands of progressive organizations, all operating within their issue-area silos. Since the end of the Vietnam War, activists have created a cornucopia of organizations covering hundreds of issues, from climate change and toxics to healthcare, education, poverty, homelessness, immigration, peace, LGBT, AIDS, abortion, police injustice, prison reform, drug decriminalization and nuclear weapons.

Each of these organizations is engaged in a constant struggle to raise money to support its work and staff. Each must appeal to private philanthropic organizations by writing detailed proposals with lists of deliverables. The philanthropic foundations, in turn, contain their own issue areas, specialized staff, and underlying interests. All this only reinforces the organizational silos: Each group works on its own set of issues, following to-do lists that come from their foundation proposals.

We are our deliverables. We are our to-do lists.

This works well if and only if the most important issues of our existence fall within many silos. But today, even as runaway inequality runs roughshod through the siloed terrain, stopping the financial strip-mining of our economy is on very few to-do lists. Many activists still do not understand how our economy has structurally changed since 1980.

Even the great crash of 2008 didn't crack the silos. For the first time since 1929, the entire financial system was in collapse. Trillions of dollars were handed out to Wall Street. Unemployment hit record post-Depression levels.

The crash revealed the horrors of Wall Street. The bailouts laid bare how government would come to the rescue of financial elites at our expense. The "recovery" reveals how money continues to go to the super-rich as inequality accelerates and catastrophic climate change looms.

Had we been ready, the collapse would have been the perfect moment for a broad-based movement to challenge Wall Street.

Instead, our silos held their ground as if taking on Wall Street was on someone else's to-do list. As a result, we got the Obama campaign and the Tea Party.

And then came Occupy Wall Street, seemingly out of nowhere. A loosely organized group around the media website Ad Busters called for the event and thousands came, then tens of thousands. In short order there were 900 encampments (modern day Hoovervilles[1]) around the world. Still our silos rarely joined the fray.

The failure of spontaneous uprisings

As you already know, mass upheavals are not the same as organized mass movements. Occupy Wall Street was, in part, built upon inherent distrust of hierarchical organizational structures. Instead, it believed in the transformative power of spontaneous uprisings. It believed that the people in the parks could keep the anti-Wall Street movement going by making all their most important strategic decisions by mass consensus. They called it "horizontal" organizing.

At first it was a joyous victory for the power of the human spirit. Young people were standing up to the power of Wall Street. It was inspirational. But it could not build a sustainable organizational structure. It seemed blind to the fact that there were millions of Americans all across the country who believed in the message and who wanted to participate, but who were not going to sleep in the parks. Who would reach them? What could the rest of us do? How would we be organized?

Horizontally or not at all.

If millions of us wanted to participate in Occupy Wall Street, then it was up to us to figure out how to do it on our own. That is the creed of spontaneous uprisings.

Unfortunately, spontaneity was no match for Mother Nature

---

1   Large shanty towns of the unemployed during the Great Depression, ironically named after President Herbert Hoover.

and the destructive power of local governments that found many ways to remove the encampments as winter settled in. What was Occupy Wall Street's survival strategy?

As with spontaneous combustion in nature, unless fed, the flame will go out.

Missed moment

Occupy Wall Street showed us that an anti-Wall Street movement had great resonance across the country – even across much of the world. Had it broadened into a formal national organization, something powerful might have emerged with staying power. But Occupy Wall Street didn't want formal organizations, and our many silo organizations, for the most part, stood back and watched.

Perhaps, the rest of us were too deferential. "Occupy didn't want us involved," one union leader told me. So what? Aren't we all the 99 percent? Shouldn't it have been everyone's movement, not just Occupy's?

We still owe Occupy Wall Street an enormous debt of gratitude for putting the 1 percent in full view. It proved that such a movement could be built, and it showed the power and necessity of idealism. It showed how hungry we are for a new culture that builds our spirits and our sense of solidarity with others. But for all that, Occupy wasn't able to build a lasting organization.

Bernie Sanders' 2016 campaign for president unleashed new possibilities. Just like Occupy Wall Street, it seemed to come out of nowhere and surprised the entire country. The 74-year-old, self-declared socialist senator from Vermont has gained an enormous following, especially among young people, as he attacks Wall Street, the "billionaire class" and the "corrupt campaign finance system." He has called for a "political revolution" to carry the campaign forward after the 2016 elections. And he has attracted millions of small donors who may be hungry to fund and participate in such a movement.

But, will it be built? Or will we quickly return to our silo to-do lists? It's up to you.

American populism

The populist movement of the late nineteenth century – the National Farmers Alliance and Industrial Union – is a movement worth studying.[2] This may have been the last time in American history that a large, dynamic, democratic movement tried to wrest financial control away from the private banking industry.

After the Civil War, farmers in the South and Midwest were suffering mightily from tight monetary policies set by Wall Street, which had gained total control of the U.S. money supply, and therefore over the availability and price of credit. The burden of obtaining loans to buy farms and maintain them was enormously onerous for millions of farmers. The price of farm goods was falling while the cost of loan repayments escalated under the big banks' tight money policies.

This financial oppression led to a movement to take control of the money supply away from private bankers while at the same time building new cooperatives to store produce, sell livestock and organize the markets farmers depended upon. The vital day-to-day practice of these cooperatives led to a mass democratic culture that stood in defiance against the new corporate capitalism then being organized and operated by financial elites.

The Farmers Alliance organized itself into state and county organizations, with national journals and national conventions. The Alliance fielded six thousand "lecturers" to conduct grassroots education to spread the word and to bring grassroots insights back to state and national leaders.

As you review carefully this monumental struggle, which lasted over 30 years, you will understand why spontaneous uprisings are

---

2 See Lawrence Goldwyn's masterful account, *The Populist Moment: A Short History of the Agrarian Revolt in America* (Oxford University Press, 1978).

unlikely to succeed against Wall Street, and why careful long-term organizing is so badly needed.

One of the biggest problems we all face lies within our own heads. We are all creatures of the prevailing political culture that undermines mass political involvement, reinforces domination by financial elites and justifies inequality. The populists built the cooperatives which gave its people an alternative day-to-day experience in democratic rule.[3] It also gave them the confidence to demand and fight for democratic control of finance at every level. The Bank of North Dakota, the only public bank in the U.S., grew from this new culture.

Building an alternative political culture will be among your biggest challenges. Siloed movement activists have spent their entire lives within a particular organizing framework and structure that focuses on achieving relatively short-term deliverables. Few of us work on big-picture education and on large-scale transformative organizing projects. Fewer still are directly challenging the power of Wall Street. That means that much of our current organizing culture does not have the patience for the long-term, self-conscious democratic movement-building that is necessary to halt runaway inequality. We also don't yet have the collective vision and strategy we need to do all this.

Silo organizers counter this critique by saying that such big picture movements are too vague, too indefinite and well beyond the scope of what can be funded through the philanthropic community. They are correct.

Building a new movement is an indefinite project that could take a generation to blossom. It is unlikely to sit comfortably on many foundation dockets. It will not have the specificity of our current batch of deliverables.

---

3   This differs substantively from the Saul Alinski organizing approach which dominates so many progressive organizations. The populists always discussed the biggest issues of the day. They had confidence that their people would understand why an alternative to Wall Street was needed and why cooperatives were essential to their lives.

What it does have going for it is the chance of success. But this kind of statement only makes sense if we face up to the fact that our current silo structure is failing. Collectively our current to-do lists are simply no match for runaway inequality. We are losing. We've got to try something different.

Therefore, your job will be to change our siloed political culture and create a new organizing life that captures us, that provides us with a sense of movement and self-confidence just as the Populists did over a century ago and as the Sanders campaign is doing now. A major problem will be to create day to day practice that reflects our ideals, the new culture we hope to create, and our new agenda. The Populists had their cooperatives. What will we have?

Race, class, environment, peace

Our siloed generation has not been able to construct an understanding that links racial oppression, gender/sexual orientation discrimination, rising inequality, environmental destruction and the anti-war efforts. Instead, we too often argue about which issue is most important. Worse still, we create a silo around each.

This was not always the case. After WWII, radicals (communists, socialists, social democrats and others) were horrified about the brewing Cold War, the arms race, civil rights and the attacks on organized labor, starting with opposition to the Labor Management Relations Act (Taft-Hartley).[4]

Radicals believed that corporate elites and their ruthless drive for profits were behind all of these issues. At the time, many believed that capitalism itself was the root cause and eventually should be replaced by democratic socialism of some sort, although there was no across-the-board agreement about what that might look like. In any event, they had no doubt about the interconnectedness of injustice.

---

4   The labor law passed in 1947 which revoked the use of many of the tools used by labor that had led to the massive surge of organizing.

Even under the brutal assault on radicalism led by Senator Joseph McCarthy, radicals kept the interconnectedness alive. Radicals were involved in the early civil rights movement. They were in the forefront of the anti-nuclear testing movement which then evolved into the modern environmental movement and fueled the earliest efforts against the war in Vietnam.

But as that generation passed, so did our sense of inherent interconnectedness among all the oppression and destruction that comes from a system that produces runaway inequality.

Your job is to rebuild that interconnectedness – to help us all see and feel the realities that cut through our silos. Of course, the tensions around racial and gender oppression will not go away within our mass movement, let alone outside of it. But you must help us always see that we are far better off fighting together than among ourselves – that an injury to one is truly an injury to all.

Some in the environmental movement may see runaway inequality as yet another silo, while the peril of climate change is the real silo-breaker. After all, climate change poses a direct threat to humans across the globe.

Fortunately, a growing movement for climate justice is based on the understanding that economic inequality and climate change are inextricably bound together, and that these challenges need to be addressed in tandem. Financial strip-mining of our economy both accelerates climate change and undermines all efforts to ameliorate it or accommodate it. Both climate change and runaway inequality are global silo-breakers.

The ongoing political revolution

The Sanders campaign has opened up new organizing terrain. He has field-tested a new populist agenda and shifted the terms of the presidential debate. This remarkable effort shows that there's a movement waiting to be built. Here are four things you'll need to consider in order to build it.

1. A coherent, short agenda and common analysis that binds us together:

We already know that this agenda must include a vast redistribution of income and wealth from the "billionaire class" to the rest of
society. It must include concrete proposals to end racial discrimination and it must confront the fact that we're the largest police state
in the world, bar none. It must address climate change head-on.

It all has to be packed into a concise 10-point plan (or shorter)
that clearly reflects the anger we feel about the domination of the
super-rich, the rigged political system, systemic racial and ethnic
injustice, and the climate crisis. We have to find a way to blend
these issues without ripping ourselves apart.

To get there, we will need a common analysis of how financial
strip-mining and runaway inequality are harming the 99 percent.
Hopefully, this book can serve as a working draft.

2. A national educational infrastructure to spread the agenda and analysis:

The populists of the 1880s, during their anti-Wall Street revolt,
fielded 6,000 grass roots educators to spread the word about the
promise of cooperatives, public banks, progressive income taxes
and popular control over railroads and communications systems.

Given our current population, we'll need more than 30,000
grassroots educators to spread the word. Yes, social media can facilitate the process, but nothing beats face-to-face discussion of these
vital issues.

Several labor unions and community groups already have
launched such a mass economic and social justice training process.
These might serve as a model for you to use.

3. A coherent national organization with state and local chapters:

Our opponents are strong and organized. They have an iron grip
on the economy and the political process. We have to be strong
and organized too. A demonstration or two will not do the job. All

of us need to belong to a lasting organization with a common identity that concretely expresses our movement. We need to prepare for a 10- to 20-year struggle to break down their plutocratic rule. So we need you to build solid organizational structures that can sustain themselves.

We should be able to travel anywhere in the country and join in a local meeting of our new organization and engage in discussion, political activities, and events. Our organization needs its own lively culture.

Building such a structure takes people and money. The Sanders campaign shows that the people and money are there. It has amassed millions of small donors and tens of thousands of volunteers and staff who may be willing to build, join and contribute to such a formation.

4. A new movement identity:
This is perhaps the highest hurdle for all of us to clear. We need to see ourselves as movement builders. We must make our silos more porous. Each of us needs to expand our identity so that we are not just enviros, racial justice fighters, or labor activists, but also broad movement builders. Our traditional approach to coalition and alliance building is unlikely to succeed unless we place a much higher value on building a new common movement identity.

None of this will come easily. It cuts hard against the grain for many progressives – it asks us to change the way we see ourselves and the way we are organized. After all, our separate identities give us nourishment and a sense of empowerment. And our distinct identities also sometimes help us get funding, since funders themselves live and work in issue silos. This shift to broader movement-building will disrupt our to-do lists and put us into strange new organizing spaces. And organizations and individuals may vie for leadership of this new movement.

This is tough stuff. Can activists for climate justice, Black Lives Matter, the fight for a $15 minimum wage, prison reform, and union organizing all come together in a common movement? Not easily.

But the Sanders campaign has demonstrated that joining together is possible. And it is necessary: runaway inequality will stifle all of our movements unless we do band together. The elite plutocracy gives us no choice but to try.

Sometime soon, we hope that you convene the first national meeting to forge a new agenda that takes on runaway inequality, climate change, and racial injustice. Or perhaps you will need to build state by state before such a national gathering. But eventually it must have a name, and all of us must be able to join because we believe in the agenda, because we believe we must act, and because we believe in each other.

We're counting on you and we're sure you won't let us down. We'd be honored if any portion of this book could help in your educational efforts.

> In solidarity,
> Les Leopold,
> May Day, 2018

Index

Page numbers in italics refer to charts and tables.

About the Author

Les Leopold cofounded and directs the Labor Institute in New York City, a nonprofit educational organization that designs programs on occupational health and safety, the environment and economics for unions and community groups. He is the author of the award-winning biography *The Man Who Hated Work and Loved Labor: The Life and Times of Tony Mazzocchi* (2006). He has also written two books on the financial crisis: *The Looting of America: How Wall Street's Game of Fantasy Finance Destroyed Our Jobs, Pensions, and Prosperity, and What We Can Do About It* (2009), and *How to Make a Million Dollars an Hour: Why Hedge Funds Get Away with Siphoning Off America's Wealth* (2013).

He currently designs, conducts and shares economic educational programs to help fight runaway inequality. He can be reached at LesLeopold@aol.com.

About the Book

All proceeds from sales of *Runaway Inequality* go to the Labor Institute's National Economics Educational Campaign – not the author personally.

Acknowledgements

We wish to thank David Dembo, Peter Holm, Lilah Leopold and Laura McClure for their expert research, editing, design and illustrations. We also wish to thank Jan Frel and Don Hazen for encouraging us to test many of the book's themes on Alternet.org. Also, many thanks to Arturo Archilla, Sally Silvers, Rodrigo Toscano and Jim Young of the Labor Institute for supporting and sponsoring this work. And we wish to thank Chester Leopold for inspiring the author by his deep dedication to the fight for justice and fairness, and Sharon Szymanski for her day-to-day commitment to the cause of worker education as well as her loving support.